Between-Election Democracy

The Representative Relationship After Election Day

P. Esaiasson and H. M. Narud

ecpr_{PRESS}

First published by the ECPR Press in 2013

Paperback edition first published by the ECPR Press in 2014

The ECPR Press is the publishing imprint of the European Consortium for Political Research (ECPR), a scholarly association, which supports and encourages the training, research and cross-national co-operation of political scientists in institutions throughout Europe and beyond.

ECPR Press
University of Essex
Wivenhoe Park
Colchester
CO4 3SQ
UK

Typeset by Anvi

Printed and bound by Lightning Source

British Library Cataloguing in Publication Data

A catalogue record for this book is available from the British Library

Hardback ISBN: 978-1-907301-98-8

Paperback ISBN: 978-1-910259-39-9

www.ecpr.eu/ecprpress

ECPR – *Studies in European Political Science* is a series of high-quality edited volumes on topics at the cutting edge of current political science and political thought. All volumes are research-based offering new perspectives in the study of politics with contributions from leading scholars working in the relevant fields. Most of the volumes originate from ECPR events including the Joint Sessions of Workshops, the Research Sessions, and the General Conferences.
Books in this series:

Europeanisation and Party Politics
ISBN: 9781907301223
Edited by Erol Külahci

Great Expectations, Slow Transformations: Incremental Change in Post-Crisis Regulation
ISBN: 9781907301544
Edited by Manuela Moschella and Eleni Tsingou

Interactive Policy Making, Metagovernance and Democracy
ISBN: 9781907301131
Edited by Jacob Torfing and Peter Triantafillou

Perceptions of Europe
ISBN: 9781907301155
Edited by Daniel Gaxie, Jay Rowell and Nicolas Hubé

Personal Representation: The Neglected Dimension of Electoral Systems
ISBN: 9781907301162
Edited by Josep Colomer

Political Participation in France and Germany
ISBN: 9781907301315
Oscar Gabriel, Silke Keil, and Eric Kerrouche

Political Trust: Why Context Matters
ISBN: 9781907301230
Edited by Sonja Zmerli and Marc Hooghe

Practices of Inter-Parliamentary Coordination in International Politics: The European Union and Beyond
ISBN: 9781907301308
Edited by Ben Crum and John Erik Fossum

Please visit www.ecpr.eu/ecprpress for up-to-date information about new publications.

Contents

List of Figures and Tables   vii

Contributors   xi

Preface   xv

Chapter One: Between-Election Democracy: An Introductory Note
Peter Esaiasson and Hanne Marthe Narud   1

Chapter Two: Communicative Responsiveness and Other Central Concepts in Between-Election Democracy
Peter Esaiasson, Mikael Gilljam and Mikael Persson   15

Chapter Three: Is Anyone Listening?
The Perceived Effectiveness of Electoral and Non-Electoral Participation
Sofie Marien and Marc Hooghe   35

Chapter Four: Issue Uptake in the Shadow of Elections
Audrey André, Sam Depauw and Kris Deschouwer   53

Chapter Five: Nominations, Campaigning and Representation: How the Secret Garden of Politics Determines the Style of Campaigning and Roles of Representation
Rune Karlsen and Hanne Marthe Narud   77

Chapter Six: Institutional Incentives for Participation in Elections and Between Elections
Henrik Serup Christensen   103

Chapter Seven: Political Parties in the Streets: The Development and Timing of Party-Sponsored Protests in Western Europe
Swen Hutter   127

Chapter Eight: Signalling Through Voting Intention Polls Between Elections
Ann-Kristin Kölln and Kees Aarts   151

Chapter Nine: 'We Need to Decide!': A Mixed Method Approach to Responsiveness and Equal Treatment
Liz Richardson   171

Chapter Ten: The Impact of Social Movements on Agenda Setting: Bringing the Real World Back In
Roy Gava, Marco Giugni, and Frédéric Varone   189

Index   209

List of Figures and Tables

Figures

Figure 4.1: A model of issue uptake in the legislative arena by
elected representatives   56

Figure 5.1: Nomination control, electoral system and styles of campaigning
and representation   81

Figure 5.2: Dimensions of nomination systems   82

Figure 5.3: Who should decide the composition of the list and the final
ranking of candidates by party affiliation? Top three candidates in the
seven parties   89

Figure 5.4: The communicative focus of the candidate's campaign. Mean
on a scale from 0 (individual focus) to 10 (party focus)   91

Figure 5.5: Representational style of the candidates. Proportion of
candidates who say that representatives should vote in accordance
with their party rather than their constituency voters. All candidates
and top three placed candidates. By party affiliation   94

Figure 6.1: The predicted probability of participation   118

Figure 7.1: The long-term development of party-sponsored protests in
Germany, 1950–2002   139

Figure 7.2: The distribution of party-sponsored protests over the electoral
cycle, 1975–2005   143

Figure 8.1: Triad of communication between voters and representatives
in the course of an electoral cycle   153

Figure 8.2: Modified path analysis of vote (intention) for government
party and satisfaction with government policies, 2006–2010   165

Figure 8.3: Logistic regression analyses of vote (intention) for government
party, satisfaction with government policies, and satisfaction with the
functioning of the economy 2006–2010   166

Figure 10.1: Hypothesised paths to agenda setting   191

Figure 10.2: Development over time of dependent and independent
variables for asylum policy   198

Figure 10.3: Development over time of dependent and independent
variables for unemployment policy   198

Figure 10.4: Estimates from structural equation model for agenda setting
on asylum policy (standardised solution)   201

Figure 10.5: Estimates from structural equation model for agenda setting
on unemployment policy (standardised solution)   202

Tables

Table 2.1: A summary of the contours and boundaries of BED phenomena   22

Table 2.2: Means of responsiveness judgments by citizens and
representatives (0–10)   26

Table 2.3: Responsiveness items predict evaluation of the government
and trust in politicians. OLS regression   27

Table 3.1: Means and ranking of the perceived effectiveness of
participation   41

Table 3.2: Cross-national differences in perceived effectiveness of electoral
and non-electoral participation   43

Table 3.3: Explaining MPs' views of the effectiveness of electoral
participation   45

Table 3.4: Explaining MPs' views of the effectiveness of non-electoral
participation   46

Table A.3.1: PartiRep survey among Members of Parliament   48

Table 4.1: A summary of the hypotheses regarding issue uptake in the
legislative arena   59

Table 4.2: Summary statistics (mean and standard deviation) of the
dependent and independent variables   62

Table 4.3: The individual effects of conceptions of representation and
behaviour in the district   65

Table 4.4: The combined effect of conceptions of representation and
behaviour in the district   68

Table 4.5: Predicted counts of uptake levels on the basis of minimum
and maximum values of the independent variables   69

Table A.4.1: Case selection: Response rates and district magnitude   72

Table 5.1: Who should decide the composition of the list and the final
ranking of candidates? All candidates and the top three candidates   89

Table 5.2: The effect of age, gender, list placement and list ranking opinion
for candidate communicative focus. Multivariate linear regression analysis
(N = 900)   91

Table 5.3: The representational focus of the candidates by party affiliation, as a percentage   92

Table 5.4: The effect of age, gender, list placement, list ranking opinion and candidate focus for representatives primarily representing the party multivariate logistic regression (N = 901)   93

Table 5.5: The effect of age, gender, list placement, list ranking opinion and candidate focus on candidates' views of representational style (MPs should vote in accordance with the party). Multivariate logistic regression (N = 880)   95

Table 6.1: Country scores for the institutional linkages (Coded 0–1 high openness)   111

Table 6.2: Multilevel analysis of effect of institutional openness on electoral, institutionalised and non-institutionalised participation   113

Table 6.3: Multilevel analysis of effect of five institutional linkages on electoral, institutionalised and non-institutionalised participation   114

Table 6.4: Multilevel analysis of effect of institutional linkages on electoral, institutionalised and non-institutionalised participation when controlling for individual level characteristics, parsimonious models   116

Table A.6.1: Coding of variables and descriptive statistics   121

Table 7.1: Conceptual differences of the protest arena and the electoral arena   129

Table 7.2: The long-term development of protests sponsored by political parties   138

Table 7.3: The long-term development of protests sponsored by Social Democratic parties   141

Table 7.4: Party-sponsored protests during election campaigns, 1975–2005   143

Table 7.5: The impact of electoral cycle and event characteristics on party sponsorship, 1975–2005   144

Table 8.1: Participation by voting and non-electoral participation distinguished by key characteristics   155

Table 8.2: Non-electoral participation and polling distinguished by key characteristics   156

Table 8.3: Panel wave characteristics   161

Table 8.4: Reported voting behaviour, 2006 and 2010 (percentages of total number of respondents)   162

Table 8.5: (Recalled) vote change and satisfaction with government policies   162

Table 8.6: Satisfaction with government policies 2007–2009   163

Table 8.7: Loglinear Markov chain models of reported vote/vote intention for government party   164

Table 9.1: Prioritisation experiment – overall rankings of requests   180

Table 9.2: Prioritisation experiment – overall averages and rankings by information-poor or -rich letters   181

Table 9.3: Prioritisation experiment – Wilcoxon rank-sum test for intervention groups   182

Table 10.1: Effects of selected independent variables on agenda setting on asylum policy (negative binomial regression coefficients)   199

Table 10.2: Effects of selected independent variables on agenda setting on unemployment policy (unstandardised regression coefficients)   200

Contributors

KEES AARTS is Professor of Political Science and Scientific Director of the Institute for Innovation and Governance Studies (IGS), University of Twente.

AUDREY ANDRÉ is a postdoctoral researcher at the University of Antwerp. As Aspirant of the FWO-Vlaanderen, she defended her PhD at the Vrije Universiteit Brussel. Her research focuses on the impact of electoral institutions on parties', legislators' and voters' behaviour. Key findings have been published in *Party Politics, Acta Politica, West European Politics,* and the *Journal of Elections, Public Opinion & Parties.*

HENRIK SERUP CHRISTENSEN is an Academy of Finland Postdoctoral Researcher at the Department of Political Science at Åbo Akademi University in Turku, Finland. His research interests include political participation and how the proliferation of new forms of citizen involvement affects the functioning of democracy. His current research project examines the causes and consequences of the spread of political disenchantment in representative democracies.

SAM DEPAUW is Assistant Professor and Postdoctoral Researcher at the Vrije Universiteit Brussel. His research concentrates on legislative and electoral studies. He has published extensively on political representation and party discipline in *West European Politics*, the *Journal of Legislative Studies, Acta Politica,* and *Party Politics.* Sam Depauw has coordinated the PartiRep comparative legislator survey in fifteen European democracies.

KRIS DESCHOUWER is Research Professor of Politics at the Vrije Universiteit Brussel. His research focuses on political parties, elections, regionalism and federalism; democracy in divided societies; and political representation. He is the central coordinator of the PartiRep research project on Political Participation and Representation in Modern Democracies (http://www.PARTIREP.eu). Kris Deschouwer has been co-editor of the *European Journal of Political Research* (2003–2009) and authored the book *The Politics of Belgium* (Palgrave, 2012).

PETER ESAIASSON is Professor of Political Science at the University of Gothenburg. His main areas of interest are empirical democratic theory, election campaigns, and the political consequences of ethnic diversity.

ROY GAVA is a PhD candidate at the Department of Political Science and International Relations, University of Geneva. He participates in the Swiss Policy Agendas Project and is currently finishing a doctoral dissertation on banking regulation. His research interests include comparative public policy, internationalisation and the regulation of financial services.

MIKAEL GILLJAM is Professor of Political Science at the University of Gothenburg. His main areas of interest are public opinion and democracy, political representation, local government, and election studies.

MARCO GIUGNI is a Professor at the Department of Political Science and International Relations and Director of the Institute of Social and Political Research (RESOP) at the University of Geneva, Switzerland. His research interests include social movements and collective action, immigration and ethnic relations, unemployment and social exclusion.

MARC HOOGHE is a Professor of Political Science at the University of Leuven (Belgium) and a Visiting Professor at the universities of Mannheim (Germany) and Lille (France). He has published extensively on political participation and social capital, and holds an ERC Advanced Grant to investigate the democratic linkage between citizens and the state.

SWEN HUTTER is a researcher and reader in Comparative Politics, University of Munich. He is a 2012/2013 Max Weber Fellow at the European University Institute. His research interests include social movements, political parties and cleavage structures. Hutter studied political science at the Universities of Zurich and Växjö (Sweden) and holds a PhD from the University of Munich. He co-authored a book with Hanspeter Kriesi *et al.* on *Political Conflict in Western Europe* (Cambridge University Press) and his revised dissertation on *New Cleavages and Protest Politics in Western Europe* is forthcoming with the University of Minnesota Press.

RUNE KARLSEN is a Postdoctoral Fellow at the Department of Political Science at the University of Oslo, and a Senior Researcher at the Institute for Social Research, Oslo. His research interests include elections, campaigning, and political communication.

ANN-KRISTIN KÖLLN is a PhD student in political science at the Institute for Innovation and Governance Studies at the University of Twente. She is also a member of the European Social Survey team in the Netherlands. Previously, she has studied and worked at the University of Münster, University of Warwick, and University of Gothenburg. Her research interests are in party politics, representative democracy, and survey methodology.

SOFIE MARIEN is a postdoctoral researcher at the Centre for Citizenship and Democracy at the University of Leuven. Currently, she studies the development of political trust in the framework of a postdoctoral grant from the Research Foundation Flanders (FWO). Her research interests include trust, participation, representation, and comparative politics. Previously, her work has been published in, among others, the *European Journal of Political Research*, *Electoral Studies*, *Political Studies* and *Intellligence*.

HANNE MARTHE NARUD was Professor of Political Science at the University of Oslo. She died in July 2012. Her research focused on political representation, political parties and voting behaviour.

MIKAEL PERSSON is a doctoral student at the University of Gothenburg. His primary areas of interest are political behaviour and public opinion. His journal articles have appeared in *Political Behavior*, the *European Journal of Political Research, European Political Science Review*, the *International Journal of Public Opinion Research, Party Politics, West European Politics, Legislative Studies Quarterly*, the *Journal of Elections, Public Opinion and Parties, Scandinavian Political Studies,* and *Politics*.

LIZ RICHARDSON is a Senior Lecturer in Politics at the University of Manchester, and a Visiting Fellow in the Centre for Analysis of Social Exclusion (CASE) at the London School of Economics and Political Science (LSE). She conducts research on citizen participation, local politics and local government, public services, and public policy. She has an interest in methodological innovation including participatory research approaches and experimental methods.

FRÉDÉRIC VARONE is Professor of Political Science at the University of Geneva. His current research interests include comparative public policy, programme evaluation and public sector reforms.

Preface

This book originates from a workshop at the ECPR Joint Sessions in St Gallen in April 2011, which was co-directed by Hanne Marthe Narud and myself. However, the chain of events that led to its publication started several years ago when my colleague Mikael Gilljam initated a discussion on the representative relationship after Election Day under the Swedish term *mellanvalsdemokrati*. Within the realms of the *Multidisciplinary Research Group on Opinion and Democracy* (MOD) at the University of Gothenburg, our ideas about the topic developed gradually. To broaden perspectives, I asked Hanne Marthe Narud to join in on an application for a workshop at the St Gallen meeting. The workshop lived up to expectations with participants engaging in open-minded discussions. Several of us agreed that we had a common interest and that we wanted to pursue our respective ideas under a common framework. The book began to take its final form in connection with a follow-up conference at the University of Gothenburg in October 2011.

Many individuals and institutions have provided valuable help during the process. Acknowledgments are presented in connection with respective chapters, but I would like to express special thanks to the anonymous reviewer and to Peter Kennealy at ECPR Press for motivating us all to think even harder about the project. Thanks also to the MOD Director Lena Wängnerud for agreeing that a follow-up conference was a good thing to support financially, and to Veronica Norell for handling the practicalities of the conference.

This preface could, and should, have ended here. However, fate wanted it differently. Some months after the St Gallen meeting Hanne Marthe was diagnosed with life-threatening cancer. With characteristic strength and good humour she continued her engagement in the book project, but on 20 July 2012 the illness finally overcame her. Everyone who has had the opportunity to interact with Hanne Marthe knows how much she is missed. This book is dedicated to her memory.

Peter Esaiasson
Gothenburg, September 2013

In memory of Hanne Marthe Narud

Chapter One

Between-Election Democracy:
An Introductory Note

Peter Esaiasson and Hanne Marthe Narud

Representative democracy is a complex system of government. It fuses two ideas from vastly different origins – 'democracy' and 'representation' (Dahl 1989; Keane 2009). The democratic system of government created by ancient Athenians was egalitarian but not representative. Tellingly, Athenians did not even have a word for representation (Pitkin 2004; Ober 2008). By contrast, representative institutions emerged in Medieval Europe during a time without egalitarian values. While the story of the dual origin of representative democracy is often retold, the consequence of fusing the two ideas has recently reappeared as a topic of interest for political theorists. Noting that each idea has contributed independently to the fusion, it is suggested that representative democracy should be understood as a distinct system of government which is both egalitarian and elitist (Manin 1997; Urbinati 2006; Disch 2011). The system is egalitarian in that each citizen contributes equally to the selection of representatives. It is elitist because selection by elections is inherently advantageous for the resourceful; because the selected few can shape the preferences of the represented; and because it is an act of submission to entrust others with the power to decide common matters.

Taking a radical position, Bernhard Manin (1997) contends that the representative system of government was originally designed 'in explicit opposition to government by the people', and that 'its central institutions have remained unchanged'. Other theorists advance more favourable evaluations of the democratic qualities of representative systems (*see* Urbinati and Warren 2008 for a review of the literature). Common in all contributions to the discussion is the urge to rethink standard assumptions about the relationship between representatives and the represented.

When compared to the standard account of contemporary democratic government, according to which electoral institutions preserve the core principles of a democratic rule by the people (Dahl 1971, 1989), the claim that representative democracy is indeed a dual system in its own right may appear surprising. However, when read from this perspective, the dual character of representative democracy is already captured by Hanna Pitkin's influential definition of representation from the 1960s: 'Representation means acting in the interest of the represented, in a manner responsive to them' (Pitkin 1967). In this context at least, the two key components in the definition are 'interest' and 'responsive'. Clearly, since objective interest is different from subjective preference, representatives are not bound by instructions from the represented at a particular point in time. Equally clear is that the demand for responsiveness means that representatives cannot remain disconnected from citizens' opinions.

A clarifying stipulation added by Pitkin indicates how the key components might combine to produce representation in the real world: '[Representatives] must not be found persistently at odds with the wishes of the represented, *without good reason* in terms of their interest, *without a good explanation* of why their views are not in accord with their interests' (1967) [emphasis added]. The stipulation implies that elected representatives are free to follow their own best judgment in how to act, even when citizens disagree about the right course of action, but while exercising their privilege, representatives are obliged to provide convincing justifications for their actions.

More generally, the dual view of democratic representation suggests that the representative relationship should be seen as a two-way process that involves continuous interactions between representatives and the represented (Alonso *et al.* 2011). Citizens and their organisations express demands that motivate representatives to respond but representatives also take actions that generate responses from citizens (Mansbridge 2003). In this dynamic relationship, electoral mechanisms – the right to select good leaders and to punish bad ones in general elections – are important checkpoints but they do not by themselves secure that government actions are driven by citizen preferences (Manin 1997; Mansbridge 2003; Disch 2011).

To see why electoral mechanisms fall short of securing a bottom-up representative relationship, consider that the back and forth communication between representatives and the represented allows representatives to shape citizen opinion to conform to their own preferences (Mansbridge 2003; Disch 2011). According to the traditional account, representatives should be responsive to citizens rather than the other way around (Disch 2011). However, if elected representatives manage to create the opinions of the represented, we face a situation in which representatives, and not the represented, give direction to the relationship (Eulau and Karps 1977). As argued by Lisa Disch (2011), to the extent that this reversed relationship materialises it becomes difficult to maintain that citizen preferences are 'the principal force' in the representative relationship (Sunstein 1991), and that citizen opinions are the 'bedrock for social choice' (Page and Shapiro 1992).[1]

The reasoning above lays out the theoretical background for the volume *Between-Election Democracy – The representative relationship after Election Day*. Challenged by the notion that the system of government known as 'representative democracy' is perhaps more elitist than is commonly assumed, contributors to the volume seek new approaches to empirical studies on the relationship between citizens and their chosen representatives.

Our joint effort focuses on the way in which representatives and citizens interact between elections during the course of mandate periods. That the interactions of interest take place *between* elections, rather than *at* elections, is

---

1. With reference to social choice theory, Riker (1982) makes a similar argument. For opposing views in this old debate, *see* Key (1966: xiv); Granberg and Holmberg (1988: 11, 218).

theoretically meaningful. In accordance with an observation originally made by Jean Jacques Rousseau, we assume that the representative relationship changes character after Election Day. At elections, the relationship is about the citizens' choice of leaders for the coming years. Once the election is over, however, the gravity of the relationship shifts towards the actions of representatives in their role as authoritative decision makers.

Below we explicate our reasons for studying the representative relationship in between elections, and how our approach adds to previous research in the field. The final sections of this brief introductory chapter present the individual contributions to the volume and discuss the relevance of the suggested approach in light of the sum of the contributions.

The representative relationship between elections

Empirical research on democratic representation has long recognised that different mechanisms apply at elections and between elections (*see* Arnold and Franklin 2012 for an effective review of the literature). In this research, the representational mechanism associated with elections is *electoral turnover* (Arnold and Franklin 2012). Citizens can bring public policies in line with their preferences by voting for responsible parties and representatives that share their values and views on specific policies, and/or by retrospectively rewarding good representatives and punishing bad ones (Ranney 1954; Miller and Stokes 1963; Converse and Pierce 1986; Klingemann *et al.* 1994; Miller *et al.* 1999; Powell 2004; Achen and Bartels 2004; Golder and Stramski 2010; Naurin 2011). In turn, the mechanism associated with representation between elections is *responsiveness*. According to the responsiveness mechanism, representation is achieved when representatives, in 'rational anticipation' of electoral repercussions, adapt public policies to changes in public demand (Stimson *et al.* 1995), or when citizens adjust their preferences alongside policy (Soroka and Wlezien 2010).

In a corresponding way, political participation research differs between citizen activities inside and outside of the electoral process (Verba *et al.* 1978). Voting and campaign activity are the primary modes of participation associated with elections. In addition, contacting and manifestations are two common modes of participation between elections (*see*, for example, van Deth *et al.* 2007).

Empirical representation research, furthermore, acknowledges the controversial claim that representative democracy is perhaps more elitist and directed from above than is commonly assumed. When phrased in the language of empirical research, the issue of interest is the direction of causality in the representative relationship. Following the lead of Page and Shapiro (1983, 1992); Stimson *et al.* (1995); and Wlezien (1995), this research assesses whether responsiveness processes are directed from above (the relationship is determined by leaders) or from below (the relationship is determined by citizen opinion). Further research examines the extent to which government is responsive to the expressed opinions of all groups of citizens, or whether affluent citizens are more often listened to (Gilens 2005; Bartels 2008; Enns and Wlezien 2011). Similarly, a major concern for participation research is to identify the extent to which citizens speak with equal voices in their communications with government officials (*see*, for example, Verba *et al.* 1995).

Thus, the rich and sophisticated empirical research that targets the representative relationship provides insights on many of the questions recently raised by political theorists. Nevertheless, the working hypothesis for this volume is that we can make advances by relaxing the assumption that representative democracy is essentially a system of government in which the people govern themselves, and by stressing even harder that the representative relationship changes its character after Election Day.

We call to mind that the representative relationship revolves around two different tasks: a) through elections, to empower a select few with the right to make authoritative decisions; and b) for that select few to actually make those authoritative decisions. In a representative system, citizens are directly involved only in the former task, whereas the latter is performed by elected representatives (and by government officials acting on delegations made by the representatives). Referring to these tasks, we distinguish two modes in the representative relationship: *the election mode*, in which citizens select their leaders for the coming mandate period, and *the between-election mode*, in which the elected few exercise the power delegated to them. Our interest lies specifically in the representative relationship in the between-election mode.

To generate new research questions, we highlight two ways in which the representative relationships change character after elections. First, as noted in participation research (Verba *et al.* 1978), and perhaps less clearly in empirical research on representation, the shift between the two modes comes with consequences for the substantive character of the representative relationship. In the election mode, during the process of authorisation, interactions between citizens and their prospective representatives centre on a multitude of policy matters which are discussed more or less simultaneously. In the between-election mode, during the processes of authoritative decision-making, interactions are content specific. This provides representatives with a clearer signal about citizens' wishes and views (*see* Christensen; and Kölln and Aarts in this volume). Concretely, each interaction between citizens and representatives will address an individual issue such as: raising the property tax, regulating the financial market, reducing social security systems (alluding to the book cover) or waging war with a foreign country.

Second, the shift between modes is consequential for the relative power of the respective actor. In the election mode, the collective of citizens formally have the upper hand. In the between-election mode, representatives dominate the relationship; citizens can only *try* to affect the actions of representatives by communicating their wishes and views, and the threat of sanctions at future elections is their primary means of power. This shift of status, we argue, affects how we view the representative relationship.

Referring to their subordinate position between elections, Rousseau famously maintained that citizens vote themselves slaves on Election Day. While provocative, there is a grain of truth to this expression. In principle, between elections the actions of representatives are bound only by what is stipulated in law and not by the expressed opinions of citizens (*see*, for example, Alonso *et al.* 2011). Electoral mechanisms for citizen control, like mandating and accountability through sanctions and rewards, are part of the calculus of representatives (Mayhew 1974; Arnold 1992), but they are not institutional guarantees for adaptive behaviour. In a similar vein, systematic monitoring from citizen organisations may put elected governments 'permanently on their toes' (Keane 2011), but it does not fundamentally alter the representative relationship as understood here. Indicative of the independence of representatives, in most political systems it is impossible for citizens to recall their authorisation in advance of the next election (Cronin 1999).

The strong position of representatives between elections is further emphasised if we follow revisionist political theorists and relax the assumption of a close kinship between Athenian style direct democracy and modern forms of representation. If we no longer hold it axiomatically true that public opinion is, and should be, 'the principal force' in the representative relationship, then this allows electoral mechanisms to be largely inconsequential for the representative relationship. For instance, as will be discussed below, responsiveness processes can be understood as distinctly top-down affairs in which representatives justify their actions but do not adapt to the policy positions of citizens.

The contribution of the volume

Building on the above reasoning, the present volume contributes in three ways to previous research on the representative relationship. First, by thinking broadly about between-election phenomena thus understood, we seek to integrate research literature that studies representative relationships as parallel to each other. The suggested approach helps to clarify that relevant between-election phenomena are studied within research that does not explicitly target political representation. We argue that to think in terms of between-election representation clarifies that the study objects of this literature overlap substantially, which, in turn, facilitates integrated findings.

In particular, we propose that some highly relevant literature has been loosely related to representative democracy because electoral mechanisms are marginally pertinent to the situations they study. Illustratively, in this research, actors who make authoritative decisions are labelled 'politicians', 'policy makers', or 'decision makers' rather than 'representatives'. Once it is acknowledged that these decision makers are representatives (or are acting on delegation from elected representatives), more bodies of literature can contribute substantial insights and theoretical perspectives to the study of the representative relationship between elections.

A chief example of underutilised findings is research on social movements and protest politics.[2] As respectively discussed in this volume by Henrik Serup

---

2. *See* Giugni 1998; Walgrave and Rucht 2009; and Amenta *et al.* 2010 for reviews.

Christensen, Swen Hutter, and Roy Gava, Marco Giugni and Frédéric Varone, a central focus of this research is how citizen organisations influence political decision-making. Although findings from social movement research are informative about representative relationships between elections, they are seldom integrated with research that targets representation. In a similar vein, governance research (Pierre 2000; Sørensen and Torfing 2005), and research on policy feedback mechanisms (Soss and Schram 2007; Campbell 2012), deal with between-election phenomena without explicitly referring to them as such. Furthermore, in Chapter Ten, Gava, Giugni and Varone show how agenda-setting theory (Baumgartner and Jones 2009) relates to responsiveness between elections. Yet another body of literature that can speak more directly to our understanding of representative relationships is political participation research, which has, throughout the years, remained surprisingly loosely coupled with representation theory (*see* Teorell 2006).

The second contribution of our approach relates to the identification of relevant phenomena to study. We believe that a broad between-election approach helps to identify questions that have remained unanswered, or even unidentified, in previous representation research. An example in kind is the chapter by Sofie Marien and Marc Hooghe which observes that, despite many studies on how citizens' political actions influence representatives, we know little about how representatives perceive different forms of participation. Another gap in the literature is identified by Audrey André, Sam Depauw and Kris Deschouwer who draw on a concept from deliberative democratic theory ('issue uptake') to capture the sources from which representatives gather information between elections. In Chapter Nine, Liz Richardson departs from the issue-specific character of representative interactions to analyse how representatives prioritise between interest organisations that contact them for support.

The third contribution of our approach examines 'responsiveness', the primary mechanism for citizen influence on government decision-making between elections. As typically understood, responsiveness is a bottom-up process in which representatives adapt public policies to match public opinion; when citizens change, so do representatives. Other research acknowledges that the process may run the other way, from representatives to citizens (Soroka and Wlezien 2010; Hakhverdian 2012), but responsiveness is still about policy adaptation. However, as developed in the chapter by Peter Esaiasson, Mikael Gilljam and Mikael Persson, from the between-election perspective, responsiveness requires communication, and not accommodation, in the short term. To be responsive, elected representatives must communicate their reason for action but they do not necessarily have to adapt to the current views and opinions of the represented. Empirical analysis, we argue, should acknowledge this broader conceptualisation by gathering information not only about adaptive processes but also about representatives' accounts for their actions, and citizens' reactions to these accounts.

Between-election democracy (BED)

More formally, our interest in this volume is with citizens' attempts to exercise power over authoritative decision-making by means other than voting, and with elected representatives' reactive (and pro-active) responses to the actions citizens take (or might take) to affect authoritative decision-making in the between-election mode. The focus, thus, is on the vertical relationship between elected representatives and citizens (Esaiasson and Heidar 2000). Horizontal relations between elected representatives in elected assemblies, and between elected representatives and other political decision-makers, are less central. We will use *between-election democracy* (BED) as a summary term for all relevant interactions between representatives and the represented.

Logically, the representative relationship can be studied from various points of observation, from below, from above, and from a systems perspective. When studied from below, the analysis works from the standpoint of citizens and their organisations. When studied from above, the analysis centres on the actions of representatives. Finally, when studied from a systems perspective, the focus of interest is on responsiveness processes and other types of continuous interactions between the two actors.

It should be emphasised that the distinction between 'election mode' and 'between-election mode' is central to our reasoning. As understood here, BED is less about time (between-election periods versus election campaigns) than about the purpose of contacts (influencing decision making versus the selection of representatives). Although the two modes may overlap – accountability concerns likely weigh on representatives as Election Day approaches – we believe it is analytically useful to acknowledge that representatives are principally free to follow their own best judgment when deciding common matters.

Furthermore, we intend our definition to be descriptive rather than prescriptive. We propose that empirical analysis of the representative relationship between elections should cover a broader group of phenomena than is common today but we do not advance a particular normative understanding of preferred conditions. Indeed, issues about the democratic qualities of the representative relationship are best addressed by other analytical means than the ones under consideration here.

Individual contributions

The introduction lays out our reasoning for empirical research, the remaining contributions explore the relevance of this approach. To better understand the representative relationship, each chapter presents an original analysis of BED phenomena.

Chapter Two, *Communicative Responsiveness and Other Central Concepts in Between-Election Democracy*, by Peter Esaiasson, Mikael Gilljam and Mikael Persson, is primarily conceptual. It details some matters of delineations in BED that are introduced above. In particular, it develops the idea of a communicative understanding of responsiveness which, in contrast to traditional understandings, acknowledges that responsiveness does not necessarily require adaptation from representatives, and that both majorities and minorities among the citizenry have a right to a responsive government.

The remaining eight contributions are concerned with a specific aspect of the representative relationship between elections. Each chapter looks for commonalities between different lines of research; suggests a new conceptualisation of BED phenomena; and/or addresses empirical questions that have remained unanswered in previous research. The contributions are organised under three headings: between-election democracy from above (from the perspective of representatives); from below (from the perspective of citizens); and from a systems perspective (from the perspective of continuous interactions between representatives and citizens).

Between-election democracy from above

The substantial literature that studies BED phenomena suffers from a systematic bias – the world of elected representatives is far less researched than the world of citizens. Chapter Three, *Is Anyone Listening?*, by Sofie Marien and Marc Hooghe, begins to address this imbalance. It offers a rare analysis of how elected representatives perceive the effectiveness of different forms of citizen participation. Using MP survey data from eight European countries, Marien and Hooghe find that representatives ascribe greater importance to traditional forms of participation related to elections and political parties than to alternative modes of participation like internet discussions, boycotts and illegal protests.

Chapter Four, by Audrey André, Sam Depauw and Kris Deschouwer, targets representatives' information-seeking activities with regard to the wishes and views of citizens and citizen organisations. For this purpose André *et al.* develop the concept of 'issue uptake', which originates in deliberative theory. Specifically, issue uptake refers to the sources – unorganised constituents, organised interests, the party and the mass media – from which representatives gather information for actions in parliament. André *et al.* use this concept to investigate information-seeking activities across thirteen national and regional parliaments in Europe. They find systematic differences in uptake between electoral systems and between individual representatives, and that, in turn, this uptake shapes the way representatives act in parliament.

In *Nominations, Campaigning and Representation* (Chapter Five), Rune Karlsen and Hanne Marthe Narud focus on the role of political parties and party leadership in the representative relationship. Their interest lies in the party leaders' potential to control the actions of representatives through the nomination of candidates for elected offices. Karlsen and Narud draw on agency literature to develop a specified theory that links nomination procedures before election campaigns to the conduct of candidates during campaigns and after elections during the representatives' terms in office. The viability of the theory is tested through a study on Norwegian candidates. In accordance with theoretical expectations, they find that representatives' campaign styles and role orientations are highly party centred.

Between-election democracy from below

This section of the volume shifts the attention from representatives to citizens. Chapter Six, *Institutional Incentives for Participation in Elections and Between Elections* by Henrik Serup Christensen, sets out to integrate theories of social movement research with individually oriented participation research. Christensen looks specifically at political opportunity structure theory and investigates the extent to which various indicators of institutional openness can account for individual-level variations in different modes of participation. Drawing on data from the first round of the 2002 European Social Survey, he finds that institutional openness is negatively associated with petitions, demonstrations and illegal protests. The main finding, however, is that a prominent theory within the collectively oriented social movement research is less successful in accounting for individual-level variations in political participation in and between elections.

Swen Hutter's *Political Parties in the Streets* (Chapter Seven) takes a reversed approach to theoretical integration by studying how a major actor in electoral politics engages an arena typically reserved for social movement research. Hutter's research question concerns the extent to which political parties' activities in the streets reflect electoral incentives. In other words, are political parties' protest actions between elections coloured by their participation in elections? To answer this question, Hutter draws on two longitudinal sets of protest data from Britain, France, Germany and the Netherlands. Overall, he finds that political parties quite frequently protest in the streets and that there is little support for an electoral cycle hypothesis in this regard.

Chapter Eight, *Signalling Through Vote Intention Polls Between Elections* by Ann-Kristin Kölln and Kees Aarts, lays out a theory on how citizens signal their political preferences between elections by means of political opinion polls. In developing their theory, Kölln and Aarts compare signalling through vote intention polls with other types of political participation between elections, and argue that polling is a form of non-electoral participation that deserves to be studied in its own right. Kölln and Aarts generate a set of hypotheses and test these on a multi-wave panel of Dutch voters. The hypotheses are largely supported by the data and they conclude that vote intention between elections can indeed be seen as yet another means by which citizens signal satisfaction and dissatisfaction with government parties.

Between-election democracy from a system perspective

The final section of the volume deals with dynamic aspects of the representative relationship. The experimental method is seldom used for studies on responsiveness mechanisms, but Liz Richardson's chapter *'We Need to Decide!:' A mixed method approach to responsiveness and equal treatment,* reports findings from two independent field experiments involving interest organisations and local representatives in England. Her findings show that representatives are not easily manipulated by better resourced interest organisations, and follow-up, qualitative interviews provide further insights into how representatives reason when they prioritise among competing demands. Overall, the chapter demonstrates how representatives use political and ideological cues when they go about being responsive.

Chapter Ten, *The Impact of Social Movements on Agenda-Setting: Bringing the real world back in* by Roy Gava, Marco Giugni and Frédéric Varone, theorises the impact of protest activities on the parliamentary agenda. Precisely, they develop a theory that bridges social movement research and agenda-setting research, two bodies of literature that focus on BED phenomena but from different perspectives. Following a review of the respective literature, Gava *et al.* set up a model for research that includes the following variables: protest activities, political alliances, public opinion and real-world indicators. Their suggested model adds a control variable to social movement theory ('real-world indicators'), and a mediator variable to agenda-setting theory ('protest activities'). Gava *et al.* also provide a first empirical test of the model. Results from two Swiss case studies are mixed, but overall factors from agenda-setting research (primarily real-world indicators) exert a stronger impact on parliamentary agendas than protest activities. Their preliminary empirical conclusion is that representatives 'appear to be more influenced by "objective" conditions than by protest activities'.

Looking beyond the current volume

Before turning to individual chapters, we will briefly evaluate the prospect of the BED approach proving useful for future research on the relationship between citizens and their representatives. In light of the analytical perspectives and empirical findings presented in the chapters that follow, is it fruitful to pursue the ideas under discussion?

We argue that the answer to this question is in the affirmative. The potential for integrating findings from different lines of research is demonstrated in the chapters by Christensen, Hutter, and Gava *et al.*, respectively, which all relate representation research to social movement research. There is every reason to believe that further insights can be gained from developing their respective analytical perspectives and from searching for commonalities between representation research and other parallel literature such as governance research and policy feedback theories.

Other contributions illustrate the benefits of asking new questions about the representative relationship between elections. Marien and Hooghe remind us of the need to study the representative relationship from the perspective of elected representatives. Similarly, Richardson, as well as Gava *et al.*, show that studies that focus on the representative relationship from a dynamic systems perspective may generate important findings. Richardson, furthermore, exemplifies the relevance of looking at responsiveness dynamics with regard to specific political issues and representation at levels other than the nation state. Moreover, ambitious analytical ideas like 'issue uptake' (André *et al.*), signalling through vote intention polls' (Kölln and Aarts), and 'linking nominations, campaigning and representational style' (Karlsen and Narud) generate intriguing questions for empirical research.

Finally, the idea of communicative responsiveness (Esaiasson *et al.*), opens up an array of research questions about the actions of representatives, as well as the consequences that follow from these actions. For instance, if communicative responsiveness is seen as a procedural requirement for fair representation between elections, we need to learn more about how communicative responsiveness actions from representatives are perceived by those affected by them.

Several decades ago, one of the leading figures in the first generation of empirical scholars in the field referred to representation as a 'puzzle' (Eulau 1967). To cultivate the BED approach along the lines laid out in this volume is yet another attempt to grapple with the representative system in all its wonderful complexity.

References

Achen, C. and Bartels, L. (2004) 'Blind retrospection. Electoral responses to drought, flu, and shark attacks', Estudio/Working Paper 2004/199, June 2004.

Alonso, S., Keane, J. and Merkel, W. (2011) 'Editors' introduction: Rethinking the future of representative democracy', in Alonso, S., Keane, J. and Merkel, W. (eds) *The Future of Representative Democracy*, Cambridge: Cambridge University Press.

Amenta, E., Caren, N., Chiarello, E. and Su, Y. (2010) 'The political consequences of social movements', *Annual Review of Sociology*, 36: 287–307.

Arnold, C. and Franklin, M. (2012) 'Introduction: Issue congruence and political responsiveness', in Arnold, C. and Franklin, M. (eds), *Assessing political representation in Europe*, (special issue) *West European Politics*, 35: 1217–25.

Arnold, D. (1992) *The Logic of Congressional Action*, New Haven, Conn.: Yale University Press.

Bartels, L. (2008) *Unequal Democracy: The political economy of the new gilded age*, Princeton, NJ: Princeton University Press.

Baumgartner, F. and Jones, B. (2009) *Agendas and Instability in American Politics* (2nd edn), Chicago: Chicago University Press.

Campbell, A. L. (2012) 'Policy makes mass politics', *Annual Review of Political Science*, 15: 333–51.

Converse, P. and Pierce, R. (1986) *Political Representation in France*, Cambridge, Mass.: Harvard University Press.

Cronin, T. (1999) *Direct Democracy: The politics of initiative, referendum, and recall*, Cambridge, Mass.: Harvard University Press.

Dahl, R. (1971) *Polyarchy: Participation and opposition*, New Haven, Conn.: Yale University Press.

—— (1989) *Democracy and Its Critics*, New Haven, Conn: Yale University Press.

Disch, L. (2011) 'Toward a mobilisation conception of democratic representation', *American Political Science Review*, 105: 100–14.

Enns, P. K. and Wlezien, C. (eds) (2011) *Who Gets Represented?*, New York: The Russell Sage Foundation.

Erikson, R., MacKuen, M. and Stimson, J. (2002) *The Macro Polity*, Cambridge: Cambridge University Press.

Esaiasson, P. and Heidar, K. (2000) 'The age of representative democracy', in Esaiasson, P. and Heidar, K. (eds) *Beyond Westminster and Congress: The Nordic experience*, Columbus: Ohio State University Press.

Eulau, H. (1967) 'Changing views of representation', in de Sola Pool, I. (ed.) *Contemporary Political Science: Toward empirical theory*, New York: McGraw Hill.

Eulau, H. and Karps, P. (1977) 'The puzzle of representation', *Legislative Studies Quarterly*, 2: 233–54.

Gilens, M. (2005) 'Inequality and democratic responsiveness', *Public Opinion Quarterly*, 69: 778–96.

Giugni, M. (1998) 'Was it worth the effort? The outcomes and consequences of social movements', *Annual Review of Sociology,* 24: 371–93.

Golder, M. and Stramski, J. (2010) 'Ideological congruence and electoral institutions', *American Journal of Political Science,* 54: 90–106.

Granberg, D. and Holmberg, S. (1988) *The Political System Matters: Social psychology and voting behavior in Sweden and the United States,* Cambridge: Cambridge University Press.

Hakhverdian, A. (2012) 'The causal flow between public opinion and policy: government responsiveness, leadership, or counter movement', in Arnold, C. and Franklin, M. (eds) *Assessing political representation in Europe,* (special issue) *West European Politics,* 35: 1386–1406.

Keane, J. (2009) *The Life and Death of Democracy,* London: Simon and Schuster.

— (2011) 'Monitory democracy?', in Alonso, S., Keane, J. and Merkel, W. (eds) *The Future of Representative Democracy,* Cambridge: Cambridge University Press.

Key, V. O. (1966) *The Responsible Electorate,* Cambridge, MA: Harvard University Press.

Klingemann, H-D., Hofferbert, R. and Budge, I. (1994) *Parties, Policies, and Democracy,* Boulder, CO: Westview Press.

Manin, B. (1997) *The Principles of Representative Government,* Cambridge: Cambridge University Press.

Mansbridge, J. (2003) 'Rethinking representation', *American Political Science Review,* 97: 515–28.

Mayhew, D. (1974) *Congress: The electoral connection,* New Haven, Conn.: Yale University Press.

Miller, W., Pierce, R., Thomassen, J., Herrera, R., Holmberg, S., Esaiasson, P. and Wessels, B. (1999) *Policy Representation in Western Democracies,* Oxford, UK: Oxford University Press.

Miller, W. and Stokes, D. (1963) 'Constituency influence in Congress', *American Political Science Review,* 57: 45–56.

Naurin, E. (2011) *Election Promises, Party Behaviour, and Voter Perceptions,* Basingstoke: Palgrave Macmillan.

Ober, J. (2008) 'The original meaning of "democracy": Capacity to do things, not majority rule', *Constellation,* 15.

Page, B. and Shapiro, R. (1983) 'Effects of public opinion on policy', *American Political Science Review,* 77: 175–90.

— (1992) *The Rational Public: Fifty years of trends in Americans' public preferences,* Chicago: University of Chicago Press.

Pateman, C. (1970) *Participation and Democratic Theory,* Cambridge: Cambridge University Press.

Pierre, J. (ed.) (2000) *Debating Governance: Authority, steering, and democracy,* Oxford: Oxford University Press.

Pitkin, H. (1967) *The Concept of Representation,* Berkeley and Los Angeles: University of California Press.

—   (2004) 'Representation and democracy: Uneasy alliance', *Scandinavian Political Studies*, 27: 335–42.

Powell, G. B. (2004) 'The chain of responsiveness', *Journal of Democracy*, 15: 91–105.

Ranney, A. (1954) *The Doctrine of Responsible Party Government*, Urbana, IL: University of Illinois Press.

Riker, W. (1982) *Liberalism Against Populism: A confrontation between the theory of democracy and the theory of social choice*, San Francisco: W.H. Freeman.

Sørensen, E. and Torfing, J. (2005) 'The democratic anchorage of governance networks', *Scandinavian Political Studies*, 28: 195–218.

Soroka, S. and Wlezien, C. (2010) *Degrees of Democracy: Politics, public opinion, and policy*, Cambridge: Cambridge University Press.

Soss, J. and Schram, S. (2007) 'A public transformed? Welfare reform as policy feedback', *American Political Science Review*, 101: 111–27.

Stimson, J., Mackuen, M. and Erikson, R. (1995) 'Dynamic representation', *American Political Science Review*, 89: 543–65.

Sunstein, C. (1991) 'Preferences and politics', *Philosophy and Public Affairs*, 20: 3–34.

Teorell, J. (2006) 'Political participation and three theories of democracy: A research inventory and agenda', *European Journal of Political Research*, 45: 787–810.

Urbinati, N. (2006) *Representative Democracy: Principles and genealogy*, Chicago: Chicago University Press.

Urbinati, N. and Warren, M. (2008) 'The concept of representation in contemporary democratic theory', *Annual Review of Political Science*, 11: 387–412.

van Deth, J., Montero, J. R. and Westholm, A. (eds) (2007) *Citizenship and Involvement in European Democracies: A comparative perspective*, London: Routledge.

Verba, S., Nie, N. and Kim, J-O. (1978) *Participation and Political Equality: A seven-nation comparison*, Cambridge: Cambridge University Press.

Verba, S., Schlozman, K. L. and Brady, H. (1995) *Voice and Equality: Civic voluntarism in American politics*, Cambridge, Mass: Harvard University Press.

Walgrave, S. and Rucht, D. (2009) *Protest Politics: Demonstrations against the war on Iraq in the US and Western Europe*, Minneapolis: University of Minnesota Press.

Wlezien, C. (1995) 'The public as thermostat: Dynamics of preferences for spending', *American Journal of Political Science*, 39: 981–1000.

Chapter Two

Communicative Responsiveness and Other Central Concepts in Between-Election Democracy

Peter Esaiasson, Mikael Gilljam and Mikael Persson

This book examines how the representative relationship works between elections, when elected representatives exercise their right to decide common matters, and those affected by the decisions can only try to influence decision making. As was laid out in the introduction, the effort is inspired by recent advances in representation theory which portray representative democracy as a system of government in its own right, different in kind from direct democracy (Manin 1997; Mansbridge 2003; Disch 2011; Urbinati 2006). Essential for our approach to the topic, these theories depict the representative relationship as bidirectional and frequently under the command of representatives, rather than as unidirectional and ultimately controlled from below.

The introductory chapter mapped out the basis of our approach to between-election democracy (BED). This chapter continues the discussion on how to conceptualise and study the representative relationship in the between-election mode. The aim is to further substantiate claims that the BED approach contributes to research in the field.

Specifically, the introductory chapter identified three ways in which the approach enhances our common understanding of the representative relationship: it facilitates integration of lines of research that study the representative relationship parallel to each other; it identifies new empirical questions; and it suggests a re-conceptualisation of the crucial notion of 'responsiveness'. Of relevance for the two initial claims, the first section of the chapter deals with questions of delineation. In operational terms, which phenomena reasonably qualify as relevant for BED? More precisely, the section discusses operational definitions in empirical research and relates them to some of the themes under discussion among representation theorists.

The chapter then turns to the conceptualisation of responsiveness. That elected representatives are responsive to the wishes and views of the represented is generally considered a necessary condition for democratic representation (Pitkin 1967; Dahl 1971). This section explicates the reasons for adopting a communicative understanding of responsiveness, and provides an initial empirical test of its relevance on data pertaining to both citizens and members of parliament. A third and final section offers concluding remarks.

Between-election democracy: Operational criterion

According to the definition offered in Chapter One, BED is about citizens' attempts to exercise power over authoritative decision-making by means other than voting, and elected representatives' reactive (and proactive) responses to the actions citizens take (or might take) to affect authoritative decision-making in the between-election mode. While this gives a general idea about the relevant real-world phenomena, a number of questions arise as we strive to make our approach useful for empirical analysis.

The discussion centres on four components which figure in most theoretical accounts of political representation (Dovi 2011): *some part that is representing* (who are the representatives?); *some part that is being represented* (who are the represented?); *something that is being represented* (what is the substance of the representative relationship?); and *a setting within which the activity of representation is taking place* (which are the relevant institutional arrangements?).

Who are the representatives?

Representation theory is increasingly concerned with non-electoral venues for representation in which self-authorised agents make representative claims (Saward 2006). A major task for this research is to develop a general theory of representation that is independent of the precise institutional arrangements for the authorisation of representatives (Rhefeld 2006). The BED approach looks exclusively at electoral authorisation and therefore has a narrower scope. However, by directing attention towards self-authorised representatives, theorists are opening up new avenues for empirical research. For example, contrasting elected representatives with self-authorised representatives will provide a much needed reference point for estimates of how electoral authorisation affects the representative relationship.

Electoral authorisation, thus, is the first criterion for identifying the relevant representatives. An additional criterion refers to the unit of analysis, whether it is individual representatives or collectives of representatives in party groups and/or decision-making institutions. Because electoral authorisation is tied to territorially defined electoral districts, the critical question here concerns the formal bonds between representatives and the represented. If formal authorisation is a requirement for inclusion in this criterion, the relevant representatives are those who stand in a direct electoral relationship with the represented. In single-member district electoral systems the unit of analysis would be individual representatives, and in multi-member electoral systems it would be small groups of representatives. However, if one takes a more relaxed approach to formal authorisation, analytical interest may lie with larger collectives of elected representatives that lack electoral relations with specific groups of citizens.

Notably, this is an area in which representation theory has been struggling to make the formal conform with the observed (Urbinati and Warren 2008). Standard representation theory focuses on territorially defined electoral districts which, in the case of the US, translates to a dyadic relationship between representatives and the represented from a specified electoral district. However, since many political matters are non-territorial in character, theorists agree that this approach leaves crucial real-world relationships unaccounted for (Urbinati and Warren 2008). It can be noted that Jane Mansbridge's (2003) recent typology over forms of representation covers both territorial and non-territorial types of relationships: 'promissory', 'anticipatory', and 'gyroscopic' representation is about territorial (dyadic) relationships, whereas 'surrogate' representation is about non-territorial (collective) relationships. Tellingly for the limitations that come with a focus on territorially defined electoral districts, the term 'surrogate' indicates a relationship in which the representative cannot fully play their part.

Empirical research in the field has been less hampered by constitutional formalities. The line of research which originates in the work of Warren Miller and Donald Stokes (1963), focuses on individual representatives and their relation to specific districts (*see also* Achen 1977; Fenno 1978; Converse and Pierce 1986). Other lines of research study the collectives of representatives that are not formally tied to a specific group of authorising citizens. For instance, policy responsiveness research compares public opinion data with measures of policy outputs that result from collective decision-making institutions (Erikson *et al.* 2002; Soroka and Wlezien 2010). Within research that targets representation (rather than responsiveness), Herbert Weissberg (1978) was one of the first to distinguish between dyadic and collective representation. In the contexts of PR electoral systems, party collectives and collective representative bodies have always been the focal interest for representation research (e.g. Holmberg 1974, 1989; Thomassen 1976, 1994). Moreover, ever since their introduction in the US election studies in the 1950s, survey measures of voters' perceived system responsiveness have usually targeted government institutions as collectives (Chamberlain 2012).[1]

From a BED perspective, both formal (individual) and informal (collective) relationships are relevant. However, since most authoritative decisions are made collectively, the primary interest is directed towards the joint actions of representatives within decision-making institutions, and hence towards informal representative relationships.

The final criterion for identification of the relevant representatives relates to the complexities of authoritative decision-making in developed societies. Representative systems require the delegation of decision-making power in multiple steps: elected representatives make appointments, and those appointees, in turn, make further appointments (Mansbridge 2012). Therefore, a central operational question is how far along the line of delegation empirical studies should walk.

---

1. A typical survey item to measure perceived responsiveness runs as follows: 'People like me don't have any say about what the government does'. To our knowledge, no study has probed the responsiveness of individual representatives: 'People like me don't have any say about what my representative does in parliament/the US Congress'.

At some point in the process that transforms policy proposals into policy outcomes the line of delegation is stretched so thin that the relationship between decision makers and citizens changes character (input-politics turn into output-politics) (Naurin 2011). It is hardly meaningful to suggest generally applicable boundary conditions but the issue deserves attention. Consider for example that contacts with civil servants and other bureaucrats are included in the standard repertoire of political activities within participation research (e.g. Teorell *et al.* 2007). From a BED perspective, this type of participation that researchers study touches the periphery of the representative relationship.

Who are the represented?

According to the standard account of representation, the relevant citizens are those who are in a dyadic electoral relationship with specific representatives. By this criterion, BED analyses should depart from citizens' territorial residence and focus on their interactions with designated representatives. Indeed, as discussed above, a main feature of the standard account is that inhabitants of a certain place elect agents to act on their behalf in the representative assembly (Castiglione and Warren 2008). However, since BED centers on collective political decision-making, all citizens' political actions become relevant. Hence, the criterion for inclusion must centre around political action that influences authoritative decision-making, not the formal electoral relationship with representatives.

For BED analyses, territorial ties are best understood as variables for research and not as factors of delineation. To exemplify, a task for empirical research is to estimate the extent to which formal territorial ties affect citizens' propensity to engage in political actions between elections. Furthermore, as defined here, the BED approach applies to citizen actions beyond nation state borders. For instance, European mass protests against US plans to wage war against Iraq can reasonably be conceived as relevant BED phenomena.

In addition to geography, at least two more factors are important when identifying applicable groups of citizens. First, it should be acknowledged that most citizen actions to influence authoritative decision-making are collective in character; organisation is the means through which individual citizens try to influence representatives in the between-election mode (Rosanvallon 2008). From this it follows that organised activities to protest unwelcome political conditions are BED phenomena.[2]

The operational question here is which parts of associational life – civic associations or interest groups – constitute the represented in the representational relationship? Precisely, what types of organisations with political goals are instruments for citizen influence, and what types of organisations are agents for

---

2.   See Amenta *et al.* (2010) for a discussion on pertinent questions within social movement research: Under what conditions do citizens form protest groups? What are the conditions that trigger overt protests? How effective are different types of protests at influencing political decisions?

other causes? We see little reason to suggest precise lines of demarcation. However, it appears reasonable to view market actors like business organisations and trade unions as well as professional lobbying organisations as different in category from citizen associations.

The final factor of importance relates to the role of political parties. Fundamental institutions for modern, representative democracy, parties are intimately linked to elections (Dalton *et al.* 2011) but they are also mediators between citizens and the state outside the electoral realm (Rucht 1996; Kitschelt 2003; Hutter in this volume). The role of parties is further complicated by their dual function in the representative process. In contrast to social movements, whose main function is to express citizen grievances, parties are two-way mediators. On the one hand they provide citizens with an arena for participation in the decision-making process; on the other hand they are organisations for top-down political communication (Rosenblum 2008; Karlsen and Narud in this volume).

The role of parties in BED analysis requires careful consideration.[3] To capture citizen involvement we need to differentiate between parties as arenas for participation and as organisations for top-down communication. Furthermore, within the arena function we should differentiate between party activities in the election mode and in the between-election mode. Citizen engagement in campaign activities like donating money and working on campaigns is part of the election mode of the representative relationship, whereas party engagement outside campaigns is relevant for BED relationships. Reflecting upon operational details of participation research, it can be noted that scholars working within the US context tend to focus on campaign aspects of party engagement (*see* Verba and Nie 1972) while scholars from other national contexts typically highlight broader forms of engagement (*see* Teorell *et al.* 2007).

What constitutes the representative relationship?

Representation theories disagree over the substance of representation. Is it about the objectively defined interests of the represented or about subjectively defined preferences and demands (Disch 2011)? This distinction is actually less important here. (It will, however, appear below in the discussion on responsiveness.) Rather, our suggested approach is concerned with manifest behaviour and with the beliefs and evaluations associated with that behaviour.

As conceived here, representation is a dynamic process that involves continuous interactions between representatives and the represented: representatives take actions (make decisions) that generate supportive and non-supportive reactions from citizens and citizens express demands that require responses from representatives (Mansbridge 2003; Urbinati 2006; Disch 2011). When the representational process is understood in this way, a broad array of manifest activities qualify as relevant phenomena.

---

3. Interestingly, theorists still struggle to identify a positive role for political parties in normative accounts of the representative relationship (Urbinati and Warren 2008).

Viewed from below – from the perspective of citizens – BED encompasses all ways in which citizens communicate their preferences, opinions and demands to representatives. Participation research conceptualises individual activities in terms of contacts, manifestations, party engagement and protests (*see*, for example, Verba *et al.* 1995; Teorell *et al.* 2007; Christensen in this volume; Marien and Hooghe in this volume). Correspondingly, from the organisational perspective, social movement research observes a steadily growing 'repertoire of contention' (Tilly 2008).

It can be noted that political consumerism – to boycott and buycott in order to influence market actors' ethical conduct (Stolle *et al.* 2005) – stands in a complicated relationship with BED. Because it primarily targets market actors a strict application of the criterion of electoral authorisation implies that political consumerism falls outside the category of relevant phenomena. However, to the extent that political consumerism aims to generate political pressure on market actors, it is comparable with other forms of participation.

Viewed from above – from the perspective of representatives – the relevant activities by representatives involve decision making as well as efforts to keep informed about citizen opinions and to shape public opinion. Reflecting on an imbalance in empirical research, it can be noted that these forms of elite actions are less thoroughly conceptualised than citizen activities (but *see* Audrey *et al.* in this volume).

Relevant activities, moreover, go beyond the modes of participation. Crucially important in representation theory (Pitkin 1967; Mansbridge 2003; Urbinati 2006; Disch 2011), but less often observed in empirical representation research, are the communicative and deliberative aspects of the representative relationship. Thus, we can ask, what specific demands are made by citizens, how are these demands motivated, and how do representatives justify their reasons for actions in controversial matters? This aspect of the discussion is further developed in the following section on responsiveness.

Furthermore, the representative relationship in the between-election mode involves beliefs and evaluations associated with activities from each side of the relationship. When viewed from below, relevant beliefs and evaluations concern, for example, the competence and integrity of elected representatives. The extensive empirical research into the political trust and support of the citizenry testifies to the importance generally ascribed to this aspect of the representative relationship (e.g. Dalton 2004). When viewed from above, corresponding beliefs and evaluations concern, for example, representatives' views on the motives for citizen engagement in politics and the effectiveness of various forms of citizen participation. Reflecting once more on the lack of empirical research on representatives, there is only scarce systematic evidence on topics like these (such as from Esaiasson and Holmberg 1996; Gilljam *et al.* 2012; Marien and Hooghe in this volume).

A final criterion for inclusion is one that deals with the dynamics of representative relationships. As it evolves in the real-world, BED is about authoritative decision-making on specific political issues; representatives and citizens communicate over matters like increased taxes, welfare state retrenchments and the siting of unwelcome public facilities. Moreover, each decision-making process goes through stages like issue identification, policy formulation, decision, implementation and evaluation. Each issue and each stage are instances of relevant phenomena and, accordingly, merit empirical attention.

Examining research in the field, it seems clear that the modal analytical approach is to generalise across issues and stages. For instance, participation research typically maps citizen engagement during a prolonged period of time (with questions such as: 'for each activity below, tell me if you have done it in the past twelve months'), and trust research probes citizens' global evaluations of institutions, actors and processes ('overall, how satisfied are you with the way in which democracy works in your country?'). There are good theoretical and practical reasons for these kinds of analytical generalisations. However, to fully capture the dynamic character of between-election democracy, there is a need for complementary analytical approaches that study the communication between citizens and representatives on specific issues as well as within and/or across stages.

Where are the relevant settings?

Between-election democracy takes place within the setting of a formal representative system: an assembly of representatives are authorised through elections to make binding decisions in common matters, and while in power – in the between-election mode – they communicate with citizens about legitimate ways to exercise their privileged right. Such representative systems are not only found at the level of nation states but also at sub-national levels, in regions and local communities. Moreover, the European Union provides a real-world example of a supra-national representative system. All of these representative systems are relevant settings for BED research (*see*, for example, Richardson in this volume).

Summary overview

Table 2.1 summarises the contours and boundaries of the representative relationship in the between-election mode. The landscape that emerges is wide, but it is also well researched in different bodies of literature. If useful for empirical analysis, the suggested approach will help to integrate findings from several lines of research (which, to date, proceeded parallel to one another), as well as identify questions that have remained unanswered in previous empirical research. The chapters that follow exemplify how this can be achieved. Additional suggestions for research have been made throughout the section above, including more emphasis on deliberative processes in the representative relationship; on analyses from the perspective of representatives ('from above'); on representative processes at the sub-national level; and on the dynamics related to decision-making on specific issues, along with the comparison between self-authorised and election-authorised representatives.

Table 2.1: A summary of the contours and boundaries of BED phenomena

Components of the representative relationship	Criteria for inclusion
Who are the representatives?	Elected representatives (including one or more lines of delegation)
	AND
	Collectives of representatives in decision-making institutions
	OR
	Individual representatives from a specific electoral district
Who are the represented?	Individual citizens that take political action (unbounded by territorial factors)
	OR
	Civic organisations for political action (but not market organisations and professional lobbyists)
	OR
	Political parties as arenas for citizen participation
What constitutes the relationship?	Actions taken in relation to representative decision-making by citizens and by representatives
	OR
	Generalised and particular beliefs and evaluations about these actions, the actors who take them, and the representational system in which the actors operate
	AND
	All phases of decision-making processes (identification, formulation, decision, implementation and evaluation)
What are the relevant settings?	National, sub-national and supra-national representational systems

Communicative responsiveness

Responsiveness is a central component in the representative relationship in the between-election mode. It is central because it addresses the paradoxical character of the representative relationship: representatives have the right to decide common matters according to their own best judgment, but in exercising their privilege they must act to preserve the autonomy of the represented (Pitkin 1967; Powell 2004; Dovi 2011). Responsiveness is the mechanism through which this complex relationship is maintained between elections.

This section discusses how responsiveness should be conceptualised within the BED framework. The basic idea of responsiveness is straightforward: representatives should take the views of the represented into account when they decide common matters. In dispute, however, is the nature of this relationship. Is the process distinctly bottom-up, running from citizens to their representatives, or is it best understood as dynamic and interactive?

According to a (standard) bottom-up understanding, responsiveness occurs when representatives adjust to match majority positions among the citizenry; as the citizens change their views, so do the representatives. Dating back to the seminal work on constituency representation by Miller and Stokes (1963) and by Achen (1977), this bottom-up conception is the typical approach in empirical research (e.g. Jennings 2009; Lax and Phillips 2009) and in research that theorises about the traditional understanding of the representative relationship (e.g. Przeworski *et al.* 1999). While not always explicitly stated, responsiveness is similarly understood in most research on social movements and protest politics (e.g. Klandermans and Roggeband 2009).

The bottom-up approach to responsiveness is appealing as it corresponds to the notion that representative government should 'form and implement policies that the citizens want' (Powell 2004). This notwithstanding, it fits poorly with the understanding of the representative relationship that underlies the BED approach. To see why, consider that the bottom-up approach assumes that citizens' policy preferences are exogenous to the representative process (Kuklinski and Segura 1995) and, more generally, that citizen preferences are the starting point for the representative relationship. As discussed in Chapter One, these assumptions are questioned by representation theorists. One reason for this is that the approach sits uneasily with the inherently elitist characteristics of the representative process identified by revisionist theorists (e.g. Manin 1997). Moreover, as observed by Lisa Disch (2011), empirical findings about preference formation 'defy this static portrait of preferences together with this linear dyadic model of influence'. Disch (2011) goes on to conclude that 'there is an emerging consensus that political representation need not and cannot take preferences as its starting place and ground'.

For reasons like these, some representation theorists advance a dynamic understanding of the representative relationship in which representatives take an active role in shaping (or trying to shape) citizen preferences and views. For example, Mansbridge's forward-looking 'anticipatory representation' allows representatives to change (and potentially manipulate) voter preferences (2003).[4]

When representatives are ascribed the freedom to shape citizens' opinions, we argue, responsiveness takes on a new meaning. A specification of responsiveness

---

4.   Within empirical research, Soroka and Wlezien's (2010) 'thermostatic model of opinion and policy' only considers such public preferences that are responsive to changes in policy. Their model, thus, deals with the problems of fickle attitudes among the citizenry, but it does not address the question of the manipulation of public opinion by the elite.

along these lines already appeared in Hanna Pitkin's classic *The Concept of Representation* (1967). Importantly, in Pitkin's account the starting place for representation is the interest of citizens and not their views and preferences: '[r]epresentation here means acting in the interest of the represented' (1967). By emphasising citizen interests rather than their current preferences, the definition assures representatives autonomy in the representative relationship. To preserve the necessary balance between the two parts a qualification is added: representatives 'must not be found persistently at odds with the wishes of the represented *without good reason* in terms of their interest, *without a good explanation* of why their wishes are not in accord with their interest' (Pitkin 1967, emphasis added). In concrete terms, thus, representatives are ascribed the freedom to go against public opinion, but also the duty to give convincing accounts of their actions to the represented.

When understood in this way, we maintain, responsiveness is a promise of communication, not of adaption in the short term. Representatives are obliged to communicate their reason for action, but not necessarily to adapt to the current views and opinions of citizens and groups of citizens. Citizens have an independent and active role in the process, first by expressing their wishes and views to representatives, and then by reacting to the way in which representatives account for their actions. By implication, representatives and the represented may disagree over responsiveness. Provided that representatives can account for their actions, they can reasonably claim to be 'responsive'. At the same time, the represented might disapprove of the accounts presented to them and, accordingly, perceive the representatives to be 'unresponsive'.

In keeping with the BED approach, a communicative understanding of responsiveness identifies a broad group of phenomena for empirical research. Specifically, and in addition to the important work on adaptive processes (e.g. Wlezien 2004; Soroka and Wlezien 2010), interest is directed towards representatives' accounts of their actions, and to citizen reaction to these accounts.

Precisely, under a communicative understanding, representatives can be responsive towards citizens in different ways. For example, they can follow a bottom-up route to responsiveness by partly or completely adapting to the current preferences of citizens. Alternatively, they can inform themselves about the wishes and views of citizens and thereafter explicate their reasons for nevertheless holding firm to their own initial views. From this it follows that responsiveness involves at least three types of manifest behaviour on the part of representatives: they act to keep themselves informed about citizen opinion (they listen), they provide accounts for their decisions (they explain); and they decide policy matters in accordance with citizens' current preferences (they adapt).[5]

---

5. Partly overlapping with the typology suggested here, Paul Schumaker (1975) draws on policy-making theory to distinguish between five types of responsiveness: access, agenda, policy, output and impact responsiveness. Similar to the topic of 'agenda responsiveness' is Hobolt and Klemmensen's (2008) study of 'rhetorical responsiveness'.

Moreover, each act of responsiveness generates a reaction from citizens in terms of responsiveness judgments, namely: the extent to which representatives are perceived as having (i) kept themselves informed about citizen wishes and views; (ii) presented credible accounts for their decisions; and (iii) adapted their policy decisions to the wishes of citizens.

This reasoning generates a number of empirical questions, some of which are new for representation research. An important but little-researched question regards the conditions under which critical citizens will be satisfied with less than policy adaption from their representatives. Responsiveness can be seen as a procedural requirement for legitimate representation; representatives can legitimately decide common matters only if they are somehow responsive to the represented. It is well known from the literature on procedural fairness that perceived procedural fairness facilitates legitimacy in the implementation phase of politics (e.g. Tyler 2006), but the importance of procedures for policy legitimacy is less well researched (Esaiasson *et al.* 2012).

The majority-minority distinction

A communicative conceptualisation of responsiveness, furthermore, allows the theoretically crucial distinction between majorities and minorities to enter the analysis. In traditional responsiveness research the fundamental empirical question is the extent to which representatives change policy positions in the direction of the majority: if a majority of citizens want immigration policies to be more restrictive, do public policies change accordingly? In effect, representatives are held accountable to one voice of the citizens, the one of the majority.

However, in case representatives are responsive towards the view of the majority they are by implication unresponsive towards minority views (towards those who want immigration policies to be more generous). Given that the principle of equal treatment ascribes all citizens a right to a responsive government, this is unsatisfactory. While representatives cannot possibly accommodate both policy camps, they can communicate their reasons for their actions to all parties. Consequently, empirical analyses of responsiveness should cover representatives' explanations (or lack of explanations) for their policy decisions, as well as reactions to these explanations among both policy majorities and minorities.

To concretise, the modal finding in representational research is that governments tend to adapt majority positions among citizens (e.g. Soroka and Wlezien 2010). Government adaption is also found within social movement research (Amenta *et al.* 2010), this is particularly the case if social movements' claims are supported by public opinion (Burstein and Linton 2002). While the finding that governments are generally responsive towards expressions of public will is significant for our understanding of representative democracies, missing from these lines of research are the reactions of those who would prefer governments to pursue different policies. A crucial question here is the extent to which policy minorities are willing to accept the unwelcome decision from their elected representatives (e.g. Levi 1997; Tyler 2006; Anderson and Mendes 2006; Esaiasson 2011).

An empirical illustration

To begin exploring the possibilities for research on communicative responsiveness we report findings from surveys with a representative sample of Swedish citizens and Swedish members of parliament. To capture responsiveness judgments, participants were asked to evaluate the extent to which the incumbent right-center coalition government, during their four-year term in office, had 'found out about the wishes of citizens' (they listened); 'explained their policies to citizens' (they explained); and 'tried to accommodate the wishes of citizens' (they adapted). The question, thus, targets the sitting government, and asks for generalised evaluations across all policy issues during the election period. However, it could just as well have targeted elected politicians in general, and/or a specific policy-decision process. Responses were registered on an eleven-point scale running from 0–10 with designated endpoints and a designated midpoint. Both surveys were conducted in connection with the 2010 parliamentary election.[6]

At this early stage of empirical examination, the main concern is that the suggested measure generates meaningful, non-random, responses. Table 2.2 shows the means for each responsiveness judgment by political affiliation in the respective survey.

As is often the case with attitudinal data, elected representatives are more polarised than citizens (Holmberg 1989). Moving on to comparisons within their respective political camp, representatives from the government parties agree less with their citizen supporters than representatives from opposition parties (government representatives perceive the government to be much more responsive

Table 2.2: Means of responsiveness judgments by citizens and representatives (0–10)

	Listen	Explain	Adapt
Citizens			
Opposition supporters (n=267)	3.7	5.0	3.8
Government supporters (n=302)	5.9	6.8	6.4
All (n=651)	4.8	5.9	5.1
Representatives			
Opposition representatives (n=168)	4.5	4.8	4.4
Government representatives (n=140)	8.0	6.9	8.0
All (n=308)	6.2	5.8	6.1

---

6. Both surveys were conducted by the Swedish National Election Study, the parliamentary survey in cooperation with the Multidisciplinary Opinion and Democracy (MOD) research group at the University of Gothenburg. Principal investigators were Henrik Oscarsson and Sören Holmberg (the election study); and Lena Wängnerud, Peter Esaiasson, Mikael Gilljam, and Sören Holmberg (the parliamentary study). For further information about the studies, *see* http://www.valforskning. pol.gu.se (accessed 15 June 2013).

than do their citizen supporters). In short, the results indicate that responsiveness beliefs are affected by prior attitudes, and, consequently, that both citizens and representatives engage in directional, motivated reasoning when assessing the responsiveness of the current government (Kunda 1990; Redlawsk 2002; Taber and Lodge 2006). However, precisely because they rely on their prior attitudes, it is also clear that neither category of respondents answer in random.

The three responsiveness items are strongly interrelated (the average simple correlation coefficient is 0.65 and 0.67 among citizens and representatives respectively). This suggests that respondents largely rely on a single underlying evaluative criteria relating to the likeability of the government. However, at the same time, and as evidenced by regression coefficients shown in the first column of Table 2.3, each responsiveness item contributes independently to citizen evaluation of the government.

Since the survey targets the incumbent government, it is expected that responsiveness judgments are weaker related to general trust in politicians. As reported in the second column of Table 2.3, results confirm this expectation. Nevertheless, both 'listening' and 'adapting' contribute significantly to general political trust.

Moreover, from a substantial point of view it can be noted that 'listening' and 'adapting' contribute more to citizen evaluations than 'explaining'. In other words, citizens seem to care more about whether the government tries to find out about their concerns and accommodate their wishes than about efforts to explain policies. Apparently, attempts to motivate different policies come across more like acts of persuasion than like responsible deliberation.

Table 2.3: Responsiveness items predict evaluation of the government and trust in politicians. OLS regression

	Evaluation of government (-5 to +5)	Trust in politicians (1–4)
Listen	0.31***	0.09***
	(0.054)	(0.016)
Explain	0.20***	0.00
	(0.047)	(0.014)
Adapt	0.40***	0.04**
	(0.056)	(0.017)
Constant	-2.85***	2.00***
	(0.230)	(0.070)
Observations	608	606
R^2	0.46	0.16

Note: Standard errors in parentheses; * $p < 0.10$, ** $p < 0.05$, *** $p < 0.01$

Referring to scattered empirical evidence from the US case, Mansbridge (2003) is pessimistic about the possibilities for representatives to explain a vote against the expressed opinions of their constituents. Likewise, Richard Fenno (1978) notes that House representatives rarely try to educate their constituents on dilemma situations they face in Washington. The results presented here tell a similar story in a different political context.

Overall, this brief empirical illustration suggests that a communicative understanding of responsiveness can help to generate new insights about the representative relationship between elections.

Concluding remarks

This chapter focuses on interactions between citizens and their representatives in the between-election mode. In light of contemporary representation theory, the chapter discusses a number of operational matters and questions about delineations. The primary contribution of the chapter, however, is a new and broader conceptualisation of responsiveness, a key component in the representative relationship between elections.

The new conceptualisation stresses the communicative aspects of responsiveness. To be responsive, elected representatives must communicate their reasons for action but they do not necessarily have to adapt to the current views and opinions of the represented. It is suggested that empirical analysis should acknowledge this broader conceptualisation by gathering information not only about adaptive processes but also about representatives' accounts for their actions, and citizens' reactions to these accounts.

Adding further analytical leverage, the notion of communicative responsiveness brings to the fore the distinction between majority and minority citizen support. Although crucially important for democratic theory, this distinction is often absent in empirical research on responsiveness and on government reactions to social movements claims. Accordingly, empirical analysis should acknowledge that all citizens, and not only those who are part of the policy majorities, are crucial to responsiveness processes.

The tendency among empirical researchers to overlook the majority-minority distinction, we note, cannot be attributed to democratic theorists in the field. Robert Dahl, whose *Polyarchy* (1971) and *Democracy and Its Critics* (1989) are standard references in empirical research on responsiveness, carefully maintains the majority-minority distinction: '[a] democratic government provides an orderly and peaceful process by means of which a majority of citizens can induce the government to do what they most want it to do and to avoid doing what they most want it not to do' (Dahl 1989, emphasis added). Referring to precisely this passage, Powell (2004) writes less precisely about 'policies that the citizens want'. For their part, Manin *et al.* (1999) talk about 'policies that are signalled as preferred by citizens'. Similarly, in their work on the opinion-policy relationship, Stimson *et al.* (1995) refer to 'public sentiments'. In a corresponding way, social movement research avoids addressing that protesting citizens sometimes – perhaps frequently – constitute a minority with intense preferences (Burstein 1998).

As discussed in the introductory chapter, our definition of BED is descriptive rather than prescriptive. In line with this ambition, the discussion in this chapter aims to facilitate empirical research on the representative relationship between elections. However, like all conceptualisations related to democratic theory (Thomassen 1994), the idea of BED evokes questions on normative standards. Are there one or more standards from which we can tell whether the representative relationship functions better or worse from a normative point of view? To begin discussions on this intricate topic, we make two provisional suggestions about the criteria for judging the democratic quality of BED.

First, we suggest that citizens' judgments should weigh heavily in normative evaluations. In particular, considering their importance for the functioning of democratic societies, global political trust and other subjective legitimacy judgments should be ascribed primary importance (e.g. Levi 1997; Hetherington 2005). Despite many years of research on citizens' trust of representatives and democratic governments (e.g. Dalton 2004), there is still limited systematic knowledge about how global political trust is affected by citizens' interactions with representatives between elections. For example, to what extent do people generalise from situations in which specific representatives act in more or less communicative ways?

Second, turning to intrinsic democratic values, 'equality' stands out as particularly relevant for BED research. The vast literature on citizen participation (Verba and Nie 1972; Verba et al. 1995) and the growing empirical literature on government cue taking (Gilens 2005; Bartels 2008; Enns and Wlezien 2011), asks the central question – to what extent do citizens of unequal resources speak with equal voices when common matters are decided? The BED framework potentially contributes to this research by directing attention to the interactive character of the representative relationship.

Between elections it is the task of the few elected representatives to handle the many conflicting, complex demands that arise in societies. We know from the empirical literature on citizen participation that resourceful individuals express their views more clearly than those who are less privileged, and that resources are more important for non-electoral forms of participation. The better the selected few handle the difficult task of weighting different interests, the higher the quality of democracy, both at elections and between elections.

References

Achen, C. (1977) 'Measuring Representation: Perils of the correlation coefficient', *American Journal of Political Science*, 21: 808–15.

Alonso, S., Keane, J. and Merkel, W. (2011) 'Editors' Introduction: Rethinking the future of representative democracy', in Alonso, S., Keane, J. and Merkel, W. (eds) *The Future of Representative Democracy*, Cambridge: Cambridge University Press.

Amenta, E., Caren, N., Chiarello, E. and Su, Y. (2010) 'The political consequences of social movements', *Annual Review of Sociology,* 36: 287–307.

Anderson, C. and Mendes, S. (2006) 'Learning to lose: Election outcomes, democratic experience, and political protest potential', *British Journal of Political Science,* 36: 91–111.

Bartels, L. (2008) *Unequal Democracy: The political economy of the new gilded age*, Princeton, NJ: Princeton University Press.

Burstein, P. (1998) 'Bringing the public back in: Should sociologists consider the impact of public opinion on public policy?', *Social Forces,* 77: 27–62.

Burstein, P and Linton, A. (2002) 'The impact of political parties, interest groups, and social movement organizations on public policy: Some recent evidence and theoretical concerns', *Social Forces*, 81: 380–408.

Castiglione, D. and Warren, M. (2008) 'Rethinking democratic representation: Eight theoretical issues', paper presented at *Rethinking Representation*, Bellagio, 30 September - 3 October 2008.

Chamberlain, A. (2012) 'A time-series analysis of external efficacy', *Public Opinion Quarterly,* 76: 117–30.

Converse, P. and Pierce, R. (1986) *Political Representation in France,* Cambridge, Mass.: Harvard University Press.

Cronin, T. (1999) *Direct Democracy: The politics of initiative, referendum, and recall*, Cambridge, Mass.: Harvard University Press.

Dahl, R. (1971) *Polyarchy: Participation and opposition*, New Haven, Conn.: Yale University Press.

— (1989) *Democracy and Its Critics*, New Haven, Conn: Yale University Press.

Dalton, R. (2004) *Democratic Challenges, Democratic Choices: The erosion of political support in advanced industrial democracies*, Oxford: Oxford University Press.

Dalton, R., Farrell, D. and McAllister, I. (2011) *Political Parties and Democratic Linkage, How parties organize democracy*, Oxford: Oxford University Press.

Disch, L. (2011) 'Toward a mobilisation conception of democratic representation', *American Political Science Review,* 105: 100–14.

Dovi, S. (2011) 'Political Representation', *The Stanford Encyclopedia of Philosophy (Winter 2011 Edition)*, Edward N. Zalta (ed.) Online. Available at: http://plato.stanford.edu/archives/win2011/entries/political-representation/> (accessed 1 February 2013).

Enns, P. and Wlezien, C. (eds) (2011) *Who Gets Represented?*, New York: The Russell Sage Foundation.

Erikson, R., MacKuen, M. and Stimson, J. (2002) *The Macro Polity*, Cambridge: Cambridge University Press.

Esaiasson, P. (2011) 'Electoral losers revisited: How citizens react to defeat at the ballot box', *Electoral Studies,* 30: 102–13.

Esaiasson, P., Gilljam, M. and Persson, M. (2012) 'Which decision-making arrangements generate the strongest legitimacy beliefs? Evidence from a randomised field experiment', *European Journal of Political Research,* 51: 785–808.

Esaiasson, P. and Holmberg, S. (1996) *Representation From Above: Members of Parliament and representative democracy in Sweden*, Aldershot: Dartmouth.

Fenno, R. (1978) *Home Style: House members in their district,* Little, Brown.

Gilens, M. (2005) 'Inequality and democratic responsiveness', *Public Opinion Quarterly,* 69: 778–96.

Gilljam, M., Persson, M. and Karlsson, D. (2012) 'Representatives' attitudes toward citizen protests: The impact of ideology, parliamentary position and experiences', *Legislative Studies Quarterly,* 37: 251–68.

Giugni, M. (1998) 'Was it worth the effort? The outcomes and consequences of social movements', *Annual Review of Sociology,* 24: 371–93.

Hetherington, M. (2005) *Why Trust Matter:. Declining political trust and the demise of American liberalism*, Princeton: Princeton University Press.

Hobolt, S. B. and Klemmensen, R. (2008) 'Government responsiveness and political competition in comparative perspective', *Comparative Political Studies,* 41: 309–37.

Holmberg, S. (1974) *Riksdagen representerar svenska folket. Empiriska studier i representativ demokrati*, Lund: Studentlitteratur.

—   (1989) 'Political representation in Sweden', *Scandinavian Political Studies,* 12: 1–36.

Jennings, W. (2009) 'The public thermostat, political responsiveness and error-correction: Border control and asylum in Britain, 1994–2007', *British Journal of Political Science,* 39: 847–70.

Kitschelt, H. (2003) 'Landscapes of political interest intermediation. Social movements, interest groups, and parties in the early twenty-first century', in Ibarra, P. (ed.) *Social Movements and Democracy*, New York: Palgrave Macmillan.

Klandermans, B. and Roggeband, C. (2009) *Handbook of Social Movements Across Disciplines,* Berlin: Springer Verlag.

Kuklinski, J. and Segura, G. (1995) 'Endogeneity, exogeneity, time, and space in political representation', *Legislative Studies Quarterly,* 20: 3–21.

Kunda, Z. (1990) 'The case for motivated reasoning', *Psychological Bulletin,* 108: 480–98.

Lax, J. and Phillips, J. (2009) 'Public opinion and policy responsiveness', *American Political Science Review,* 103: 367–86.

Levi, M. (1997) *Consent, Dissent, and Patriotism,* Cambridge: Cambridge University Press.

Manin, B. (1997) *The Principles of Representative Government,* Cambridge: Cambridge University Press.

Mansbridge, J. (2003) 'Rethinking representation', *American Political Science Review,* 97: 515–28.

— (2011) 'Clarifying representation', *American Political Science Review,* 105: 621–30.

— (2012) 'On the importance of getting things done', *PS: Political Science and Politics,* 45: .

Miller, W. and Stokes, D. (1963) 'Constituency influence in Congress', *American Political Science Review,* 57: 45–56.

Naurin, E. (2011) *Election Promise, Party Behaviour and Voter Perceptions,* Basingstoke: Palgrave Macmillan.

Page, B. and Shapiro, R. (1992) *The Rational Public: Fifty years of trends in Americans' policy preferences,* Chicago: University of Chicago Press.

Pitkin, H. (1967) *The Concept of Representation,* Berkeley and Los Angeles: University of California Press.

Powell, G. B. (2004) 'The chain of responsiveness', *Journal of Democracy,* 15: 91–105.

Przeworski, A., Stokes, S. and Manin, B. (eds) (1999) *Democracy, Accountability and Representation,* Cambridge: Cambridge University Press.

Redlawsk. D. (2002) 'Hot cognition or cool consideration: Testing the effects of motivated reasoning on political decision making', *Journal of Politics,* 64: 1021–44.

Rehfeld, A. (2006) 'Towards a general theory of representation', *Journal of Politics,* 68: 1–21.

Rosanvallon, P. (2008) *Counter-Democracy: Politics in an age of distrust,* Cambridge: Cambridge University Press.

Rosenblum, N. (2008) *On the Side of the Angels: An appreciation of parties and partisanship,* Princeton: Princeton University Press.

Rucht, D. (1996) 'The impact of national contexts on social movement structures: A cross-movement and cross-national comparison', in McAdam, D., McCarthy, J. D. and Zald, M. (eds) *Comparative Perspectives On Social Movements: Political opportunities, mobilizing structures, and cultural framings,* Cambridge: Cambridge University Press.

Saward, M. (2006) 'The representative claim', *Contemporary Political Theory,* 5: 297–318.

Schumaker, P. (1975) 'Policy responsiveness to protest-group demands', *Journal of Politics,* 37: 488–521.

Soroka, S. and Wlezien, C. (2010) *Degrees of Democracy: Politics, public opinion, and policy,* Cambridge: Cambridge University Press.

Stimson, J., MacKuen, M. and Erikson R. (1995) 'Dynamic representation', *American Political Science Review,* 89: 543–65.

Stolle, D., Hooghe, M. and Micheletti. M. (2005) 'Politics in the super-market: A three nation pilot survey on political consumerism as a form of political participation', *International Review of Political Science,* 26: 245–69.

Sunstein, C. (1991) 'Preferences and politics', *Philosophy and Public Affairs,* 20: 3–34.

Taber, C. and Lodge, M. (2006) 'Motivated skepticism in the evaluation of political beliefs', *American Journal of Political Science,* 50: 755–69.

Teorell, J. (2006) 'Political participation and three theories of democracy: A research inventory and agenda', *European Journal of Political Research,* 45: 787–810.

Teorell, J., Torcal, M. and Montero, J. R. (2007) 'Political participation: Mapping the terrain', in van Deth, J., Montero, J. R. and Westholm, A. (eds) *Citizenship and Involvement in European Democracies: A comparative perspective*, London: Routledge, 2007.

Thomassen, J. (1976) *Kiezens en gekozen in een representatieve demokratie*, Alphen aan den Rijn: Samson.

—   (1994) 'Empirical research into political representation. A critical reappraisal', in Klingemann, H.-D., Stöss, R. and Weßels, B. (eds) *Politische Klasse und politische Institutionen. Probleme und Perspektiven der Elitenforschung*, Opladen: Westdeutscher Verlag.

Tilly, C. (2008) *Contentious Performances*, Cambridge: Cambridge University Press.

Tyler, T. (2006) 'Psychological perspectives on legitimacy and legitimation', *Annual Review of Psychology,* 57: 375–400.

Urbinati, N. (2006) *Representative Democracy. Principles and genealogy*, Chicago: Chicago University Press.

Urbinati, N. and Warren, M. (2008) 'The concept of representation in contemporary democratic theory', *Annual Review of Political Science,* 11: 387–412.

Verba, S. and Nie, N. (1972). *Participation in America: Political democracy and social equality*, New York: Harper and Row Publishers.

Verba, S., Schlozman, K. L. and Brady, H. (1995) *Voice and Equality: Civic voluntarism in American politics*, Cambridge, Mass: Harvard University Press.

Weissberg, H. (1978) 'Evaluating theories of congressional roll-call voting', *American Journal of Political Science,* 22: 554–77.

Wlezien, C. (2004) 'Patterns of representation: Dynamics of public preferences and policy', *Journal of Politics,* 66: 1–24.

Chapter Three

Is Anyone Listening?
The Perceived Effectiveness of Electoral
and Non-Electoral Participation

Sofie Marien and Marc Hooghe

Within recent democratic theory literature, continuous communication between citizens and representatives and comprehensive forms of deliberation among citizens are considered as essential to ensure the quality of democratic governance (Mansbridge 2003; Urbinati and Warren 2008). While elections are an important mechanism for citizens to get information across, communication is certainly not restricted to the moment of elections. Citizens engage in various activities between elections in order to put issues on the political agenda, influence their representatives and try to keep them accountable. During previous decades, the political participation repertoire of citizens in Western democracies has expanded considerably (Dalton 2008; Stolle and Hooghe 2011). Much more frequently than in the past, citizens now use various forms of non-electoral participation to ensure their voices are heard in the political decision-making process. However, as Rousseau aptly put it, people are only free at the moment of their vote, after this they can be considered as slaves governed by the will of others. While citizens have the final say during elections, between elections citizens can only try to influence the politicians they elected into office.

To date we do not know whether non-electoral forms of participation are an effective method for informing and influencing elected representatives. To gain an insight into this question, we study the opinions of elected representatives regarding the perceived effect of various electoral and non-electoral forms of participation on political decisions. Do representatives ascribe importance to non-electoral forms of participation? Within this chapter this question is addressed, thereby providing a better understanding of this crucial aspect of between-election democracy. First, we will briefly expand on the importance of participation between elections and address the question of the effectiveness of political participation. Subsequently, we present the results of a recent survey on the perceived effectiveness of several forms of participation among Members of Parliament in eight countries. The main results are summarised in the concluding section.

The importance of citizen participation

The equal incorporation of the interests of all social groups within political representation is at the core of the democratic ideal (Dahl 1989; Dworkin 2000). To reach this ideal all relevant perspectives of an issue should be taken up within the political debate. Because the information content of the vote is rather low, it is difficult to communicate particular preferences and interests in this manner. Therefore, extensive interactions between the represented and representatives between elections are crucial (Urbanati and Warren 2008). Through these interactions, interests are defined and citizens are offered the possibility to agree with or object to representative claims that are made by elected politicians (Saward 2006; Severs 2010). In a well-functioning democracy all citizens affected by a decision made by the political system should have the opportunity to have their voices heard in the decision-making process (Habermas 1962; Young 2000; Dahl 1989).

In this regard, Rosanvallon (2006) has argued that democracy works best if citizens are not only voters but also act as quality-controllers between elections. He considers it as a democratic duty of citizens to scrutinise government and hold politicians accountable both at and between elections. The latter ideal can be attained if citizens are vigilant and closely monitor government to ensure government functions properly and is responsive to their interests. The fundamental idea goes back to Bentham's dictum: 'the more strictly we are watched, the better we behave'. In brief, this line of thought can be summarised as: 'le peuple ne peut rester libre et commandant que s'il dispose d'une sorte de "réserve de défiance", pour s'opposer si nécessaire au pouvoir qu'il a lui-même consacré' (Rosanvallon 2006).[1] Thus, we can conclude that the better the communication between citizens and representatives, the better the quality of the representation will be. Negotiation and deliberation between represented and representatives between elections can be considered as critical for good representation. Political participation serves as an important tool for citizen input in the democratic process and it enables citizens to pressure politicians to take this information into account when making political decisions (Mansbridge 2003; Verba, Schlozman and Brady 1995).

In practice, we see that citizens do indeed engage in all kinds of activities to inform representatives about their preferences and interests. Yet participation in elections has declined during the previous decades. While, in the past, elections and political parties might have been a preferred mechanism for imparting information, citizens increasingly have the feeling that these institutions no longer adequately fulfil this function. Voters have become progressively more volatile and political parties seem to be unable to convince their voters that their actions in government have been in voters' interests (Fox 2009). As a result, citizens have been looking for other forms of participation between elections – especially non-institutionalised participation modes. More people than ever before take part in demonstrations, and the background characteristics of protesters have gradually become mainstreamed (Norris et al. 2005). For petitions and other forms of non-institutionalised participation, the same trend can be observed (Marien et al. 2010). It has even been demonstrated that various acts of political consumerism (both buying and boycotting products and services for ethical or political reasons) have

1. 'The people could not remain free and in control unless they maintained a sort of "reservoir of mistrust" in order to mount, if need be, effective opposition against the government they themselves have consecrated.' Rosanvallon (2008).

now become a fixed element of the political participation repertoire of citizens (Micheletti 2004), while Internet activism has also become an important element of the action repertoire, especially for young citizens (Hooghe and Vissers 2009; Lynch 2011; Oser *et al.* 2013).

We also know that a diverse set of opinions is presented to decision makers since non-electoral participation is not just the method preferred by 'the happy few'. While gender and age gaps have been observed in electoral and institutionalised participation, the emerging forms of participation also attract previously excluded groups such as younger age cohorts and women (Stolle and Hooghe 2011). Nevertheless, in almost all modes of participation those with high education levels are much more active than those with low education credentials, and this implies that this elite group has more possibilities than the rest of the population to have its voice heard by the political system (Marien *et al.* 2010).

While most scholars perceive the expansion of the participation repertoire as a positive development, some scholars have voiced concerns. Some of the non-electoral forms of participation could be considered as less demanding and more individual which could lead to the expression of ill-considered and predominantly self-interested demands (Esaiasson 2010). Moreover, van Deth (2003, 2009) has formulated the argument that stretching the definition of participation leads to the risk that the label loses its meaning, and that almost all forms of involvement can be considered to be political. A related problem is the question of whether non-electoral forms of participation actually succeed in providing a linkage mechanism between citizens and the political system. This linkage would require that citizens can use these forms: a) to get information across to politicians about their preferences and demands; and b) to ensure that they can also exert pressure on those political decision-makers to take these preferences into account (Verba *et al.* 1995). Given this is the case, an important area for investigation is whether non-electoral forms of participation enable citizens to get their message across and hold decision makers accountable.

We should acknowledge in this regard that effectiveness is not the only concern in the study of participation. Political participation also has expressive and symbolical meanings, and participation acts do not necessarily have to aim at reaching policy changes (Hosch-Dayican 2010). These kinds of symbolic and cultural meanings have already been well documented in the literature (Norris 2002; Zukin *et al.* 2006). The question about the effectiveness of the non-electoral participation repertoire, however, has received far less research attention. While it has to be noted that participation can have both expressive and instrumental motivations, in general it can be assumed that participants in some way or another want to change something in politics or society. Only when their participation method is seen as effective does it allow them to have an impact on the process of political decision-making. Moreover, participation that is perceived to be ineffective can have detrimental consequences on policy satisfaction and political trust. In addition to the perception of 'voice', the perception of influence is crucial in fostering political trust and satisfaction. As Ulbig (2008) states: 'A loud voice falling on deaf ears is not as important as a quieter one spoken to someone who is listening'.

We do have access to a number of case studies showing that, in some instances, non-electoral forms of participation can lead to success. In specific cases, demonstrations and other forms of contentious politics certainly have had a strong effect on political decision-making (Tarrow 2011; Christensen and Strømsnes 2010). These exceptional cases, however, do not inform us about the routine effectiveness of participation acts. There can be little doubt that events like the May 1968 revolt in Paris, the marches of the Civil Rights Movement, or the Arab Spring revolts in Egypt and Tunisia have had a huge political and social impact. In practice, however, this can hardly be labelled a routine form of citizens' input into the political system and in decision-making processes. It would be erroneous, therefore, to assume that these kinds of case studies could inform us about the possibility that these non-electoral forms of participation will develop into a strong and enduring linkage mechanism between citizens and the political system.

A noteworthy exception is the study of Verba and Nie (1972) on the responsiveness of local leaders (i.e. elected representatives, business leaders, local newspaper publishers, etc) in sixty-four American communities. They found that the policy priorities of local leaders were more in line with active citizens than with passive citizens. The policy priorities of local leaders were also more in line with the citizens in communities with high participation rates. In communities characterised by disagreement on policy priorities, high rates of voting and campaign activity were associated with high levels of agreement between local leaders and citizens on policy priorities. However, contact and communal activity led to a larger discrepancy between the views of leaders and citizens. This led Verba and Nie (1972) to conclude that in communities with more disagreement on policy priorities, non-electoral modes of participation are likely to result in a decrease of responsiveness of leaders to the community as a whole, given the distorted input they receive.

In this study, we address this topic by asking elected representatives to judge the effectiveness of electoral participation and various forms of non-electoral participation. This will provide us with an insight of elected representatives' beliefs about the forms that contacts with citizens may take. We can assume that the potential and effectiveness of non-electoral participation will be hindered if representatives do not think it is worthwhile to spend too much attention on them. We do not wish to concentrate on a number of highly exceptional cases as it is clear that a number of demonstrations and uprisings in the past have led to huge political consequences. The question, however, is whether the insights from these highly exceptional cases can be generalised toward more routine uses of non-electoral participation.

This study will also shed light on representatives' perceptions about the workings of representative democracy today (the traditional view of the representative process puts elections at centre stage and ascribes little importance to interactions between elected representatives and the represented between elections). During campaigns representatives make promises about the future governing period and, by means of elections, citizens authorise representatives to fulfil these promises (Mansbridge 2003). More recent views on representation, however, take into account the importance of retrospective voting and, as a result, emphasise the importance of citizens' preferences at the next elections. This kind of anticipatory representation requires substantial information about the preferences of the represented. Therefore, communication between represented and representative between elections becomes crucial as it enables representatives to anticipate the preferences of the represented and influence them (Mansbridge 2003).

In sum, while the more traditional view attaches less importance to non-electoral forms of citizen participation, the more recent understanding of representation ascribes much more importance to citizen participation between elections.

Data and methods

We use the PARTIREP survey in which Members of Parliament from thirteen countries were questioned about their opinions on electoral participation and various forms of non-electoral participation. In every country the aim was to collect representative data about Members of Parliament, both in the national parliament and (in federal states) in regional parliaments.[2] Between March 2009 and December 2010, all members of the selected legislatures were contacted at least three times, employing a variety of methods: legislators typically received an introductory letter and email inviting them to participate in a web-based survey. They further received at least two online reminders and were offered the option to either fill out a printed questionnaire or be interviewed (excluding 'hard' refusals). A final invitation was by telephone in many countries. We limited ourselves to those eight countries with at least 100 respondents. Response rates and sample sizes can be found in the Appendix to this chapter.[3]

The Members of Parliament were asked to rate the effectiveness of ten different political participation acts, on a scale of one to seven. The text of the question was: *'Citizens can do different things in order to try to have an impact on political decisions. Could you rate the following acts on how effective they are in order of influencing political decisions?'* We operationalise electoral participation as voting in elections. Non-electoral participation includes nine acts of participation between elections, namely: demonstrations, signing petitions, illegal demonstrations, obtaining media attention, taking part in Internet discussions, contacting a politician (either by letter or email), boycotting products and being active in a political party.

2.   We thank Kris Deschouwer and Sam Depauw *et al.* for coordinating this large data-gathering project and granting us access to this dataset.

3.   Even when limiting ourselves to these countries, it will be noted that 634 MP's originated from Switzerland, as in that country all cantonal parliaments were included in the survey. When calculating figures for the overall sample, however, a weighting will be applied.

Results

In Table 3.1 the mean averages of the perceived effectiveness questions are presented. Looking at what representatives consider an effective means of influencing the decision-making process, there seems to be a strong consensus that taking part in elections is by far the most effective means of influencing political life. Only among the Belgian representatives does the score (on a one to seven scale) fall below six, which might be related to specific characteristics of the Belgian electoral system.[4] Despite the fact that participation repertoires have expanded considerably, and despite the importance of non-electoral forms of political participation, representatives apparently still consider taking part in elections as the single most effective form of participation.

Working in a political party is also considered by the representatives to be a very effective tool with which citizens can influence public policy. Across the various countries, working in a political party is seen as the second or third most effective way to influence public policy. Only in Portugal can a different pattern be observed, with representatives rating five other activities as more effective than party activism. In all other countries, however, representatives tend to hold to the notion that political parties play an important role in the process of interest mediation, despite the fact that within the population the motivation to become a member of a political party has continuously declined, especially among younger age cohorts (Whiteley 2011). Apparently, the representatives strongly believe in those activities that give themselves the centre stage in politics. It seems that they agree on a rather traditional view of representation, with elections and political parties as the two most important tools for citizen influence.

Further, representatives also clearly pay a lot of attention to the potential impact of the mass media. Earlier studies have already shown that professional politicians assume that the mass media has an enormous impact, both on their own functioning and on public opinion in general (van Aelst *et al.* 2008).

Next to elections, political parties, and featuring in the media, contacting politicians by mail or email is rated as highly efficacious in various countries. Especially in the United Kingdom, representatives consider contact as an effective form of influence with a mean score of 5.26 on the one to seven scale. As a result, contact is ranked as the third most effective activity in the United Kingdom. Contacting a politician by writing a letter is considered to be slightly more effective than contact by email. In Italy, contact is perceived to be less effective compared to other activities citizens can undertake.

Also, the perception of demonstrations differs substantially across the various countries. While demonstrations are seen as the third most effective form of citizen influence in Italy (after elections and political party work), this act is seen as far

---

4.   The federal country of Belgium is divided into two distinct electoral systems, with the effect that Dutch-speaking citizens cannot vote for French-speaking parties, and *vice versa*. As such, it could be argued that the effect of the vote is diluted, as citizens can only have an impact on half of the composition of parliament (and subsequently also of the ruling majority and the government).

Table 3.1: *Means and ranking of the perceived effectiveness of participation*

	All	Austria	Belgium	Germany	Hungary	Italy	Portugal	Switzerland	UK
Vote	6.27 (1)	6.32 (1)	5.99 (1)	6.4 (1)	6.23 (1)	6.07 (1)	6.3 (1)	6.37 (1)	6.13 (1)
Political party	5.58 (2)	5.61 (3)	5.35 (3)	6.05 (2)	5.02 (3)	5.62 (2)	4.61 (6)	5.88 (2)	5.52 (2)
Media	5.35 (3)	5.77 (2)	5.56 (2)	5.1 (3)	5.77 (2)	4.95 (4)	5.27 (2)	5.44 (3)	5.00 (5)
Contact by letter	4.73 (4)	5.06 (5)	4.77 (4)	5 (5)	4.23 (4)	3.85 (8)	4.46 (7)	4.3 (5)	5.26 (3)
Contact by e-mail	4.68 (5)	5.2 (4)	4.51 (6)	4.86 (6)	4.17 (5)	3.95 (7)	4.62 (5)	4.36 (4)	5.06 (4)
Demonstration	4.61 (6)	4.62 (6)	4.56 (5)	5.04 (4)	3.92 (7)	5.2 (3)	5.09 (3)	3.99 (8)	4.45 (6)
Petition	4.26 (7)	4.24 (9)	3.65 (8)	4.79 (7)	3.99 (6)	4.18 (6)	4.97 (4)	4.27 (6)	3.79 (7)
Online forum	4.01 (8)	4.33 (8)	3.74 (7)	4.38 (8)	3.36 (8)	4.25 (5)	4.12 (8)	3.78 (9)	3.29 (9)
Boycott	3.82 (9)	4.48 (7)	3.41 (9)	4.28 (9)	3.12 (9)	3.45 (9)	3.26 (9)	4 (7)	3.75 (8)
Illegal protest	2.43 (10)	2.4 (10)	2.86 (10)	2.34 (10)	2.02 (10)	3.36 (10)	2.41 (10)	2.44 (10)	1.97 (10)

Source: PARTIREP MP survey 2009–2010.
Note: Perceived effectiveness of participation acts by Members of Parliament. The figures in the second column are weighted by parliamentary party group in each parliament. The weight coefficient also corrects for the substantial overrepresentation of Swiss MPs in the total sample.

less effective than other activities in Switzerland and Hungary. Also, in Portugal, demonstrations are considered relatively effective. Hence, while demonstrations are the sixth or seventh most effective activity in the majority of the countries, in the two southern European countries demonstrations take third place in the effectiveness ranking, which is in line with previous research documenting a more confrontational political action repertoire in these southern countries.

The results in Table 3.1 also show that representatives agree on the means of participation that are least effective: boycotting, Internet discussions and illegal protests. In all countries illegal protests and boycotts are seen as the least effective of all activities presented to the representatives. By itself this can be seen as problematic since we know that these activities are on the rise in Western societies. Some authors even assume that these new forms of participation can have a strong impact on the way democratic societies will function in the future (Earl *et al.* 2010; Lusoli *et al.* 2006; Micheletti and Stolle 2008; Shah *et al.* 2007). While it is clear that these forms of engagement have a huge democratic potential, we can observe that representatives still consider them to be less effective. To the extent that Members of Parliament function as gatekeepers to the political system (and thus will be less inclined to allow in information that is based on these forms of participation), this could imply that citizens that are engaged in these forms will, in the end, have less influence than they hoped for.

Members of Parliament in the various countries all seem to think about citizen input - and representation in general – in rather traditional terms. Great importance is attached to elections, political parties and contact with politicians, while less attention is paid to new forms of citizen participation. If we are experiencing a 'democratic deficit', as is often claimed (Norris 2011), one of the causes might be that citizens are increasingly using methods that are considered, by representatives, to be less effective for establishing a linkage between citizens and the political system.

Despite these similarities in representatives' beliefs about the forms contact with citizens may take, Table 3.1 also points at cross-national differences in these beliefs. An analysis of variance reveals significant differences in the perceptions of the effectiveness of electoral and non-electoral participation across the eight countries. We consider voting in elections as electoral participation, and non-electoral participation as several activities citizens can engage in to try to communicate with, and influence, elected representatives between elections. The latter includes: demonstrations, signing petitions, illegal demonstrations, obtaining media attention, taking part in Internet discussions, contacting a politician (either by letter or email), boycotting products and being active in a political party.

In Table 3.2 the results of subsequent *post-hoc* tests that give us an insight into the nature of this cross-national variation are represented. These comparisons reveal that Belgian representatives' perception of electoral participation significantly differs from that of German and Swiss representatives (cells with 'X'). German and Swiss representatives rate the effectiveness of electoral participation as extremely high, while Belgian representatives give a slightly lower score. Nevertheless, in addition, Belgian representatives consider electoral participation as the most

Table 3.2: Cross-national differences in perceived effectiveness of electoral and non-electoral participation

	Austria	Belgium	Germany	Hungary	Italy	Portugal	Switzerland	UK
Belgium								
Germany		X						
Hungary								
Italy								
Portugal								
Switzerland		X						
UK								
Mean election	6.32	5.99	6.40	6.23	6.07	6.30	6.37	6.13
Mean between election	4.63	4.28	4.64	3.95	4.33	4.30	4.25	4.25

Source: PARTIREP MP survey 2009–2010.
Note: the results of the post-hoc tests (Games-Howell procedure) are represented. The grey cells represent a significant difference between two countries in the perceived effectiveness of between-election participation. The cells with 'X' represents a significant difference between two countries in the perceived effectiveness of participation in elections.

effective channel for influence with a mean of six on the one to seven scale. Further, German representatives also give higher effectiveness scores to non-electoral participation than representatives in other countries (grey cells). Austrian representatives too are more positive about citizens' opportunities to influence public policy in between elections. The differences in effectiveness perceptions between representatives from Austria and Germany, on the one hand, and from Belgium, Hungary, Italy, Portugal, Switzerland and the UK, on the other, are significant. Hungarian representatives are the most negative about the possible impact of non-electoral forms of participation. The mean score of 3.95 is significantly lower than means of the other countries.

Also, within countries, representatives can differ in their assessment of the effectiveness of electoral and non-electoral forms of participation. It might be that the younger generation of representatives pays more attention to non-electoral forms of political expression than the older representatives. Previous research has also pointed to ideology and parliamentary position as important determinants of representatives' attitudes towards citizen participation (Gilljam *et al.* 2012). In Tables 3.3 and 3.4 we investigate the factors that influence the perceptions of representatives towards electoral and non-electoral participation. The dependent variables in these analyses are the perceived effectiveness of electoral participation (Table 3.3) and a sum-scale of the perceived effectiveness of the nine non-electoral participation acts (Table 3.4).

First, we investigate perceptions regarding electoral participation. The Ordinal Logistic Regression model in Table 3.3 predicts the likelihood that respondents will have answered that electoral participation is very effective. None of the socio-demographic characteristics can predict the likelihood that Members of Parliament will have more positive opinions towards the effectiveness of electoral participation. Men, women, higher and lower educated, younger and older MPs all agree that electoral participation is an extremely effective tool with which citizens can influence political decisions. MPs with a right-wing orientation are slightly more likely than MPs with a moderate ideological orientation to state that electoral participation is very effective. MPs in government and in opposition equally think that electoral participation is very effective. Finally, the results show that MPs in Belgium, Italy and Switzerland are slightly less likely than MPs in Austria to rate electoral participation as very effective. However, the difference that could be explained by these variables is rather low as there is a strong consensus across all groups on the potential of participation in elections to influence political decisions.

The results of the OLS regression analysis of non-electoral participation in Table 3.4 show that female MPs believe that non-electoral participation is more effective than their male counterparts do. Contrary to the expectations, the younger generation of MPs does not significantly differ from the older generation in their evaluation of the effectiveness of non-electoral participation. Hence, a process of generational replacement among Members of Parliament will not be sufficient to change representatives' views on the role of non-electoral participation within the representative process. Similarly to the findings of a study among Swedish local representatives, left-wing representatives are more likely to rate the effectiveness

Table 3.3: Explaining MPs' views of the effectiveness of electoral participation

	Estimate	S.E.	Wald	Sig.
Women	-0.243	0.148	2.695	0.101
Age (ref. 60+)				
–40	0.175	0.219	0.641	0.423
41–50	-0.049	0.188	0.068	0.794
51–60	0.039	0.183	0.047	0.829
Education level (ref. university degree)				
Primary and or secondary education	0.358	0.221	2.619	0.106
Non-university higher education	0.042	0.180	0.054	0.816
Left-right position (ref. right)				
Left	-0.199	0.143	1.937	0.164
Moderate	-0.398	0.202	3.906	0.048
Party in government	-0.166	0.132	1.594	0.207
Countries (ref. group: Austria)				
Belgium	-0.636	0.277	5.249	0.022
Germany	0.131	0.271	0.233	0.629
Hungary	-0.173	0.300	0.332	0.564
Italy	-0.659	0.297	4.918	0.027
Portugal	-0.015	0.301	0.002	0.961
Switzerland	-0.047	0.317	0.022	0.881
UK	-0.686	0.303	5.120	0.024
Adj. R^2	0.049			

Source: PARTIREP MP survey 2009–2010. N= 1,733.
Note: Entries are the result of an Ordinal Logistic Regression. The thresholds of this analyses are for value 1 (not at all effective) = -6.066; value 2 = -5.601; value 3 = -4.552; value 4 = -3.200; value 5 = -1.985; value 6 = -0.664. Weighted by parliamentary party group in each parliament. The weight coefficient also corrects for the substantial overrepresentation of Swiss MPs in the total sample.

of non-electoral election participation higher than right-wing representatives (Gilljam *et al.* 2012). Also, opposition parties are more likely than government parties to rate the possibilities for citizen influence between elections as higher.

Finally, as already presented in Table 3.2, there are cross-national differences in the perceptions of non-electoral participation. Controlling for all these variables, Hungarian MPs are still more negative about the influence citizens can have on political decisions by engaging in various activities between elections. Also, MPs from the United Kingdom are more negative about citizen influence between elections than MPs from Austria.

Table 3.4: Explaining MPs' views of the effectiveness of non-electoral participation

	Estimate	S.E.	β	t	Sig.
Women	0.207	0.057	0.122	-3.605	0.000
Age	-0.004	0.002	-0.058	-1.747	0.081
Education level (ref. university degree)					
Primary and or secondary education	0.034	0.084	0.014	0.403	0.687
Non-university higher education	0.051	0.069	0.027	0.738	0.460
Left-right position	-0.039	0.010	-0.126	-3.793	0.000
Party in government	-0.145	0.051	-0.094	-2.853	0.004
Countries (ref. group: Austria)					
Belgium	-0.127	0.108	-0.058	-1.180	0.238
Germany	0.132	0.103	0.077	1.288	0.198
Hungary	-0.435	0.114	-0.179	-3.800	0.000
Italy	-0.124	0.117	-0.049	-1.062	0.288
Portugal	-0.129	0.115	-0.051	-1.126	0.261
Switzerland	-0.173	0.120	-0.069	-1.438	0.151
UK	-0.255	0.119	-0.095	-2.148	0.032
Cte.	4.849	0.163		29.739	0.000
Adj. R^2	0.112				

Source: PARTIREP MP survey 2009–2010. N = 1,733.
Note: Entries are the result of an Ordinary Least Squares Regression. Weighted by parliamentary party group in each parliament. The weight coefficient also corrects for the substantial overrepresentation of Swiss MPs in the total sample.

Conclusion

Within the recent representation literature, interactions between representatives and the represented between elections are considered to be crucial in order to arrive at good representation. Over the past decades, the increasing popularity of various forms of non-electoral participation has been documented in the participation literature. It has even been shown by now that activities such as demonstrations, petitions, Internet activism and various acts of political consumerism have become a fixed element of the political participation repertoire of citizens (Micheletti 2004; Oser *et al.* 2013). Participation enables citizens to communicate their preferences to decision makers and to pressure them into taking this information into account. In effect, the crucial principle underlying every democracy entails that 'all affected by collective decisions should have an opportunity to influence the outcome' (Urbinati and Warren 2008: 395).

Thus far, we do not know much about the effectiveness of non-electoral participation. Therefore, in the current chapter, we have used new survey material to investigate how elected representatives perceive the effectiveness of different forms of participation. In particular, the perceived effectiveness of electoral participation and non-electoral participation were compared. The results show that the representatives in eight European countries strongly agree that elections are still the most powerful means that citizens have available to exert pressure on the political decision-making process. Despite all the shortcomings of the electoral process, and the fact that it can convey just a limited amount of information to the political system, there is no reason to doubt the primacy of the electoral system as such. Ultimately, the power of citizens continues to depend on the fact that during elections they can express their approval of political decision makers, or send them home.

However, when citizens want to send more detailed information about their preferences to the political system, a more extended action repertoire is required. In this regard, working in political parties is considered to be a very effective tool. Quite a strong consensus among representatives also emerges on the actions that do not work, or are seen as least effective: illegal protest, Internet discussions and boycotts. Elected representatives seem to be inclined to attach the lowest levels of efficacy to these acts in all countries.

Hence, across all eight investigated countries, representatives turn out to have a rather traditional view on useful ways to communicate with citizens. They all attach much more importance to elections, political parties, contacting politicians and appearing in the media than to less institutionalised forms of interaction. This is rather sobering with regard to theories that predict that political consumerism or Internet activism would become a central focus of citizens' involvement and protest (Bennett 2003).

We can conclude that the results of this study seem to suggest that citizens are increasingly engaging in activities that elected representatives ascribe less importance to. Elected representatives still look at the representative process in rather traditional terms, with elections and political parties as the main avenues of interaction between citizens and representatives. However, we know that citizens increasingly refrain from participating in elections, joining political parties and more institutionalised forms of interaction (Hajnal and Lee 2011). Yet the current analysis suggests that developing a functional equivalent for party activism might not be straightforward. While, for citizens, political parties have lost their meaning, politicians themselves clearly still perceive parties as a privileged mechanism for linking citizens and the state.

Acknowledgment

This research project was made possible by the generous support of the Belgian Federal Science Policy as part of the Inter University Attraction Pole PartiRep (http://www.partirep.eu). Sofie Marien also gratefully acknowledges the support received as a postdoctoral researcher of the Research Foundation Flanders (FWO). We also wish to thank the participants of this book project and the reviewers of ECPR Press for their valuable feedback.

Appendix

Table A.3.1: PartiRep survey among Members of Parliament

Country	Sample size	Response rate (%)
Austria	233	35
Belgium	165	39
Germany	279	28
Hungary	99	26
Italy	128	15
Portugal	118	33
Switzerland	604	25
United Kingdom	107	17
Total	1,733	

References

Bennett, L. W. (2003) 'Communicating global activism', *Information, Communication, and Society*, 6: 143–68.

Christensen, D. A. and Strømsnes, K. (2010) 'Democracy or do-ocracy: The activist group "Byen Vår" and the mobilisation against clear channel in Bergen', in Amnå, E. (ed.), *New Forms of Citizen Participation: Normative implications*, Baden-Baden: Nomos.

Dahl, R. A. (1989) *Democracy and Its Critics*, New Haven CT: Yale University Press.

Dalton, R. J. (2008) 'Citizenship norms and the expansion of political participation', *Political Studies*, 56: 76–98.

Dworkin, R. (2000) *Sovereign Virtue: The theory and practice of equality*, Cambridge: Harvard University Press.

Earl, J., Kimport, K., Prieto, G., Rush, C. and Reynoso, K. (2010) 'Changing the world, one webpage at a time: Conceptualizing and explaining internet activism', *Mobilization*, 15: 425–46.

Esaiasson, P. (2010) 'Is citizen involvement always a plus?', in Amnå, E. (ed.), *New Forms of Citizen Participation: Normative implications,* Baden-Baden: Nomos

Fox, R. (2009) 'Engagement and participation: What the public want and how our politicians need to respond', *Parliamentary Affairs*, 62: 673–85.

Gilljam, M., Persson, M. and Karlsson, D. (2012) 'Representatives' attitudes toward citizen protests: The impact of ideology, parliamentary position and experiences', *Legislative Studies Quarterly*, 37: 251–68.

Habermas, J. (1962) *Strukturwandel der Öffentlichkeit*, Neuwied: Luchterhand.

Hajnal, Z. and Lee, T. (2011) *Why Americans Don't Join the Party: Race, immigration, and the failure (of political parties) to engage the electorate*, Princeton: Princeton University Press.

Hooghe, M. and Vissers, S. (2009) 'Reaching out or reaching in? The use of party websites during the 2006 electoral campaign in Belgium', *Information, Communication, and Society*, 12: 691–714.

Hosch-Dayican, B. (2010) *Political involvement and democracy: How benign is the future of post-industrial politics?*, unpublished thesis, Enschede: Twente University Press.

Lusoli, W., Ward, S. and Gibson, R. (2006) '(Re)connecting Politics? Parliament, the public and the Internet', *Parliamentary Affairs*, 59: 24–42.

Lynch, M. (2011) 'After Egypt: The limits and promise of online challenges to the authoritarian Arab state', *Perspectives on Politics*, 9: 301–10.

Mansbridge, J. (2003) 'Rethinking representation', *American Political Science Review*, 97: 515–28.

Marien, S., Hooghe, M. and Quintelier, E. (2010) 'Inequalities in non-institutionalised forms of political participation: A multilevel analysis of 25 countries', *Political Studies*, 58: 187–213.

Micheletti, M. (2004) *Politics, Products and Markets: Exploring political consumerism, past and present*, New Brunswick: Transaction.

Micheletti, M. and Stolle, D. (2008) 'Fashioning social justice through political consumerism, capitalism, and the Internet', *Cultural Studies*, 22: 749–69.

Norris, P. (2002) *Democratic Phoenix: Political activism worldwide*, Cambridge: Cambridge University Press.

— (2011) *Democratic Deficit: Critical citizens revisited*, Cambridge: Cambridge University Press.

Norris, P., Walgrave, S. and Van Aelst, P. (2005) 'Who demonstrates? Antistate rebels, conventional participants, or everyone?', *Comparative Politics*, 37: 189–206.

Oser, J., Hooghe, M. and Marien, S. (2013) 'Is online participation distinct from offline participation? A latent class analysis of participation types and their stratification', *Political Research Quarterly*, 66(1): 91-101.

Rosanvallon, P. (2006) *La contre-démocratie. La politique a l'âge de la défiance*, Paris: Seuil.

— (2008) *Counter-democracy: politics in an age of distrust*, Cambridge University Press, New York.

Saward, M. (2006) 'The representative claim', *Contemporary Political Theory*, 5: 297–318.

Severs, E. (2010) 'Representation as claims-making: Quid responsiveness?', *Representation*, 46: 411–23.

Shah, D., McLeod, D., Kim, E., Young Lee, S., Gotlieb, M., Ho, S. and Breivik, H. (2007) 'Political consumerism. How communication and consumption orientations drive "Lifestyle Politics"', *Annals of the American Academy of Political and Social Science*, 611: 217–35.

Stolle, D. and Hooghe, M. (2011) 'Shifting inequalities: Patterns of exclusion and inclusion in emerging forms of political participation', *European Societies*, 13: 119–42.

Tarrow, S. (2011) *Power in Movement: Social movements and contentious politics*, 3rd edn, Cambridge: Cambridge University Press.

Ulbig, S. G. (2008) 'Voice is not enough: The importance of influence in political trust and policy assessments', *Public Opinion Quarterly*, 72: 523–39.

Urbinati, N. and Warren M. E. (2008) 'The concept of representation in contemporary democratic theory', *American Review of Political Science*, 11: 387–412.

Van Aelst, P., Brants, K., Van Praag, P., De Vreese, C., Nuytemans, M. and van Dalen, A. (2008) 'The fourth estate as superpower? An empirical study of perceptions of media power in Belgium and the Netherlands', *Journalism Studies*, 9: 494–511.

van Deth, J. (2003) 'Vergleichende politische Partizipationsforschung', in Berg-Schlosser, D. and Müller-Rommel, F. (eds), *Vergleichende Politikwissenschaft*, Opladen: Leske and Budrich.

—   (2009) Is creative participation creative democracy?', in Micheletti, M.
         and McFarland, A. (eds), *Creative Participation: Responsibility-taking
         in the political world,* Boulder: Paradigm Publishers.
Verba, S. and Nie, N. H. (1972) *Participation in America: Political democracy
         and social equality*, Chicago: University of Chicago Press.
Verba, S., Schlozman, K. L. and Brady, H. (1995) *Voice and Equality,* Cambridge:
         Harvard University Press.
Whiteley, P. (2011) 'Is the party over? The decline of party activism and
         membership across the democratic world', *Party Politics,* 17: 21–44.
Young, I. M. (2000) *Inclusion and Democracy*, Oxford: Oxford University Press.
Zukin, C., Keeter, S., Andolina, M., Jenkins, K. and Delli Carpini, M. (2006) *A
         New Engagement? Political participation, civic life, and the changing
         American citizen*, Oxford: Oxford University Press.

Chapter Four

Issue Uptake in the Shadow of Elections

Audrey André, Sam Depauw and Kris Deschouwer

People are hard to find, Richard Fenno (1978) noted. Driving past row after row of apartment houses, he reports one congressman saying: 'They have no rotary clubs or groups like that. It's just a bunch of houses. [...] I don't know how you would campaign there'. He does not know how to represent them either. People frequently do not know much about politics or policies, and are reluctant to learn more. Entrepreneurial representatives have considerable discretion in the claims they make that this or that is in the constituents' interest (Saward 2010). In the legislative arena they raise the issues and concerns that they believe – but cannot be entirely certain – will be more advantageous for them in the next election (Manin 1997).

There is frequently a tension between what is advantageous for the party and what is advantageous for the individual representative (Carey and Shugart 1995). That is, there is an assumption that the 'shadow of elections' looms over the representative relationship and that much of what elected representatives do in the legislative arena cannot be separated from the conditions under which they compete for re-election. The issues that representatives take up in the legislative arena are ones they select, in part, for self-interested (i.e. electoral) reasons.

People are hard to find, but some people are not (Fenno 1978). Organised interests lobby elected representatives to take up their proposed legislation, to introduce their questions and their amendments. Every day the mass media confront millions of people, and representatives for that matter, with concerns in the privacy of their own homes. Whose issues and concerns the elected representatives take up in the legislative arena, we demonstrate, are chosen on the basis of (i) the actual images and ideas representatives have about representation and (ii) their actions in the local area between elections.

Conceptions of representation, Hanna Pitkin (1967) observed, are intimately intertwined with notions of representatives' and people's abilities and the nature of people's interests. Previous studies have not been very successful in linking representatives' conceptions of trustees and delegates to the electoral circumstances, on the one hand, or to their policy responsiveness, on the other (*see* Jewell 1970; Thomassen 1994). Instead we relate issue uptake by elected representatives to their conceptions of representation from above and representation from below, of *ex-ante* representation and *ex-post* representation (Andeweg and Thomassen 2005). For this purpose we rely on the self-reported estimates of how frequently representatives in thirteen advanced industrial democracies take up constituents' concerns in the course of new legislation, amendments to legislation, or parliamentary questions, and contrast them to their estimated uptake from other prominent societal actors: organised interests, the party and the mass media. The argument will proceed in four steps. The first section illustrates that frequent contact with constituents holds a central position in recent democratic theory. The second section presents the theoretical foundations underpinning the consequences that representatives' conceptions of representation have for their uptake. The third section introduces the PARTIREP cross-national survey and the operationalisation of the dependent and independent variables. The fourth section demonstrates what representatives think about representation and how their conceptions influence the issues they take up in the legislative arena. We conclude in the fifth section.

On connection and disconnection

It is a 'social fact' of representative government that representatives do not know much about the constituents in whose interests they claim to act, and that constituents, for their part, frequently do not know where their interests lie (Hardin 2004). Many constituents in advanced industrial democracies do not feel connected to their elected representatives: they have not met them and feel they are out of touch with constituents (e.g. Curtice and Shively 2009). Constituencies are increasingly heterogeneous and issues more short-lived. The erosion of longstanding cleavages in society has wrested from governments, parties and representatives the blueprints for their 'representative claims' and the interests that they claim to be responsive to (Andeweg 2003; *see also* Saward 2010). Party identifications and confidence in political institutions are waning in the electorate across most advanced industrial democracies, whereas electoral volatility is increasing (Dalton 2004; Dalton *et al.* 2000). The trend towards individualisation has only underlined the fact that people typically have multiple social identities, some salient but most latent (Bishin 2009). Through position-taking political parties, and individual representatives, draw public awareness to those identities that are most beneficial to them (Manin 1997; *see also* Mayhew 1974). That is, constituents frequently learn where their interests lie from the 'self-interested' (or, rather, re-election-seeking) communications of representatives (Disch 2011; see also Bullock 2011; Shaffner 2005).

Pitkin (1967) noted that political representation must always bring with it the possibility of disagreement between constituents and their representatives. Nonetheless, disagreement normally ought not to arise. Democratic theorists increasingly (re)emphasise that it is critical in this respect that constituents are offered every opportunity to state their views and voice their opposition. Frequent personal contact with their elected representatives between elections is one common manner in which this can be achieved. Jane Mansbridge (2003), for instance, measures the quality of anticipatory representation by the quality of deliberation between constituents and their representatives in between elections. Lisa Disch (2011) uses the notion of reflexivity to judge representation by the polity's mobilisation of manifest and latent dissent among constituents. It hinges on the presence of regular and structured opportunities to voice disagreement and for such disagreement to be taken into account. Suzanne Dovi (2007) also seeks to separate good from bad representatives on the basis (amongst others) of the relations they maintain with all constituents, promoting constituents' participation in public deliberation and enabling them to forge informed opinions. Andrew Rehfeld (2005: 124) reluctantly admits that 'there are few ways better than physical proximity to enable citizens to deliberate about politics'.

Frequent contact brings with it access to the representative, Fenno (1978) explains, and the promise of access in the future. In the short run, constituents get to present their case to their representatives and demonstrate how public policies negatively affect them. The knowledge to run modern society is spread thin across a great number of government agencies, organisations and individuals – each with private information on the basis of their situation in life and past experiences (Fearon 1998). Previous studies regarding casework have emphasised how information gathered in this manner can be used in administrative self-correction, questioning administrative procedures and corrective legislation (Elling 1979; Rawlings 1990).

In the long run, frequent contact builds trust: the feeling that the representative makes him/herself available to them adds to his/her trustworthiness in the eyes of constituents. Should disagreement arise, constituents feel that they can go and speak to their representative (Fenno 1978). We shall demonstrate that, for their part, representatives differ in their propensity to take up concerns raised in this manner in the legislative arena. Differences between representatives and constituents are related to their conceptions of representation and their actions in the district, within the context of the electoral rules.

Conceptions of representation and issue uptake

Democratic representation demands that people's policy preferences somehow inform representatives' actions. The notion of issue uptake in particular relates what elected representatives do in the legislative arena to the preferences of others. The notion originated with participants in a deliberation, engaging with, and including in their own contributions, the ideas expressed by other participants (e.g. Bohman 1996). Tracy Sulkin (2005) expanded the notion of issue uptake to include other forms of position taking by congressmen in the legislative arena (e.g. bill sponsorship and floor statements), specifically regarding issues that were raised first and foremost by their challengers in the preceding election campaign. The notion of uptake used here similarly regards legislators' actions in the legislative arena but, unlike Sulkin (2005), relates them to four societal actors that may 'trigger' their actions. That is, uptake levels tap into legislators' perceptions as to who prompted them to introduce new legislation, amendments to existing legislation or parliamentary questions. In particular we focus on four societal actors – i.e. unorganised constituents, organised interests, the party and the mass media – whose concerns representatives may choose to take up.

The reason for concentrating on these societal actors is the distinction between the collective and the individual accountability of elected representatives (Carey 2009). The distinction matches the longstanding debate on political representation between scholars in Europe and the United States (Esaiasson 1999). On the one hand, collective accountability rests with political parties. Disciplined parties enact into law the mandate that was given to them in the course of the election. In this manner, voters reward or dismiss those responsible for past public policies. On the other hand, the individual elected representative is accountable to his/her constituents. His/her actions should serve their interests. But even finding out what they want him/her to do is not a simple task and the representative may rely on simple heuristics. According (for instance) to state legislative staffers in Illinois, public opinion is not the opinions that groups of individuals who share a social identity express in the course of opinion polls or sample surveys (Herbst 1998). Nor do the staffers tend to think of public opinion in terms of the individuals they meet 'just sitting in a café or listening to people talk' (Herbst 1998: 75). Public opinion is articulated by organised interests and the mass media. Both the mass media and organised interests set the agenda in the legislative arena (*see* Baumgartner and Jones 1993; Kingdon 1984; van Aelst and Walgrave 2011).

Uptake of people's preferences in the legislative arena, we argue, is shaped by the images and ideas elected representatives have about political representation and the nature of people's preferences. Uptake in the legislative arena further mirrors representatives' behaviour in the district. Legislators have often been assumed to *compartmentalise* their actions in parliament and in the constituency so that their actions in one do not have negative repercussions in the other. Thus, for example, the freedom to ignore constituents' opinions in parliament can be bought by exemplary service responsiveness in the district (Norton and Wood 1993; Bianco 1994). The notion of uptake, however, intimately interlinks what representatives do in the district and in parliament (Sulkin 2005). In many respects the act of representation cannot be separated from the conditions that representatives compete under for re-election (Fenno 1978). As illustrated in Figure 4.1, representatives think about representation and decide on actions in the district *within the context of distinct electoral rules*. But the conceptions they have about political representation *in between elections* continue to shape what representatives do in the legislative arena, irrespective of the electoral conditions.

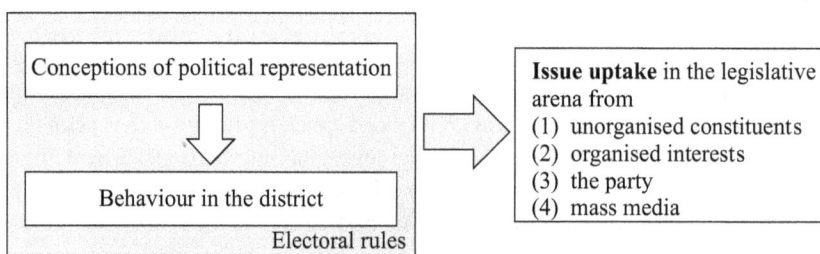

Figure 4.1: A model of issue uptake in the legislative arena by elected representatives

Uptake by representatives in the legislative arena is shaped by their personal conceptions about political representation. The actual images and ideas they have about the nature of people's preferences and the process of representation will increase their attentiveness to the preferences of some societal actors and decrease their attentiveness to others. It has long been stated that the representative's *delegate's* or *trustee's* attitude is a key determinant of the congruence between the constituency's policy preferences and the representative's roll call record (McCrone and Kuklinski 1979; Miller and Stokes 1963). This operationalisation in terms of voting behaviour has missed the key element, however, in the mandate-independence controversy (Pitkin 1967): that is, whether people's preferences are exogenous or endogenous. Rudy Andeweg and Jacques Thomassen (2005) distinguish two dimensions in the conceptions of representation. The first dimension juxtaposes representation from below to representation from above (Esaiasson and Holmberg 1996). From the bottom-up perspective of representation, people have clear and exogenous policy preferences that representatives translate into public policies. From the top-down perspective, representatives present distinct policy options to voters who then choose between them. People do not know much about policies and will form preferences only in response to what parties say and do (Manin 1997). The second dimension contrasts *ex-ante* representation to *ex-post* representation. *Ex-ante* controls, in the hands of constituents, serve to select those representatives that will implement the preferred policies once elected, whereas *ex-post* controls serve to sanction (or reward) representatives for their actions in the past (Mansbridge 2009; Fearon 1999).

The first dimension that contrasts representation from below with representation from above, as summarised in Table 4.1, is expected to be reflected in representatives' attentiveness to the party and to unorganised constituents. The second dimension that contrasts *ex-ante* with *ex-post* representation will, on the other hand, have repercussions for representatives' attentiveness to the mass media and the party. Legislators' actions in the legislative arena will more frequently originate with unorganised constituents when they believe constituents hold exogenous policy preferences, and representation is about translating these into legislation. When, contrary to this, representatives believe constituents incapable of holding exogenous policy preferences, their actions in the legislative arena will more frequently be dictated by the party (by the party's research centre, for instance).

At the same time, high uptake levels from the party are also expected to be related to *ex-ante*, promissory representation. Promissory representation is based on the policy pledges that parties make during the campaign and their ability to implement them once elected (Mansbridge 2003). Between elections, representatives are therefore beholden to faithfully translate their party manifesto into public policy.

Ex-post representation, on the other hand, is more closely associated with uptake from societal actors that react only after the fact. The mass media shape political agendas in particular by reporting the adverse outcomes of earlier policies. Taking up the issue in the legislative arena, legislators thereby seek to pre-empt the electorate's disapproval in the next election (Mansbridge 2003).

The notion of issue uptake further explicitly interlinks representatives' actions in the legislative arena with what they do in the district (Sulkin 2005). In the context of single-member districts, Fenno (1978) coined the concept of 'home style' to denote the actions in the district by which congressmen present to constituents what they do and stand for. In party-list proportional representation (PR), elected representatives likewise choose how to allocate scarce resources – their own time, if nothing else – to present themselves to voters and explain what they do in parliament. They have considerable discretion in their choice of how to relate to voters – though the 're-election constituency' that votes for them may be quite different from the geographical constituency. Even in single-member districts, after all, representatives relate differently to those who vote for them and those who do not (Fenno 1978).[1] More specifically, representatives' home styles, or the total of their actions in the district, differ as to their individual blend of one-way and two-way communication (Fenno 1978).

Representatives advertise: they seek name recognition and opportunities to set out their positions to the public (Mayhew 1974). They send out regular newsletters to constituents, are interviewed in local newspapers and on local television, and participate in debate nights. On the other hand, representatives organise frequent 'surgeries'[2] in the district, are invited to constituents' private homes to discuss issues with them and to answer their questions, and attend weddings and funerals in the local community. What they have in common is their give-and-take nature, presenting constituents with the opportunity to voice their concerns and speak their minds. What representatives do in the district and in parliament is intimately intertwined, we argue. In one arena, representatives remain ever mindful of the other: the access that representatives grant organisations and individuals in the district, for instance, frequently entails the promise of access in parliament (Fenno 1978). The actions in the legislative arena of representatives who developed home styles focusing on this give-and-take two-way communication are assumed to originate more often with unorganised constituents. Representatives who emphasise one-way communication tend to take their cue more from organised interests and the mass media whose ready-made propositions they then set out to communicate to constituents and use to mobilise wider support. Alternatively, the compartmentalisation thesis suggests that actions in the district and the legislative arena are unrelated (Norton and Wood 1993).

Representatives think about political representation and decide on their actions in the district *within the context of distinct electoral rules*. The conditions under

---

1.   What separates party-list proportional representation from single-member plurality, it has been argued (*see* e.g. Thompson 2005; Rehfeld 2005), is that individuals in party-list PR form their own constituencies using their party vote and each constituency is therefore perfectly homogeneous regarding ideology. This view, we argue, confuses the constituency in the first sense defined by Rehfeld (2005). That is, those who are eligible to vote for a representative, with the constituency in the second sense, are those who vote for him.

2.   Members of the UK House of Commons have frequent office hours in their respective constituencies where constituents can present them with any problem they may have, for example, in their dealings with public authorities. These are set up along the lines of a general practitioner's surgery. In Ireland they are called 'clinics'.

Table 4.1: A summary of the hypotheses regarding issue uptake in the legislative arena

		Unorganised constituents	Organised interests	Party	Mass Media
(1)	*Conceptions of political representation:*				
a.	representation from above	↘		↗	
b.	*ex-ante* representation			↗	↘
(2)	*Behaviour in the district:*				
a.	compartmentalisation thesis	no effect	no effect	no effect	no effect
b.	contact: one-way communication	↘	↗		↗
c.	contact: two-way communication	↗	↘		↘
d.	contact: interest groups		↗		
(3)	*Electoral rules:*				
a.	direct effect thesis: district magnitude	↘	↗	↗	↗
b.	interaction thesis: in open-list systems	↗		↘	
c.	in closed-list systems	↘		↗	

Note: Arrows indicate the expected direction of the effect

which representatives compete for re-election shape their attentiveness to different societal actors and their uptake levels in the legislative arena.

There are two competing theories in this regard. On the one hand, single-member districts prompt elected representatives to be responsive to unorganised constituents rather than organised interests in a manner that multi-member districts do not. For one, their re-election rests in the hands of the median voter rather than with partisan voters (Curtice and Shively 2009). Elected representatives will turn more to organised interests as district magnitude grows. There are two reasons for this: first, organised interests command greater numbers of voters; and second, organised interests are more about money than votes. Unpopular organised interests may even cost votes, and their candidates may need to be hidden amongst longer lists of co-partisans (Bawn and Thies 2003). Either way, elected representatives will favour catering to organised interests over unorganised constituents as district magnitude increases.

On the other hand, as John Carey and Matthew Shugart (1995) argued, district magnitude has a differential effect on the relative value of a representative's personal reputation compared to the party reputation: the scope of intra-party competition increases with district magnitude in open-list systems and decreases as districts grow in magnitude in closed-list systems. Representatives' responsiveness to unorganised constituents in particular is assumed to increase with their electoral incentive to cultivate a personal reputation (Heitshusen *et al.* 2005; but *see* Farrell and Scully 2007). Table 4.1 summarises the hypotheses and presents the expected effects.

Data: The PARTIREP cross-national survey in thirteen advanced industrial democracies

The data regarding 'uptake' have been collected as part of the cross-national PARTIREP survey among legislators in thirteen advanced industrial democracies across Europe. They include Austria, Belgium, Germany, Hungary, Ireland, Israel, Italy, the Netherlands, Norway, Poland, Portugal, Switzerland, and the United Kingdom. The PARTIREP project further undertook a cross-national survey of regional legislators in Austria, Belgium, Germany (Brandenburg, Lower Saxony, Rhineland-Palatinate and Thuringia), Italy (Calabria, Campania, Lazio, Lombardy, Tuscany and Aosta Valley), Portugal (Azores and Madeira), Switzerland (excl. Appenzell-Innerrhoden), and the United Kingdom (Scotland and Wales).

The inclusion of regional legislatures allows for more variation in terms of electoral rules and district magnitude. The cases in the selection include both open-list and closed-list electoral rules, ranging in district magnitude from single-member districts to at-large constituencies. Included are a combination of systems where preferential voting significantly affects the allocation of seats to candidates (Belgium, Ireland, Poland and Switzerland) and systems where preferential voting does not have such an effect (Israel, the Netherlands, Norway and Portugal). Then there are countries that use a combination of systems to elect the representatives of a single parliament (in the case of mixed-member systems, in Germany and Hungary), of different regional parliaments (Italy), and across levels of government (United Kingdom). Parliaments in Austria, finally, adopted PR systems with complex districting using varying electoral formulae and ballot types in the different tiers.[3]

About one in four in the selected national and regional legislatures participated in the study, totalling 1,990 responses. In the Appendix, response rates are reported per country and level of government. Lower or higher response rates are not concentrated in either open-list or closed-list electoral systems. While the numbers of national legislators responding are comparable across countries, there are marked differences between the numbers of regional legislators who responded, reflecting the constitutional structure of the countries, as well as the choice to focus on a limited number of regions in Germany and Italy. In terms of party affiliation, however, the legislators who responded do not markedly differ from the legislators in the population (except in Poland where the major parties are somewhat under-represented). To make the data more suited to our institutional research questions, weights were added by parliamentary party group in each

---

3. The Austrian Nationalrat employs a three-tiered system with preferential voting at the lowest levels (nominal voting is quite uncommon in the second tier and, as such, is ineffective). The ease of supporting an individual candidate differs markedly at both levels. While candidates are fully listed on the ballot and voters simply tick the box next to the name of their preferred candidate in the first tier, voters have to write a candidate's name in the second tier (Müller 2008). Both the second and third tiers are therefore coded as closed lists. Though reduced to two levels, the regional parliaments largely mirror the electoral system used at national level.

parliament, and a corrective was used to bring the total number of respondents in the Swiss cantonal parliaments in line with the other countries. All models were subsequently tested (both weighted and unweighted); the results reported are robust.

Operationalisations: the dependent variable

Uptake levels are defined in the PARTIREP cross-national survey as legislators' estimations of the proportion of their parliamentary initiatives that originated with each of the four societal actors in question, i.e. individual citizens, interest and action groups, the party (e.g. leadership or research centre), and the mass media.[4] Legislators' estimations need not add up to one hundred per cent.[5] Any single private member bill, floor statement, or parliamentary question may originate from the interplay between several societal actors. Moreover, the four actors of main interest by no means constitute an exhaustive list. A small minority of legislators in the selection also report drawing inspiration from their personal experience, from scientific reports and policy experts, or from other political parties at home and abroad.

As indicated in Table 4.2, approximately equal proportions (20 per cent) of the average legislator's initiatives in the legislative arena originated with the party, with organised interests, and from meeting with individual citizens. At 15 per cent the mass media inspired slightly fewer initiatives on average. More importantly, there are considerable individual and cross-national differences in the selection. Three out of four uptake levels effectively range from 0 to 100 per cent; uptake from the mass media ranges from 0 to 80 per cent. In addition, the average proportion of parliamentary initiatives derived from contact with individual constituents ranges from about 15 per cent in Germany, the Netherlands, Norway and Switzerland to over 30 per cent among Hungarian, Irish, Israeli, Italian and Polish legislators. Cross-national variation is equally pronounced regarding uptake levels from the party, organised interests and the mass media: country averages frequently range from about 5 per cent to well over 20 per cent.

Operationalisations: the independent variables

The primary explanatory variable, that is, what representatives think about representation, is captured by two dilemmas (Andeweg and Thomassen 2005). The first dilemma puts representation from below in opposition to representation from above. It constitutes a five-point scale: one end of the dilemma being whether

---

4. The exact question is: 'Of the initiatives (e.g. bills, written and oral questions) which you personally raised in parliament in the last year, roughly what proportions of these did you derive from the media, from interest groups, from within the party, from meeting with individual citizens, and from your personal experience, respectively? Could you please give a rough estimate in percentages?'

5. In order not to skew the analysis, we have excluded respondents whose sum of proportions exceeds 200. However, a robustness check of the models on the full sample yields the same results.

Table 4.2: Summary statistics (mean and standard deviation) of the dependent and independent variables

	mean	sd	min	max
uptake: unorganised constituents	19.24	18.25	0	100
uptake: organised interests	20.47	15.98	0	100
uptake: party	19.18	15.75	0	100
uptake: mass media	15.26	14.99	0	80
rep. from above	3.15	1.15	1	5
rep. *ex-ante*	3.20	1.05	1	5
contact: two-way	2.46	0.88	1	5
contact: one-way	2.82	0.84	1	5
contact: interest groups	2.86	0.83	1	5
seniority	5.21	6.55	0	54
left-right	5.05	1.96	0	10
distance (in 100km²)	1.32	1.80	0	16.91

politicians should aim to translate the political views of citizens into policy as accurately as possible, the other, whether politicians should stand clearly on their party's platform and aim to win citizen support for those views. On average, representatives holding a top-down conception of representation (41 per cent) outnumber those with a bottom-up notion (28 per cent). However, there is important variation within and across countries.

The second dilemma trades off *ex-post* representation against *ex-ante* representation. Asked for their views on the meaning of elections, 37 per cent think that politicians should account to the voters for their actions in the past, whereas 19 per cent feel that politicians should put their plans for the future to the voters. However, weighing up the alternatives in this second dimension seems to be much tougher than in the first: while 31 per cent of the respondents gravitate towards the middle of the first scale, 44 per cent consider *ex-post* and *ex-ante* controls equally important.

Elected representatives further differ as to the range of actions they take between elections in the district. They engage in advertising, position-taking and credit claiming to different degrees and with different frequencies (Mayhew 1974).

In the PARTIREP survey, representatives indicated how often they engaged in a range of actions outside the electoral campaign: the frequencies constitute a five-point scale ranging from never to once a week. The cross-national variation is considerable. Almost half of the legislators included in the survey meet with organised interests of every ilk at least once a fortnight, most often with employers' organisations or trade unions. More than half are featured in the local media at least once a fortnight. With the same frequency, 37 per cent give lectures and speak at debate nights and 29 per cent send out a personal newsletter. Their number is highest among elected representatives in Germany in particular. At least once a fortnight 41 per cent hold a surgery in the district, helping individual constituents in their dealings with public authorities. Twenty-three per cent meet local businesses and local action groups at least once a fortnight and less than 10 per cent publicise their successes in attracting businesses and obtaining government grants for the local area.

Constituency service of this kind is most common among Irish and United Kingdom legislators (*see also* Norton and Wood 1993). Polish legislators hold surgeries at least as frequently, whereas Norwegian legislators are as active in defending the economic interests of the local area. Moreover, 18 per cent attend weddings and funerals in the local area and 14 per cent meet with constituents in their private homes at least once a fortnight to talk about their wants and needs. Rather surprisingly the practice is almost as common among Israeli legislators as it is among Irish legislators.

The distinction is made between actions that focus on one-way communication, setting out the representative's position to constituents, and actions that concentrate on two-way communication. The former scale of actions includes giving lectures and speaking at debate nights, sending out a newsletter, being featured in the local media, and publicising their successes in project work; the latter scale includes attending weddings and funerals, meeting constituents in their private homes, holding surgeries, and meeting with businesses and local action groups.

Electoral incentives are measured by the decimal logarithm of district magnitude and a dichotomous indicator coded '1' for effective preferential systems and '0' for closed-list systems. In order to isolate the effect that representatives' conceptions of representation have on their uptake levels, a number of control variables are added: the level of government representatives serve, whether their party is in office or in opposition, its ideology on the left-right dimension, their seniority in parliament, and the distance of their district to the seat of parliament.

First, regional authorities are assumed to be closer to constituents than national authorities. On the one hand, regional legislators are typically elected by a constituency that is smaller in terms of population and size than the constituencies used in the general elections (Patzelt 2007). Regional legislators typically have to travel a shorter distance to the district and can consequently spend more time in the district. On the other hand, the jurisdictions of regional parliaments concentrate more on issues that are by their nature tied to a territory that is physically closer to constituents (Patzelt 2007). Because of their jurisdictions, regional legislators have to deal more frequently with local authorities and local interest groups. For both these reasons, regional legislators will more readily engage in constituency activities that bring them into frequent contact with constituents than is the case with national legislators. They will also more readily take up the issues constituents raise in those meetings than national legislators.

Second, uptake levels from the mass media are expected to be highest among opposition legislators, considering the media's propensity to concentrate on negative events. Furthermore, parties in opposition have fewer means at their disposal than parties in office to police government policies on their own initiative. Opposition parties resort more to 'fire alarm' forms of oversight, responding to information made public by other societal actors, in particular the mass media (McCubbins and Schwartz 1984).

Third, partisan conceptions of collective accountability are often expected to be stronger among the parties of the left – even though the empirical evidence is inconclusive (Converse and Pierce 1979; Jensen 1999). Fourth, elected representatives' goals and emotional incentives evolve and priorities shift over time: after a few terms in the legislature, a legislator will have established some measure of name recognition and support in the district (Fenno 1978). At the same time s/he is likely to assume extra responsibilities in the party, parliament or the executive – thereby committing him/herself to spending more time away from the district (Heitshusen *et al.* 2005). Fifth, the geographical location of the district constrains legislators' behaviour: the distance from the seat of parliament imposes practical limitations on the time legislators can spend in the district meeting constituents.

The consequences of what elected representatives think about representation

Uptake levels by representatives are count variables: that is, representatives offer rough estimates in non-negative integers (often multiples of five and ten) of the percentages of new legislation, amendments to legislation, and parliamentary questions that originated in the party; in meeting unorganised constituents and organised interests, and in the mass media. They are best analysed by means of negative binomial regression models, considering the evidence that the distributions of the dependent variables are over-dispersed (Long and Freese 2006). Percentage answers tend to sum to 100 per cent and are therefore (weakly) negatively correlated. Discussion of the results will proceed in two stages: first, elected representatives' conceptions of representation, behaviour in the district, and the electoral context will be looked at in isolation, each in turn. Then we will turn to their combined effect. The estimated negative binomial regression coefficients of the individual effects are presented in Table 4.3, their combined effect in Table 4.4. All models include the control variables and country dummies. Robust standard errors clustered at the party level account for the non-independence of observations within districts and avoid inflated levels of statistical significance (Steenbergen and Jones 2002).

Individual effects of conceptions of representation and behaviour in the district

Table 4.3 provides strong evidence for the assumption that the actual images and ideas elected representatives have about political representation guide their actions in the legislative arena in between elections. Representation-from-below conceptions tend to increase uptake levels from unorganised constituents, whereas representation-from-above conceptions tend to raise responsiveness to the party. Representation from above emphasises the view that people's preferences are

Table 4.3: The individual effects of conceptions of representation and behaviour in the district

	Unorganised constituents	Organised interests	Party	Mass Media
Representation from above	-0.089***	-0.005	0.072**	0.009
	(0.025)	(0.025)	(0.034)	(0.029)
Representation *ex-ante*	0.045*	0.003	0.046*	-0.037
	(0.023)	(0.024)	(0.026)	(0.029)
Constant	2.882***	3.351***	2.887***	2.359***
	(0.129)	(0.110)	(0.140)	(0.189)
log pseudo-likelihood	-4,491.035	-4,471.176	-4,409.306	-4,114.461
LR(df)	66.386***	28.712*	39.948***	63.512***
	(19)	(19)	(19)	(19)
Contact: two-way	0.141***	-0.085**	0.020	-0.091**
	(0.035)	(0.041)	(0.043)	(0.037)
Contact: one-way	0.002	0.041	-0.036	0.098**
	(0.037)	(0.040)	(0.047)	(0.045)
Contact: interest groups	-0.061	0.167***	0.048	-0.073**
	(0.038)	(0.045)	(0.039)	(0.036)
Constant	2.631***	2.924***	3.186***	2.392***
	(0.162)	(0.146)	(0.190)	(0.199)
log pseudo-likelihood	-4,489.572	-4,462.332	-4,412.359	-4,112.038
LR(df)	67.85***	37.556***	36.895**	65.935***
	(20)	(20)	(20)	(20)
Open list	-0.432***	0.181	0.424***	-0.157
	(0.136)	(0.153)	(0.151)	(0.181)
District magnitude	-0.160***	0.039	0.077	0.143*
	(0.027)	(0.041)	(0.071)	(0.080)
District Magnitude* Open list	0.344***	0.130	-0.163	-0.341**
	(0.100)	(0.129)	(0.127)	(0.146)
Constant	2.948***	3.323***	3.171***	2.044***
	(0.107)	(0.106)	(0.141)	(0.182)
log pseudo-likelihood	-4,493.572	-4,468.107	-4,411.397	-4,107.907
LR(df)	63.85***	31.78**	37.857***	70.066***
	(20)	(20)	(20)	(20)
Controls	Included	Included	Included	Included
Country dummies	Included	Included	Included	Included
N	1,456	1,456	1,456	1,456

Note: The table displays the estimated coefficients and standard errors from a negative binomial model. The set of predictors have been tested for multicollinearity using variance inflation factors. * $p < 0.10$; ** $p < 0.05$; *** $p < 0.01$, using two-tailed t-values.

endogenous. People typically do not know much about politics and policies, and are unwilling to learn more. They form policy preferences only on the basis of parties' self-interested political communications. Representatives who hold this view are then more likely to look to the party.

Representatives whose view more closely resembles representation from below, on the other hand, more often look to what unorganised constituents tell them and take up their concerns in the new legislation, amendments to legislation, and parliamentary questions they introduce in the legislative arena. The evidence that the second dimension of representatives' conceptions of representation affects their actions in between elections is less convincing. *Ex-ante* representation is related to high uptake from both unorganised constituents and the party. Alternatively, uptake from the mass media is highest among representatives who feel representation is about accounting to voters for actions in the past. The mass media typically concentrates on scandal, dissension and policy failure after the fact. Though the effects are in the expected direction, they do not reach conventional levels of statistical significance.

Moreover, elected representatives' actions in the legislative arena are closely interlinked with their actions in the district. The access they offer constituents and organised interests in the district clearly has consequences for their uptake in the legislative arena (Fenno 1978). In this respect there is little support for the compartmentalisation thesis: the legislators who emphasise two-way communication present higher uptake from unorganised constituents. They hold more frequent surgeries and meet more often with businesses, local action groups and constituents at social events in the local community. They take up the wants and needs heard at these meetings in the legislative arena: that is, their actions more frequently originate in meetings with unorganised constituents, and less frequently in organised interests and the mass media.

One-way communication, on the other hand, is not similarly related to lower uptake levels from the unorganised interests and higher uptake from the party. All elected representatives advertise (Mayhew 1974): they give lectures and speak at debate nights, are featured in the local media, and send out newsletters. Instead, representatives, who are most active in this kind of behaviour, are most informed in their actions by the mass media. Representatives, moreover, who meet most frequently with organised interests, also take up their concerns in the legislative arena more frequently.

The conditions that elected representatives compete under for re-election also shape their responsiveness to various societal actors between elections. The scope of intra-party competition motivates representatives to be more responsive to unorganised constituents in particular. The incentive to cultivate a personal reputation grows stronger the larger the number of co-partisan competitors they face. In open list systems the percentage of a representative's actions in parliament that directly result from meeting with constituents increases with district magnitude, whereas it decreases in closed list systems as the district grows in magnitude. Confirming Kathleen Bawn and Michael Thies' (2003) thesis, the representatives that are least responsive to organised interests are to be found in single-member districts.

Moreover, uptake from organised interests increases as the party list grows longer. However, the increase in district magnitude is even more pronounced in open list systems where, according to the Bawn and Thies' thesis, links to organised interests ought to cost rather than yield votes; the findings are more in accord with the Carey and Shugart (1995) thesis. Like parties, close ties to organised interests tend to be important in all circumstances: compared to unorganised constituents they communicate not only people's preferences, but also the intensity of their preferences (Herbst 1998). Furthermore, organised interests are key signals where public policies are failing. Therefore, the trade-off tends to be more to the detriment of uptake from the mass media than from the party or organised interests.

The combined effect of conceptions of representation and behaviour in the district

Representatives engage in communication with constituents partly for self-interested reasons, namely, seeking re-election. The conditions that they compete under for re-election affect the segments of society they are responsive to between elections. But re-election does not exhaust representatives' motivations and electoral rules do not *determine* the segments of public opinion they are responsive to. Electoral incentives' capacity to predict representatives' levels of uptake is modest at best. Table 4.4 presents these combined effects, while the predicted counts for the minimum and maximum values of the independent variables are reported in Table 4.5. The increase in uptake from meeting with constituents is modest where intra-party competition is present: from 14 to 21 per cent when district magnitude grows from 1 to 100. Uptake from constituents is the strongest in single-member districts but, in the absence of intra-party competition, uptake decreases from 22 to 16 per cent when district magnitude grows from 1 to 150. Even after controlling for the electoral context, how representatives think about representation guides their actions in the legislative arena between elections, and the effect is among the strongest found.

On the one hand, uptake levels from unorganised constituents increase from 16 to 22 per cent among representatives who feel that representation is best described as translating the political views of citizens into policy as accurately as possible, compared to those for whom people's preferences are endogenous and who, rather, seek support for their political views. Uptake levels from the party increase from 18 to 25 per cent among the latter. On the other hand, uptake levels from the party are similarly raised from 19 to 24 per cent among those favouring conceptions of *ex-ante* representation to *ex-post* conceptions. Conceptions of *ex-post* representation have a more limited effect on representatives' uptake levels from the mass media. The combined effects of representatives' conceptions of representation after controlling for their behaviour in the district and electoral context are about as strong as their individual effects. This suggests that people holding particular views of representation are not, on the whole, more likely to come forward and run for office under some electoral conditions than under other rules. Possible *sorting effects*, that is, cannot be very strong. Nor can they account for our findings.

Table 4.4: The combined effect of conceptions of representation and behaviour in the district

	Unorganised constituents	Organised interests	Party	Mass Media
Representation from above	-0.089***	0.010	0.078**	-0.011
	(0.024)	(0.025)	(0.032)	(0.029)
Representation *ex-ante*	0.043*	0.004	0.056**	-0.048*
	(0.023)	(0.023)	(0.027)	(0.028)
Contact: two-way	0.140***	-0.087**	0.028	-0.089**
	(0.035)	(0.041)	(0.043)	(0.036)
Contact: one-way	-0.003	0.039	-0.042	0.115***
	(0.037)	(0.039)	(0.046)	(0.043)
Contact: interest groups	-0.062	0.174***	0.062	-0.078**
	(0.035)	(0.047)	(0.041)	(0.037)
Open list	-0.439***	0.128	0.492***	-0.142
	(0.127)	(0.153)	(0.147)	(0.185)
District magnitude	-0.137***	0.045	0.055	0.155**
	(0.028)	(0.045)	(0.064)	(0.076)
District Magnitude* Open list	0.331***	0.183	-0.159	-0.376***
	(0.096)	(0.133)	(0.203)	(0.146)
Regional parliament	0.002	0.013	0.239***	0.103
	(0.062)	(0.075)	(0.084)	(0.095)
Seniority	-0.000	-0.004	0.000	0.007
	(0.003)	(0.004)	(0.004)	(0.007)
Left-right	0.020	-0.047***	-0.036***	0.064***
	(0.018)	(0.012)	(0.013)	(0.014)
Distance (in 100km^2)	-0.036**	-0.013	0.030*	-0.011
	(0.018)	(0.018)	(0.017)	(0.018)
Governing party	-0.052	0.002	0.112*	-0.164***
	(0.035)	(0.044)	(0.066)	(0.060)
Constant	2.989***	2.838***	2.667***	2.272***
	(0.177)	(0.176)	(0.197)	(0.241)
Country dummies	Included	Included	Included	Included
N	1,456	1,456	1,456	1,456
Log pseudo-likelihood	-4478.54	-4458.70	-4406.43	-4130.86
LR(df)	157.76***	82.38***	85.65***	148.23***
	(25)	(25)	(25)	(25)

Note: The table displays the estimated coefficients and standard errors from a negative binomial model. The set of predictors have been tested for multicollinearity using variance inflation factors. * p <0.10; ** p < 0.05; *** p < 0.01, using two-tailed t-values.

Table 4.5: Predicted counts of uptake levels on the basis of minimum and maximum values of the independent variables

	min-max value	Unorganised constituents	Organised Interests	Party	Mass media
District magnitude in closed-list systems	1	21,87	19,53	20,28	10,45
	150	16,22	21,56	22,87	14,64
District magnitude in open-list systems	1	14,09	22,19	33,16	9,06
	100	20,74	35,03	26,94	5,83
Representation from above	1	22,42	20,14	18,44	12,68
	5	15,71	20,96	25,23	12,16
Representation *ex-ante*	1	17,23	20,37	19,30	13,66
	5	20,44	20,72	24,11	11,29
Contact: two-way	1	15,75	22,90	20,84	13,88
	5	27,59	16,19	23,28	9,71
Contact: one-way	1	18,85	19,37	22,96	10,46
	5	18,63	22,66	19,44	16,53
Contact: organised interest	1	20,82	15,36	19,45	14,13
	5	16,23	30,83	24,93	10,36

Note: Entries display the predicted count at the minimum and maximum values of the explanatory variables of main interest. Shaded cells indicate that the change in predicted counts is statistically significant at the 95 per cent or 90 per cent level (dark and light grey respectively).

Control variables

In recent decades many advanced industrial democracies have introduced regional levels of government. Regional legislators are expected to be closer to constituents as a result of both smaller constituencies and the jurisdiction of regional parliaments. Representation-from-below attitudes are more common among regional legislators than among national legislators. They also engage more in two-way communication with constituents. However, after controlling for the size of constituencies, what they think about representation, and what they do in the district, few differences remain between regional and national legislators.

Other controls have the expected effect: the distance that representatives have to travel to the district decreases their uptake from meeting constituents. Left-wing party representatives introduce more amendments to legislation, new legislation, and parliamentary questions that originate with the party and organised interests (in particular, trade unions); whereas right-wing parties turn more to the mass media. Opposition parties concentrate even more on the mass media: they frequently lack other resources for finding out where policies fail. Seniority does not affect uptake levels, even if what representatives think about representation and their level of activity in the district can be expected to evolve as they serve longer in parliament (Fenno 1978).

Furthermore, there are '*cultural* repertoires' of ready-made representative claims that legislators tap into (Saward 2010). That is, there are cultural differences in what legislators think about representation and in their uptake that are, in part, shaped by conditions that legislators compete under for re-election. They reflect the accumulated wisdom of past campaigns, hard won from the 'fight for their life' campaigns that most legislators experience at some point in their career (Fenno 1978) and from observing resourceful challengers (Sulkin 2005).

Nonetheless, even then, there remain non-negligible fixed country effects in legislators' uptake. In previous sections, country differences have been largely glossed over but legislators in Ireland, Italy, Poland and the United Kingdom, for instance, share a propensity to look to unorganised constituents when acting in the legislative arena. This propensity is in line with the electoral institutions in these countries. However, even after taking them into account, the models underestimate this propensity in these countries. Electoral institutions are even less instrumental in understanding Israeli legislators' propensity to take up unorganised constituents' interests in the legislative arena – Israeli legislators are elected by a single, nation-wide constituency under closed-list proportional rules. Rather, the use of party primaries in the selection of candidates by several Israeli parties may, for instance, prompt them to take up constituents' interests (Rahat and Hazan 2001). Legislators in Norway and the Netherlands tend to concentrate on the mass media instead. Legislators in Portugal, finally, turn to the party. These patterns are in line with their favourable conceptions of representation 'from above' but are not fully explained by them.

Conclusion

Typically, only a minority of constituents have met an elected representative in the twelve months leading up to a general election: the proportion ranges from as 'many' as 19 per cent in Switzerland to as few as 5 per cent in the Netherlands (Curtice and Shively 2009). That constituents and their elected representatives frequently meet is considered critical to representative government, however, by democratic theorists and empiricists alike. It is critical that constituents have ample opportunities to challenge, and if needed, reject representatives' claims to speak and act on their behalf. Contact is further related to the belief that representatives know what people think, but not to satisfaction with democracy (Curtice and Shively 2009).

We demonstrated that elected representatives' actions in the legislative and the electoral arenas are intimately interconnected in this regard. On the one hand, electoral incentives to cultivate a personal reputation are directly related to their propensity to take up concerns voiced by unorganised constituents in parliament. That is, constituents may benefit even from self-interested representatives (Disch 2011). On the other hand, where frequent access is given to constituents, representatives more often feel constituents' concerns are reflected in their actions in parliament. Of course, frequent access is neither a necessary, nor a sufficient condition for public policy to be in people's best interests. Nevertheless, somehow, constituents' preferences seem to inform their representatives' actions. Even after controlling for electoral incentives, representatives who meet frequently with constituents during surgeries, in the privacy of constituents' homes, and at local community functions, believe that a larger proportion of their actions in parliament is directly inspired by these meetings.

Representatives, on the other hand, who frequently attend debate nights, send out newsletters, and are featured in the media, turn more often to what the mass media are reporting on. That is, those who favour 'educating' constituents (by their actions in the district) over listening to them are also less likely to act on the instigation of constituents in parliament. More importantly, what 'self-interested' representatives think about representation shapes their actions in parliament: representation-from-below beliefs are related to high levels of uptake from unorganised interests, whereas representation-from-above beliefs result in high levels of uptake from the party. *Ex-ante* representation beliefs are equally related to promissory representation by parties. Representatives communicate with constituents in the 'shadow of elections' but they decide on their actions in the legislative arena, at least in part, on the basis of the actual images and ideas they have about representation and of their actions in the district between elections.

Appendix

Table A.4.1: Case selection: Response rates and district magnitude

		mean M	min-max	resp.	pop.
Austria	nat.	7.5	1–36	56	183
	reg. (9)	6.6	1–26	173	448
Belgium	nat.	13.6	4–24	70	150
	reg. (4)	35.1	2–72	95	313
Germany	nat.	2.0	1–65	134	622
	reg. (4)	1.9	1–65	145	429
Hungary		1.9	1–64	99	383
Ireland		3.9		34	166
Israel		120	120	39	120
Italy	nat.	24.2	1–44	45	632
	reg. (6)	8.9	1–42	83	364
The Netherlands		150	150	65	150
Norway		8.9	4–17	46	169
Poland		11.2	7–19	56	460
Portugal	nat.	10.5	2–47	72	230
	reg. (2)	26.4	2–47	36	104
Switzerland	nat.	7.7	1–34	53	200
	reg. (25)	19.6	1–100	581	2,573
United Kingdom	nat.	1	1	62	639
	reg. (2)	1.5		46	189

References

Andeweg, R. (2003) 'Beyond representativeness: Trends in political representation', *European Review*, 11: 147–61.

Andeweg, R. and Thomassen, T. (2005) 'Modes of political representation: Toward a new typology', *Legislative Studies Quarterly*, 30: 507–28.

Baumgartner, F. and Jones, B. (1993) *Agendas and Instability in American Politics*, Chicago: University of Chicago Press.

Bawn, K. and Thies, M. (2003) 'A comparative theory of electoral incentives: Representing the unorganized under PR, plurality and mixed-member electoral systems', *Journal of Theoretical Politics*, 15: 5–32.

Bianco, W. (1994) *Trust: Representatives and constituents*, Ann Arbor: University of Michigan Press.

Bishin, B. (2009) *The Tyranny of Minority: The subconstituency politics theory of representation*, Philadelphia: Temple University Press.

Bohman, J. (1996) *Public Deliberation: Pluralism, complexity, and democracy*, Cambridge: MIT Press.

Bullock, J. (2011) 'Elite influence on public opinion in an informed electorate', *American Political Science Review*, 105: 496–515.

Carey, J. (2009) *Legislative Voting and Accountability*, Cambridge: Cambridge University Press.

Carey, J. and Shugart, M. (1995) 'Incentives to cultivate a personal vote: A rank ordering of electoral formulas', *Electoral Studies*, 14: 417–39.

Converse, P. and Pierce, R. (1979) 'Representative roles and legislative behavior in France', *Legislative Studies Quarterly*, 4: 525–62.

Curtice, J. and Shively, P. (2009) 'Who represents us best? One member or many?', in H. -D. Klingemann (ed.) *The Comparative Study of Electoral Systems*, Oxford: Oxford University Press, pp. 171–192.

Dalton, R. (2004) *Democratic Challenges, Democratic Choices*, Oxford: Oxford University Press.

Dalton, R., McAllister, I. and Wattenberg, M. (2000) 'The consequences of partisan dealignment', in Dalton, R. and Wattenberg, M. (eds) *Parties Without Partisans*, Oxford: Oxford University Press, pp. 37–63.

Disch, L. (2011) 'Toward a mobilisation conception of democratic representation', *American Political Science Review*, 105: 100–14.

Dovi, S. (2007) *The Good Representative,* Oxford: Blackwell.

Elling, R. (1979) 'The utility of state legislative casework as a means of oversight', *Legislative Studies Quarterly*, 4: 353–79.

Esaiasson, P. (1999) 'Not all politics is local. The geographical dimension of policy representation', in Miller, W., Pierce, R., Thomassen, J., Herrera, R., Holmberg, S., Esaiasson, P. and Webels, B. (eds) *Policy Representation in Western Democracies*, Oxford: Oxford University Press, pp. 110–36.

Esaiasson, P. and Holmberg, S. (1996) *Representation From Above: Members of parliament and representative democracy in Sweden*, Aldershot: Dartmouth.

Farrell, D. and Scully, R. (2007) *Representing Europe's Citizens? Electoral institutions and the failure of parliamentary representation*, Oxford: Oxford University Press.

Fearon, J. (1998) 'Deliberation as discussion', in Elster J. (ed.) *Deliberative Democracy*, Cambridge: Cambridge University Press, pp. 44–68.

—— (1999) 'Electoral accountability and the control of politicians: Selecting good types versus sanctioning poor performance', in Przeworski, A., Stokes, S. and Manin, B. (eds) *Democracy, Accountability, and Representation,* Cambridge: Cambridge University Press, pp. 55–97.

Fenno, R. (1978) *Home Style: House members in their districts*, Boston: Little, Brown and Co.

Hardin, R. (2004) 'Representing ignorance', *Social Philosophy and Policy*, 21: 76–99.

Heitshusen, V., Young, G. and Wood, D. (2005) 'Electoral context and MP constituency focus in Australia, Canada, Ireland, New Zealand, and the United Kingdom', *American Journal of Political Science*, 49: 32–45.

Herbst, S. (1998) *Reading Public Opinion: How political actors view the democratic process*, Chicago: University of Chicago Press.

Jensen, T. (2000) 'Party cohesion', in Esaiasson, P. and Heidar, K. (eds) *Beyond Westminster and Congress: The Nordic experience*, Columbus: Ohio State University Press, pp. 210–36.

Jewell, M. (1970) 'Attitudinal determinants of legislative behavior: The utility of role analysis', in Kornberg A. and Musolf L. (eds) *Legislatures in Developmental Perspective*, Durham: Duke University Press, pp. 460–500.

Kam, C. (2009) *Party Discipline and Parliamentary Politics,* Cambridge: Cambridge University Press.

Kingdon, J. (1984) *Agendas, Alternatives, and Public Policies*, Boston: Little, Brown and Co.

Long, S. and Freese, J. (2006) *Regression Models for Categorical Dependent Variables Using STATA*, College Station: STATA Press.

McCrone, D. and Kuklinski, J. (1979) 'The delegate theory of representation', *American Journal of Political Science*, 23: 278–300.

McCubbins, M. and Schwartz, T. (1984) 'Congressional oversight overlooked: Police patrols versus fire alarms', *American Journal of Political Science*, 28: 165–79.

Manin, B. (1997) *The Principles of Representative Government,* Cambridge: Cambridge University Press.

Mansbridge, J. (2003) 'Rethinking representation', *American Political Science Review*, 97: 515–28.

—— (2009) 'A "selection model" of political representation', *Journal of Political Philosophy*, 17: 369–98.

Mayhew, D. (1974) *Congress: The electoral connection*, New Haven: Yale University Press.

Miller, W. and Stokes, D. (1963) 'Constituency influence in Congress', *American Political Science Review,* 57:45–56.

Müller, W.C. (2008) 'Austria: A complex electoral system with subtle effects', in Gallagher, M. and Mitchell, P. (eds) *The Politics of Electoral Systems,* Oxford: Oxford University Press, pp. 397–416.

Norton, P. and Wood, D. (1993) *Back from Westminster: British Members of Parliament and their constituents,* Lexington: University Press of Kentucky.

Patzelt, W. (2007) 'The constituency roles of MPs at the federal and länder levels in Germany', *Regional and Federal Studies,* 17: 47–70.

Pitkin, H. (1967) *The Concept of Representation,* Berkeley: University of California Press.

Rahat, G. and Hazan, R. (2001) 'Candidate selection methods: An analytical framework', *Party Politics,* 7: 297–322.

Rawlings, R. (1990) 'The MP's complaints service', *Modern Law Review,* 53: 22–42.

Rehfeld, A. (2005) *The Concept of Constituency: Political representation, democratic legitimacy, and institutional design,* Cambridge: Cambridge University Press.

Saward, M. (2010) *The Representative Claim,* Oxford: Oxford University Press.

Shaffner, B. (2005) 'Priming gender: Campaigning on women's issues in US Senate elections', *American Journal of Political Science,* 49: 803–17.

Steenbergen, M. and Jones, B. (2002) 'Modeling multilevel data structures', *American Journal of Political Science,* 46: 218–37.

Sulkin, T. (2005) *Issue Politics in Congress,* Cambridge: Cambridge University Press.

Thomassen, J. (1994) 'Empirical research into political representation: Failing democracy or failing models', in Jennings, K. and Mann, T. (eds) *Elections at Home and Abroad,* Ann Arbor: University of Michigan Press, pp. 237–64.

Thompson, D. F. (2005) *Restoring Responsibility: Ethics in government, business and healthcare,* Cambridge: Cambridge University Press.

Van Aelst, P. and Walgrave, S. (2011) 'Minimal or massive? The political agenda-setting power of the mass media according to different methods', *International Journal of Press/Politics,* 16: 295–313.

Wahlke, J., Eulau, H., Buchanan, W. and Ferguson, L. (1962) *The Legislative System: Explorations in legislative behaviour,* New York: John Wiley.

Chapter Five

Nominations, Campaigning and Representation: How the Secret Garden of Politics Determines the Style of Campaigning and Roles of Representation

Rune Karlsen and Hanne Marthe Narud

Quite a few studies now exist on the nomination procedures of political parties, a process previously referred to as the 'secret garden of politics' (Gallagher and Marsh 1988). Central topics have been candidate selection methods and their political consequences, and how nominations impact on the representativeness of the elected elites (e.g. Hazan and Rahat 2010; Narud 2011). Moreover, there are numerous studies of political representation in which the interactions between the elected and the represented are discussed, analysed, and/or theorised from a variety of angles (e.g. Esaiasson and Holmberg 1996; Manin 1997; Esaiasson and Heidar 2000; Urbinati and Warren 2008; Valen and Narud 2007). Finally, in recent years a number of scholars have paid attention to the differences in campaign styles between systems. At the most basic level, a line is drawn between the candidate-centred US campaign and the party-centred Western European campaign (Plasser and Plasser 2002). Little has been done, however, to link the three subfields in which responsiveness (or lack of such) is the end product. Our aim in this chapter, therefore, is to ask: to what extent do the methods of candidate selection impact upon the style of campaigning, and consequently upon how the elected candidates define their representational roles? Implicit in our question is that we regard the three elements as parts of a dynamic process which starts with party nominations, goes on through party campaigning, and continues with political representation.

The concept of between-election democracy offers an excellent framework for our analytical purposes. It allows us to link elements of the representational process *before* the election, i.e. nominations and campaigning, to central features of what is going on *after* the election, i.e. how representatives define their representational roles. The question is how *strong* this link is; does it differ in strength as we move from one stage of the process to another? These questions are analysed in light of agency theory which takes into consideration how party-dominated institutions constrain the behaviour of individual candidates both during and between elections.

This chapter has a theoretical as well as an empirical objective. Theoretically, it aims at developing a framework that helps explain differences between countries in terms of the interactions between parties and citizens before and after elections.

As discussed by Esaiasson, Gilljam and Persson in Chapter Two, the between-election democracy perspective directs attention to the representative processes in which past and present elections have a subordinated role. Consequently, the framework put forward in this chapter links candidate behaviour related to election democracy (campaigning), with behaviour related to between-election democracy (representational focus and style).

We argue that, theoretically, campaign styles are linked to the properties of candidate selection methods, emphasising two dimensions of candidate selection: the level of inclusiveness (in terms of participation) on the one hand, and the level of decentralisation on the other. The core of the argument is that if the party controls the nomination, the candidate's campaign style will be party centred, whereas if voters control the nomination, the style will be candidate centred. We also argue that the nomination practices affect the candidates' representational role orientations. In systems where the parties nominate, candidates are more likely to consider the party their basis for representation. In systems where the voters nominate, they are more likely to consider the voters in their constituency as their representational focus. From the perspective of between-election democracy an interesting question is whether the institutional setting affects campaign styles to a greater extent than representational roles as campaigning is closer to the nomination process and the electoral system.

In the analysis we also study differences between individual candidates based on their placement on the list and their party affiliation. The acceptance of individualised behaviour might differ between parties based on their culture and traditions and this might have consequences for campaign style and representational roles. In a proportional system a number of candidates from one party in one constituency might expect to win a mandate, while a number of lower placed candidates will stand no chance of being elected. We investigate whether the higher placed candidates are more party centred than the lower placed candidates.

For the purpose of this chapter, we further elaborate our model based on a study of the parliamentary system of one individual country: Norway. In so doing, we analyse the Norwegian Candidate Study of 2009, for which we have survey items on nominations, styles of campaigning and representation. The empirical study of the Norwegian case serves two purposes. First, we investigate how far the behaviour of Norwegian candidates meets the expectations drawn from our theoretical framework, and investigate the candidates' views on the nomination process, the level of individualised campaigning, and the representational roles of Norwegian candidates. Second, we study empirically the relationship between views on nomination, campaign style and representational roles.

A schematic model of campaign styles and representational roles

In recent years the theoretical vocabulary drawn from agency theory has gained prominence in the study of representational linkages. These linkages may be described in terms of delegation from a principal to an agent which takes place in several stages of the political process: from voters to parliamentary candidates, from parliament to government, and from government to the bureaucracy.[1] Our interest concerns what goes on in the first stage of this process (the selection of parliamentary candidates) and its impact on the election campaign and representation. *Accountability*, which is the other important element in the chain of delegation, reverses this relationship, and involves requirements for reporting back and the possibility for sanctions (e.g. removing someone from office) and rewards. When delegation takes place, there is always a danger of opportunistic behaviour on the part of the agents, referred to in the literature as so-called 'agency-losses' (Kiewiet and McCubbins 1991).[2] To control such problems, principals may place certain restrictions on agent actions. These control mechanisms may be put in place *ex-ante*, i.e. before the principal delegates to an agent, or *ex-post*, i.e. after authority has been delegated (Kiewiet and McCubbins 1991; Strøm 1999, 2000). Let us further illustrate the relevance of these concepts for the purpose of our chapter.

There are two types of control mechanisms that are placed *ex-ante*. The first is the so-called *contract design*, that is, the set of rules by which the principal 'hires' the agent. In the process of candidate selection these are the set of institutions that regulate delegation from voters to representatives, i.e. the electoral system and/or the nomination process. One important question regards the extent to which the electoral laws allow for a personal vote, or at the other extreme, whether voters are faced with a closed-list system. Another is the level of institutionalisation of the procedure, that is, whether nominations are structured by formal regulations or whether they are governed by rules and procedures that are decided by the parties themselves. The other *ex-ante* control mechanisms are the *screening and selection devices* applied by the principals to identify the 'good agents' (Strøm 1999), that is, candidates with the qualifications and characteristics preferred by the selectorate. With relevance to the nomination process, these are the demands for group affiliation, local connections and other characteristics that help 'balance' the list with a variety of economic, demographic and social interests (Gallagher and Marsh 1988; Hazan and Rahat 2010; Narud 2011).

Ex-post control mechanisms, on the other hand, are the ways through which the principals are able to *monitor* and *sanction* the agents at a later stage. Monitoring is obviously constrained by the nature of parliamentary affairs, which take place on a stage that is distant from the attention of the public. In most systems the ability – and even the interest – of individual voters to keep an eye on the actions of their MPs is very limited. For most people the media would be the most important source of information – particularly before election time. It is during the electoral campaign that the candidates take their case to the electorate, thereby providing an incentive to the public to either withdraw their electoral support or to continue

---

1. For a thorough discussion on the problems of delegation and accountability in multilevel parliamentary systems, *see* e.g. Strøm 1999, 2000; Bergman *et al.* 2000; Strøm *et al.* 2003; Bergman and Strøm 2011.
2. Technically, there are two necessary conditions for agency losses: divergent preferences on the one hand, and asymmetric information on the other (Strøm 2000).

supporting the party/candidate. Hence, the voters' perceptions of their agents' performances will most likely be coloured by the incumbents' performances at election time.

The ability to *sanction* individual candidates is related to the character of the electoral system as well as to the formal and informal rules of the nomination process. Elections, defined retrospectively, are the most important sanctioning devices that voters can use to secure responsiveness from their leaders. However, defined prospectively, they are mechanisms for the selection of 'good' agents. These two understandings of elections, as Fearon (1999) points out, are by no means incompatible. Elections are means for both selection and sanctioning, and the extent to which these interact or dominate is highly conditional upon certain mechanisms of the electoral law.[3] Electoral systems in which candidates have the incentive to seek a personal vote, for instance, offer a direct and much stronger sanctioning mechanism to the voters than a strictly party-centred system. Closed list systems, therefore, put the sanctioning devices in the hands of the party activists.[4] Here, the effective principals may be the national, local, or provincial party branches – conditioned upon the level of *centralisation* of the process (*see* Figure 5.2).

The point of departure for our argument is how the various mechanisms of the nomination process may be linked to electoral campaigning and political representation under the means by which principals control their agents. The basic concepts of the agency literature offer a framework that takes into consideration how institutions shape the strategic context of parties and candidates. We know from previous studies that nominations take place within a complex network of multiple principals and multiple agents, in which nomination practices determine 'who' is accountable to 'whom' (Narud *et al.* 2002). Introducing the concept of accountability helps clarify the dilemmas facing incumbent candidates seeking reselection, thereby shedding light on the quality of responsiveness of candidates *vis-à-vis* different levels of the party.

Hence, we argue, and substantiate our arguments below, that the level of centralisation and inclusiveness in the nomination process has a bearing on the responsiveness of individual candidates (agents) concerning two aspects: the campaign style of candidates, and their role orientation as elected representatives. Therefore, we have to take into consideration that the party hierarchy consists of several levels (at least five):

---

3. Consider, for example, a system with fixed term limits in which MPs can serve only one term. Here, it is not meaningful to talk about *electoral* accountability, even though the elected representative may be accountable to some other party in other respects (e.g. to the court). Under these circumstances elections serve as mechanisms for choosing political representatives rather than as devices for control. *See* Fearon (1999) for a principled discussion about electoral accountability and the control of politicians.

4. *See* Müller (2000) for a theoretical account of the intermediate role of the party in the system of delegation.

- central party leadership
- regional party leaders
- local party leaders
- party members
- party voters

Each one of these levels encompasses a set of principals as well as agents who are accountable to one another. The ultimate principal, of course, is the individual voter, but the institutional setting determines his/her ability to sanction the elected agent, and consequently, the electoral focus of the incumbent candidates. For example, in a decentralised and party-centred system in which nominations are restricted to convention delegates, the candidates have few incentives to seek personal votes. When seeking re-selection, the focus of the incumbent would be towards the local party leaders, since they control the 'key' to his/her success. By contrast, in an open system with party primaries or preferential voting, voters are able to control reselection (and re-election), and the incumbents have the incentives to seek personal votes. In Figure 5.1 we attempt to represent the various factors discussed in one comprehensive model.

The conceptual basis for this model is the agency framework, and the principal agent relationships discussed above. 'Accountability' and 'responsiveness' are key factors. In PR systems when the party nominates and there is no possibility for preference voting, the result will be a party-centred campaign style, and the focus of representation will be the party. When the party nominates in PR systems and there is a possibility for preference voting, we argue that the campaign style

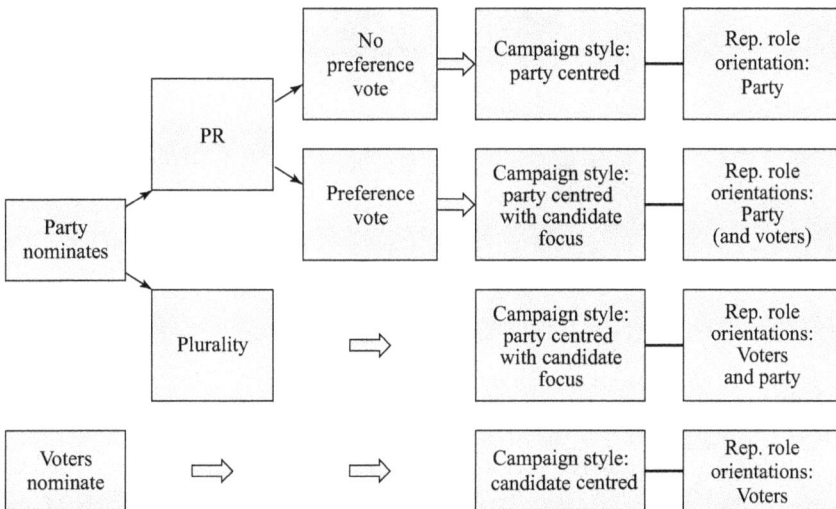

Figure 5.1: Nomination control, electoral system and styles of campaigning and representation

will be party centred but, depending on the extent of preference voting, with elements of individual focus (individualised campaigning). Here, the focus of representation will be the party first and the voters in the constituency second. We argue that when the party nominates in plurality systems the campaign style will be party centred but with elements of individual focus (individualised campaigning). However, in this case we argue that the focus of representation will be voters in the constituency first and the party second. Finally, we argue that, when voters nominate, the campaign style will be candidate centred and the focus of representation will be the voters in the constituency.

In the next section of the chapter we substantiate our model – linking the nomination procedures to the campaign styles and the representational roles of candidates.

Dimensions of centralisation and inclusiveness

As hinted at already, two dimensions in particular serve to classify the nomination systems. These are the degree of centralisation, on the one hand, and, on the other, the degree of inclusiveness (openness to participation) (Gallagher and Marsh 1988).[5] In Figure 5.2 we have combined these points into a two-dimensional continuum.[6]

Centralisation was given great attention in the seminal volume edited by Gallagher and Marsh (1988) (*see also* Katz and Mair 1992; Norris 1997; Narud *et al.* 2002; Hazan and Rahat 2010). Power over candidate selection is distributed according to national, regional or constituency agencies, and the level of system centralisation depends upon the degree of supervision exercised by these agencies over the selection procedures. Ranney (1981) concludes that by far the most common pattern is 'selection by constituency party agencies under some form

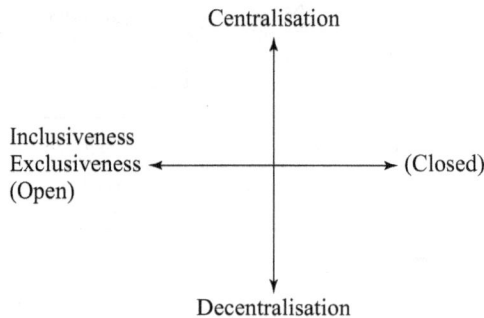

Figure 5.2: Dimensions of nomination systems

---

5. A third dimension, which we will not discuss at any length here, concerns the qualities demanded from the aspirants in the selection process.

6. Several scholars have pointed out that the two dimensions are, in some cases, interrelated (Marsh 2000; Hazan and Rahat 2010). For example, more centralised nomination procedures are normally more exclusive, even though there is no automatic correlation between the two factors.

of supervision by national or regional agencies, and the next most common is selection by national agencies after considerations or suggestions made by constituency and regional agencies'. The supervision consists of parties trying to influence the allocation of candidates (e.g. by constituency), and the placement of candidates (e.g. central *vs* local) or interfering in the positioning of candidates (e.g. on 'safe' seats). The final and most common device for supervision is the veto, i.e. the power of the national or regional party agency to withhold support of a locally selected candidate.

The level of *inclusiveness* in the process concerns who is allowed to participate. In most countries, participation in the process of candidate selection is restricted to party members and is made according to party rules. The notable exception, Ranney (1981) observes, is the US system, where party candidates are chosen in the parties' primaries and where state laws govern who can vote in these primaries. Hence, in contrast to the European parliamentary systems, candidate selection in the US is by far the most inclusive since party agencies or party officials have virtually no say in who participates in the selection of candidates. However, Bille (2001) points to the fact that in many democracies candidate selection methods are becoming more inclusive as more and more parties give their rank and file members the right to influence the selection of candidates. A case in point is the Israeli experience, as reported by Hazan and Rahat (2010) in their recent book. Over the years the Israeli parties have tried out virtually all methods of candidate selection, from the adoption of party primaries in the 1990s (Likud and Labour), to the most exclusive processes in which one rabbi or a group of rabbis decide the nominations (the ultra-orthodox parties).

The degrees of centralisation and inclusiveness of the nomination procedures are important from several perspectives and they have different implications for the styles of campaigning on the one hand, and the representational focus on the other. First of all, the two dimensions generate a multifaceted system of 'national principals' versus 'local principals', which complicates the question of agent accountability and responsiveness. Decentralised nominations put forward local agents and affect the focus of incumbent candidates seeking reselection. By contrast, centralised nominations promote national policy 'servants' with incentives to pursue a parliamentary career. In decentralised systems the party MPs face demands from the central party leadership as well as from the local party leadership. Since the local party controls reselection, the representatives must devote sufficient time to the specific problems of their constituency. On the other hand, elected representatives encounter demands from the central leadership for party discipline and cohesion in parliamentary behaviour. Thus, individual candidates may face the problem of conflicting demands from the two sets of principals. Furthermore, if voters have any say in the final ranking of candidates, the individual candidates will have incentives to seek a personal vote which, in turn, will affect the style of campaigning. Hence, the more important dimension in relation to campaigning and representational roles seems to be the *level of inclusiveness* in the nomination process rather than the level of centralisation. We will discuss the relationship between the rules of nomination, campaigning and representation in more detail below.

Nominations and styles of campaigning

As mentioned initially, in the campaign literature a line is drawn between the candidate-centred US campaign and the party-centred Western European campaign (Plasser and Plasser 2002). In the US, the campaign organisation is centred around the individual candidates. They hire a campaign manager and campaign staff; they identify their own campaign message, do their own polling, and recruit and organise volunteers in the grass-roots campaigns (Herrnson 2008). By contrast, in Western Europe, campaigning is party-centred as the party organisation is the campaign organisation. The individual candidates are part of the party-campaign organisation, and the centralising efforts of the party are highlighted as characteristic of the Western European model (Plasser and Plasser 2002).

The notion of 'individualised' campaigning refers to a situation in which the candidates campaign independently of the party with regard to a candidate-centred organisation, a candidate-focused agenda, and candidate-centred means of campaigning (Zittel and Gschwend 2008). The extent of individualised campaigning differs not only between the US and the Western European ideal types, but also among Western European systems.

The difference between presidential systems, on the one hand, and parliamentary ones, on the other, has a clear bearing on styles of campaigning (Bowler and Farrell 1992). In parliamentary systems an effective executive depends on party discipline in the legislature. Consequently, parties should be expected to be less willing to give in to reforms that provide incentives to individualised campaigning. Still, the US system is characterised as party-centred prior to the introduction of primaries (Brox and Shaw 2006), regardless of presidentialism. The electoral system has also been emphasised as important and several scholars argue that proportional systems will increase party-centred campaigning (Plasser and Plasser 2002; Swanson and Mancini 1996). According to Bowler and Farrell (1992) proportional representation list systems promote greater centralisation than plurality systems. In a similar manner, Swanson and Mancini (1996) argue that majority systems highlight the role of the individual candidate and thus promote 'personalisation'. However, Western European systems with plurality elections, most notably Great Britain and France, are best described as party centred (e.g. Plasser and Plasser 2002).

We argue that the nomination process is the best starting point for the purpose of explaining differences between countries concerning the extent of individual candidate campaigning. The introduction of the primaries in the US is considered the deciding factor for the rise of the candidate-centred US campaign as candidates set up campaign organisations and expertise independently of the party (Agranof 1972). Moreover, Rahat (2008) points out that the move from nominating committees to party primaries had important consequences for the electoral focus of the candidates in Israel. Intensified media attention increased candidates' attentiveness towards their own image and personality and also their need for professional campaign specialists. This, in turn, increased the need for campaign funding and paved the way for the growing influence of financial donors (Hofnung 2005). Hence, the Israeli case supports our basic assertion that changes in the nomination procedures of parties have consequences for the campaign strategies of parties and candidates.

The main dimension of nomination is, as already argued, the level of inclusiveness in the process, most importantly the distinction between open primaries and party-centred nominations. Based on the agency framework sketched out above, we argue that if the local party is in charge of the nominations, the candidate needs to appeal to the local base of the party in order to be reselected. By the same logic, if the central party decides, candidates will respond to the demands put forward by the central party leadership. Alternatively, if the voters decide the nominations (by open primaries), the candidates need to cater to the voters in the process of candidate selection.

In addition to the nomination process, certain aspects of the electoral systems are essential in regard to the level of individualised campaigning. Unlike earlier studies that highlight the difference between plurality and proportional systems, holding that to be the most important aspect, we emphasise the significance of a preference vote scheme: open list systems where the voters decide the final ranking of the candidates. For example, if the party controls nominations but voters have great influence on the rankings of the candidates, the individual candidates must find a balance between the attention they give the party (and the party programme) and the attention they give their own candidature.

Role orientations of representation

In the classical literature on political representation, two concepts are particularly relevant for our combined approach: the style and focus of representation. The two concepts stem from the works on the US Congress by Wahlke *et al.* (1962) who studied the role orientations of American legislators. The term 'focus' refers to those interests that the elected representatives defended, that is, 'whom' they represented. The 'style of representation' refers to the way such interests were defended, or more specifically 'how' representation took place.

Eulau and Karps (1977) suggested that the representational focus of elected representatives should be divided into three interests: territorially defined (national, regional, or local), functional (religious, economic, ethnic, and ideological), and individually defined (individual voters). The role of the party was not given much attention in these earlier works, probably because the party had a much weaker standing in the US than in the parliamentary systems of Europe. In the latter, however, the interest of the party must be added to the other three. Numerous studies confirm that the interest of the party weighs heavily when the representatives are asked to define their role as elected representatives (e.g. Esaiasson and Holmberg 1996; Esaiasson 2000; Narud and Valen 2007). In addition, the importance of the party for representational style is confirmed by the high level of party discipline in parliamentary behaviour (Strøm *et al.* 2003). Consequently, the 'responsible party model' has been the dominant theoretical paradigm for the analysis of political representation in parliamentary regimes for the last few decades (Thomassen 1994). This is a point we shall bear in mind in the subsequent empirical analysis.

The concept of role orientations fits quite neatly into our principal-agent framework. For us, the important question is how the role orientations of the elected representatives between-elections are conditioned upon the nomination procedures of the parties as well as their styles of campaigning. We argue that different types of nomination systems create different sets of principal-agent relationships which condition the representational focus and style of the candidates. In systems where the parties nominate, candidates are more likely to consider the party their basis for representation. In systems where the voters nominate, on the other hand, they are more likely to consider their constituency voters as their representational focus. An underlying factor, we claim, is the extent to which the electoral system allows for a personal vote.

Before turning to the empirical analysis, a few words about the Norwegian political system are called for.

The Norwegian case

In the Norwegian multiparty system, class, religion, geography, language, and moral issues have constituted the essential cleavages for party competition. The traditional parties formed around these cleavages, which in time have weakened – and have been supplemented by newer cleavages related to public versus private enterprise, the environment, immigration, and other issue dimensions (*see* e.g. Urwin 1997; Aylott 2011). At present, following parliamentary elections in September 2009, there are seven parties represented in parliament. Two are left-of-centre parties (the Socialist Left (SV) and Labour (AP)), three are centrist parties (the Centre Party (SP), the Christian People's Party (KRF), and the Liberals (V)), and two are right-of-centre parties (the Conservatives (H) and the Progress Party (FRP)).

Since 1952, Norway has used a modified Sainte-Laguë system of proportional representation (PR), and over the second half of the twentieth century a series of electoral reforms were implemented aiming for greater proportionality in representation. However, despite these reforms, Norwegian electoral results have ranked among the least proportional in Western Europe (Lijphart 1999), and the main beneficiaries have been the Labour Party and rural regions. Several factors explain this trend: mal-apportionment, small district magnitude, and, until 1989, the lack of any pool of supplementary (higher-tier adjustment) seats. Complex districting was introduced in 1989, first with 157 first-tier seats and a pool of eight national second-tier seats. The system was amended in 2002 (effective from 2005), when the number of adjustment seats was raised to 19, equalling the number of county constituencies, and the number of first-tier seats was reduced to 150. Consequently, the over-representation of peripheral areas has been considerably reduced and the overall partisan proportionality enhanced (Aardal 2002).

In Norway, as in Finland and Germany, election laws have regulated the process for nominating parliamentary candidates. Although the Norwegian law governing nominations was revoked when the electoral system was revised in 2002, the earlier law has had lingering effects on how parties recruit their candidates.[7] Political parties recruit candidates for parliament through local nomination processes in which local delegates meet at the nomination conventions to finalise the list. This meeting is held at the regional level. The Norwegian parties have a long tradition of leaving nominations for parliament to local party branches and locally affiliated collective organisations such as trade unions. However, the populist party on the political right, the Progress Party, is an exception because the party leader has often intervened personally in local nomination processes (Valen *et al.* 2002). Party primary elections have not been held in modern times and Norway's electoral system does not involve any form of preferential voting. The fact that the Norwegian system does not include this option provides parties with considerable control over parliamentary nominations, and the Norwegian case may accordingly be regarded as more exclusive (or rather, less inclusive) than, for instance, its Nordic neighbours (Narud *et al.* 2002). There has nevertheless been a recent tendency for some local party branches to open their nomination process to allow greater participation by registered party members, particularly among the Conservative party branches (Narud 2008).

Norwegian parties' views of desirable candidate credentials have been surprisingly stable over time (Valen 1988; Skare 1996; Valen *et al.* 2002). On the demand-side, political experience has long been regarded as crucial for a potential candidate to be judged electable and, for a candidate to be allocated a top spot on the party nomination list, his or her *local political experience* must be substantial. Qualities like political competence and personal integrity are also weighed, though they tend to be taken for granted once a person is judged electable. A potential candidate's ability to present a political message with eloquence, perform well in public, and handle the media with dexterity has been increasingly important in recent years.

In sum, the nomination procedures in both the Norwegian parties and the Norwegian electoral system have characteristics that place the Norwegian case in the top row of Figure 5.1, that is, locally dominated nominations with a high level of party control. Consequently, we expect candidates to be party centred in their campaigning and that their representational role orientations be towards the party.

Empirical analysis

We start our empirical analysis by investigating the candidates' views on the nomination process: who should decide the composition of the list and the final ranking of candidates? In the second part we study the candidates' campaign styles. In the third part of the empirical analysis we investigate the candidates' representational role orientations. The question is how well the empirical relationship between the three factors fits our theoretical expectations.

---

7. The Norwegian nomination law prescribed a nomination procedure that was not obligatory. But in order to have travel expenses paid by the state, parties had to adhere to the law which, among other things, stipulated the number of delegates who could participate in nomination meetings (Valen *et al.* 2002).

The data consists of a survey of all candidates running for election for any of the seven major parties in the 2009 parliamentary election.[8] The cohort consisted of 1,972 candidates, and the response rate was 52 per cent, leaving us with 1,015 candidates included in the study. All seven parties are more or less equally represented among the candidates, and top candidates are represented on a par with the candidates placed lower on the lists. The questionnaire covers a number of questions on campaigning, nominations and representation.

Opinions on the nomination process

In the questionnaire, the respondents were asked who should decide the composition and the ranking of the list. Consistent with what has been the norm for party nominations in Norway, the candidates mostly agree with the traditional nomination process of letting the delegates at the nomination meeting decide the composition of the party list. As Table 5.1 shows, 56 per cent of the candidates want the delegates at the nomination meeting to decide the composition of the list. However, as many as 24 per cent of the candidates want the process to be democratised, that is, they want to let the composition of the list be decided by the party members. Only 4 per cent want to go further still, and let the voters decide.

The pattern is somewhat similar with regard to the final ranking of the candidates. Almost 70 per cent hold the opinion that the delegates should decide the ranking. Only 12 per cent of the candidates want to introduce some type of preference vote scheme and let the voters decide. As we can see from the table, there is little difference based on list placement. The pattern for the top three candidates is very similar to the overall pattern. However, as Figure 5.3 reveals, the pattern differs somewhat between the top three candidates in the different parties.

The figure shows that there are substantial differences between candidates from the different parties regarding who should decide the composition of the list as well as the final ranking of candidates. The Labour Party candidates are least interested in letting the voters decide with regard to both the composition of the list and the final ranking of the candidates. None of the top three Labour candidates want to leave these issues to the voters. At the other end of the spectrum, just half of the candidates from the Christian People's Party want to leave it to the delegates. However, they are keener to involve the party members regarding the composition of the list than are the voters. When it comes to the final ranking, candidates from the Centre Party as well as from the Progress Party, the Liberal Party, the Conservative Party and the Christian People's Party are most willing to

---

8. The Norwegian Candidate Study is part of an international effort initiated by the *Mannheimer Zentrum für Europäische Sozialforschung* (MZES) to give the various national studies a cross-nationally comparable core. The project coordinator is Hermann Schmitt, MZES, University of Mannheim, Germany. The core questionnaire focuses on the relationships between the candidate, the party and the voters, with special emphasis on electoral campaigning. The Norwegian study also has various national-specific additional questions. Information about the CCS study and the network is online. Available: http://www.comparativecandidates.org/ (accessed 15 January 2013).

Table 5.1: Who should decide the composition of the list and the final ranking of candidates? All candidates and the top three candidates

	The composition of the list		The final ranking of candidates	
	All	Top 3	All	Top 3
Delegates	56	60	70	69
Party members	25	29	12	13
Nomination committee	16	9	7	4
Voters	4	3	12	14
Party leadership	0	0	1	1
N	1,002	201	1,002	202

Q: Who should decide the composition of the list?
Q: Who should decide the final ranking of the candidates?
The categories for both questions are: the nominating committee, the party leadership, delegates at the nomination meeting, party members, and the voters.

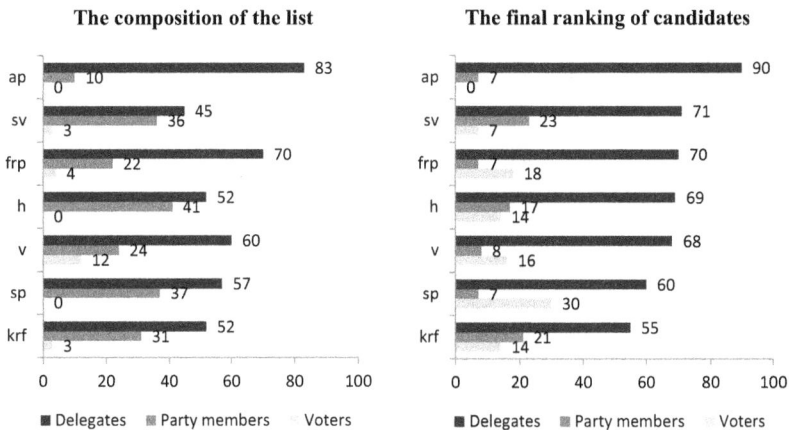

Party names: Socialist Left Party (SV), Labour Party (Ap), The Centre Party (Sp) The Christian Democratic Party (KrF), The Liberal Party (V), The Conservative Party (H) and The Progress Party (FrP).

Figure 5.3: Who should decide the composition of the list and the final ranking of candidates by party affiliation? Top three candidates in the seven parties

leave it to the voters. However, an overwhelming majority in these parties wants to leave the decision to the delegates at the nomination meeting.

We now turn to the impact of the nomination procedures on the campaign style of the parties. Since the standing of the local party conventions is so strongly anchored in the preferences of the delegates, we will first examine the position of the party *vs* that of the individual candidate for the campaign style of the Norwegian candidates.

Style of campaigning

Based on the theoretical framework presented initially, we expect low levels of individualised campaigning among candidates in Norway. The country has no provisions for a preference vote and the nomination procedures are highly dominated by the local party branches. The results presented in Figure 5.4 are in line with our expectations: the campaign focus of the Norwegian candidates is highly party centred. On a scale of 0 (candidate focus) to 10 (party focus) the mean for all candidates is 8.7, indicating a massive party focus. However, the mean value conceals interesting differences between different types of candidates.

First, list placement has an effect on the communicative focus of the candidates: the top candidates are more likely to focus on themselves than the lower placed candidates. Second, this effect is partly contingent on party affiliation. The Labour Party candidates are very much inclined to focus on the party in their communication, regardless of their list placement. To a lesser extent this is also true for the candidates from the Progress Party and for the Liberals. The top placed Conservatives and Christians, on the other hand, are more inclined to focus on their own candidacy.

Although candidate campaigning is best described as party centred, there are elements of individualised campaigning too. Hence, the question arises: is there a relationship between the wish to democratise the nomination process (i.e. increase the level of participation) and focusing on one's own candidacy in the campaign? In Table 5.2 we investigate the effect of age, gender, list placement and list ranking opinion on the communicative focus of the candidate.

Gender and list placement both have independent and significant effects on communicative focus. The male and the *higher*-placed candidates are more likely to focus on their own candidacy than female and *lower* placed candidates. We would also have expected candidates who believed that voters should decide the final ranking of the list to be more candidate focused. This, however, is not the case, and consequently there appears to be no correlation between wanting to democratise the nomination process and tendencies towards individualised campaigning.

Table 5.2: The effect of age, gender, list placement and list ranking opinion for candidate communicative focus. Multivariate linear regression analysis (N = 900)

	B	**beta**
Constant	2.496	
Age	-0.004	-0.023
Gender (female)	-0.518**	-0.125**
List placement	-0.095**	-0.228**
List ranking opinion	-0.077	-0.012
R^2	0.07	

Age is continuous from 0 (recoded from 18)
Gender: male = 0 female = 1
List placement is from first (1) to last place (0)
List ranking opinion: voters should have final say = 1, other = 0

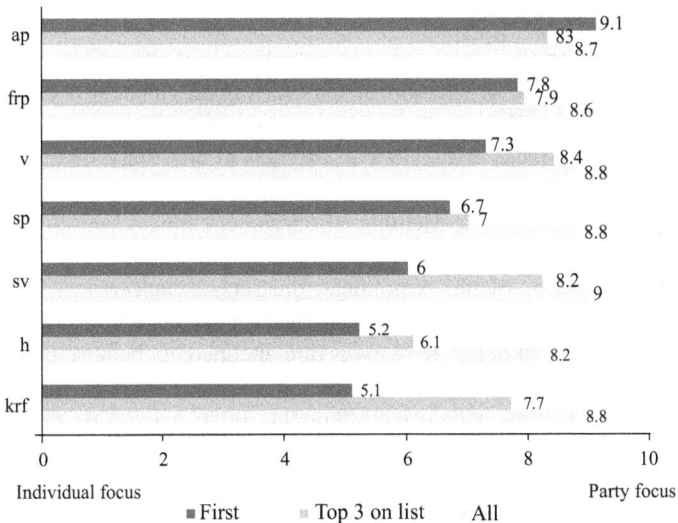

ap: 9.1, 83, 8.7
frp: 7.8, 7.9, 8.6
v: 7.3, 8.4, 8.8
sp: 6.7, 7, 8.8
sv: 6, 8.2, 9
h: 5.2, 6.1, 8.2
krf: 5.1, 7.7, 8.8

0 2 4 6 8 10
Individual focus — Party focus
■ First ▨ Top 3 on list All

Question: What was the primary aim of your campaign? Where would you place yourself on a scale running from 0 to 10, where 0 means 'to attract as much attention as possible for me as a candidate' and 10 means 'to attract as much attention as possible to my party'?

Figure 5.4: The communicative focus of the candidate's campaign. Mean on a scale from 0 (individual focus) to 10 (party focus)

Table 5.3: The representational focus of the candidates by party affiliation, as a percentage

	The party	The population	Own voters	All voters in constituency	All voters	A social group	N (100%)
SV	68	10	16	3	1	1	150
KrF	59	15	19	6	2	0	143
Ap	58	20	11	6	5	1	138
FrP	54	22	11	6	6	0	130
H	50	22	20	4	4	0	131
Sp	44	19	28	8	1	1	123
V	40	24	21	9	6	0	140
All	54	19	18	6	4	1	958

Q: There are different opinions about whom an elected Member of Parliament should primarily represent. What is your opinion? *(Please rank all of the options in decreasing order of importance. You can do this by marking the most preferred as 1, the second most as 2, and so on – up to the number 5/6).*

Focus and style of representation

Based on the theoretical framework sketched out initially and our findings so far, we expect the role orientation of the Norwegian candidates to be directed towards the interests of the party. In this section we study the candidates' views on representational focus and style with two sets of questions: first, with an item asking 'whom' a Member of Parliament should primarily represent, and second, with the question of 'how' a Member of Parliament should vote if the voters in the constituency and the party disagree. While the first question taps the general representational focus of the respondent, the second concerns representational style with particular relevance to between-election democracy.

As expected, candidates in Norway are inclined to believe that members of parliament should primarily represent the party. However, the results are not as unanimous as we would have thought. Table 5.3 reports the proportion of the candidates who believe that an MP should primarily represent one of six different groups. Fifty-four per cent of all the candidates believe that a Member of Parliament should primarily represent the party, whereas 19 per cent think that the Norwegian population should be the focus of the elected representative. Eighteen per cent believe that MPs should focus on their own voters. However, as was the case with campaigning style, we find differences between the parties. While almost 70 per cent of the Socialist Left candidates say that an elected Member of Parliament should primarily represent the party, only about 40 per cent of the Liberal Party candidates hold this view.

Table 5.4: The effect of age, gender, list placement, list ranking opinion and candidate focus for representatives primarily representing the party multivariate logistic regression (N = 901)

	Coeff.	S.E.
Age	0.02**	0.01
Gender (female)	0.28*	0.14
List placement	-0.02	0.01
List ranking opinion	-0.58**	0.22
Candidate focus	-0.01	0.03
Party dummies		
SV	0.35	0.25
Sp	-0.64**	0.26
KrF	-0.15	0.26
V	-0.74**	0.26
H	-0.32	0.26
FrP	-0.17	0.25
Constant	-0.07	0.28
Nagelkerke R^2	0.07	

**Significant at the 1 per cent level. *Significant at the 5 per cent level
Age is continuous from 0 (recoded from 18)
Gender: male = 0; female = 1
List placement is from first (1) to last place (0)
Party affiliation: reference category is Labour Party affiliation
Dependent variable representatives primarily representing the party = 1, other = 0

Do the candidates' opinions regarding democratising the nomination process and their campaign style affect their representational focus? In Table 5.4 we report the results of a multivariate analysis that investigates this question. In addition, we include age, gender, list placement and party affiliation in the model.

Age and list ranking opinion affect representational focus. Older candidates are more inclined to believe that an elected MP should primarily represent the party. Candidates who believe that voters should decide the final ranking of the lists are less inclined to emphasise the party. Campaign style, on the other hand, does not have an effect on representational focus. Consequently, it appears to be a relationship between wanting to democratise the nomination process and the representational focus, but not between opinions on the nomination process and campaign style, or between campaign style and representational focus.

Above, we have investigated the general representational focus of the candidates. The next question is: how is this translated into representational style or behaviour? Although the candidates believe that an MP should primarily

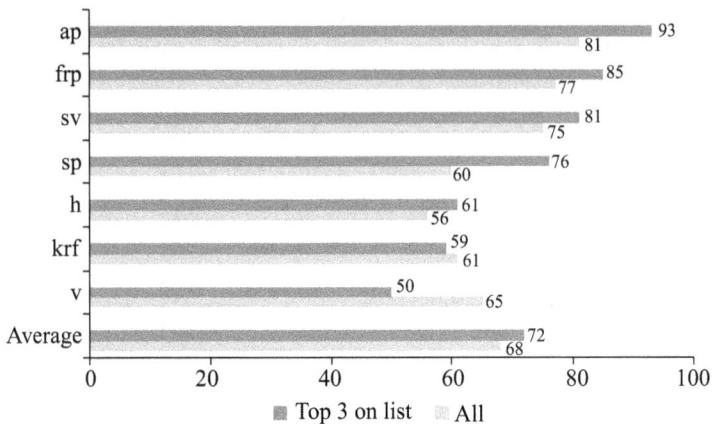

Q: How should a Member of Parliament vote in parliament if the voters in his/her constituency have one opinion and his/her party takes a different position?

Figure 5.5: Representational style of the candidates. Proportion of candidates who say that representatives should vote in accordance with their party rather than their constituency voters. All candidates and top three placed candidates. By party affiliation

represent the whole population or the voters in the constituency, when decisions are actually made in parliament they might still want the MP to vote in accordance with the party. Figure 5.5 presents the proportion of candidates who voice the opinion that an MP should vote in accordance with his or her party on an issue – even if the constituency voters take a different stand from that of the party.

Overall, the figure demonstrates that the candidates believe the MP should vote in line with his or her party. However, there are considerable differences between the parties. While 81 per cent of the Labour candidates (and 93 per cent of the top three candidates) think that the MP should vote with the party, 60 per cent of the Conservative candidates, and just 50 per cent of the Liberal candidates hold this opinion. This difference might be due to the different representational focus in the different parties, and to different cultures regarding party discipline. Table 5.5 presents the results of a multivariate analysis in which we include representational focus as an independent variable in order to test whether this factor removes the effect of party affiliation.

The results reveal that representational focus has a strong effect on the candidates' views on whether a Member of Parliament should vote in line with the party or in line with the voters in the constituency. However, candidates in the Centre Party, the Christian People's Party and the Conservative Party are more inclined to say 'vote with the voters in the constituency', even when representational focus is controlled for. This suggests that distinct party cultures that vary with regard to party discipline have an independent effect. Moreover, the

Table 5.5: The effect of age, gender, list placement, list ranking opinion and candidate focus on candidates' views of representational style (MPs should vote in accordance with the party). Multivariate logistic regression (N = 880)

	Coeff.	S.E.
Age	0.00	0.01
Gender (female)	-0.33*	0.16
List placement	0.00	0.02
List ranking opinion	0.27	0.24
Candidate focus	0.06	0.04
Representational focus	1.29**	0.16
Party affiliation		
SV	-0.67*	0.32
Sp	-1.15**	0.31
KrF	-1.29**	0.31
V	-0.78**	0.31
H	-1.42**	0.32
FrP	-0.31	0.32
Constant	0.93**	0.35
Nagelkerke R^2	0.17	

**Significant at the 1 per cent level. *Significant at the 5 per cent level
Age is continuous from 0 (recoded from 18)
Gender: male = 0; female = 1
List placement is from first (1) to last place (0)
Party affiliation: reference category is Labour Party affiliation
Dependent variable: vote with party (1) vote with voters (0)

emphasis on party discipline does not apply just to the top candidates, it is also the dominant view among the lower placed candidates (i.e. list ranking has no effect). Hence, the norm about a strong party discipline is strongly institutionalised in the various parties and goes well beyond the top parliamentary elite.

Discussion and conclusion

The aim of this chapter has been to develop a framework for analysing campaign styles and representational roles in light of the nomination practices of the political parties. In so doing, we have leaned on the conceptual framework from the agency literature, in which candidate responsiveness may be seen as a product of the means by which principals control their agents. Agent control is partly conditioned by the institutional context of parties and candidates (e.g. the electoral system), partly by the norms and practices of individual actors (e.g. the parties). We have argued that aspects of the electoral system as well as the nomination procedures will affect the responsiveness of individual candidates, measured in terms of individualised campaigning and representational role orientations. More specifically, voter influence on the nominations, plurality systems and preference vote schemes are expected to increase the level of individualised campaigning and the candidates' focus on individual voters. By contrast, party control of the nominations and proportional systems with no preference vote schemes are expected to increase a party-centred campaign style and a representational focus on the party.

We have applied this framework in a study of Norwegian candidates. Based on our knowledge of the Norwegian election and nomination systems, we expected the campaign style of the candidates as well as their representational role orientations to be highly party centred. To a great extent, these expectations have been met. The communicative focus of the Norwegian candidates is directed primarily towards the party, even though there are elements of individualised campaigning too. The top candidates are more inclined to have an individualised campaign style than lower placed candidates. This is partly contingent on party affiliation. The Labour candidates are particularly party centred in their campaigning efforts, while the Conservative candidates are more inclined to focus on their own candidacy.

In regard to representational focus and style, more than half of the candidates believe that an elected MP should primarily represent the party, and there is little difference based on list placement. The candidates' views on representational focus are reflected in their views on representational style through the question of party discipline. A great majority of the candidates believe that an MP should vote in line with the party – even if the voters in the constituency hold a different opinion.

Consequently, the empirical findings of this chapter support the arguments of the theoretical framework sketched out initially. However, our results underline that, regardless of institutional settings, campaign style and representational roles vary between candidates, especially based on party affiliation.

Although the nomination process is likely to affect both the style of campaigning and representational focus in a system, there is little support for any direct linkage between all three of them in the sense that the candidates who want to democratise the nomination process are not more candidate focused in their campaign style. Most candidates want to maintain the traditional nomination process of letting the delegates at the nomination meeting decide the composition of the party list as well as deciding the final ranking of the candidates. Nevertheless, about a fourth of the candidates want to 'democratise' the process and let the members decide the composition, and 12 per cent want to leave the final ranking of candidates to the voters. Contrary to our expectations, a more inclusive view of the nomination process does not affect the campaign style of the candidates. It does, however, affect their representational focus. By contrast, there is no direct link between campaign style and representational role orientation.

Some of the party differences deserve attention. At one end, we have the Labour Party candidates who want to leave the nomination decisions to the party delegates, and who also have the most party-centred campaign style. At the other end, we have the Christians and the Conservatives who are more willing to democratise the nomination process and who have a more individualised campaign style. The general representational focus, however, does not vary much between these parties; their views on representational style, on the other hand, do. The Labour candidates are far more inclined to vote in line with the party – even if the constituency voters hold a different view – than are the Conservatives, the candidates from the Christian People's Party and the Liberals. This difference between the parties holds true even when representational party focus is controlled for.

The observed differences probably stem from variations in the ideological and cultural background of the parties. The Conservative Party and the Liberals emerged *within* parliament and emphasised the parliamentary group and individual representation. The Labour Party, on the other hand, emerged *outside* of parliament and emphasised the importance of the party organisation and party discipline (von Beyme 1985).

From the perspective of between-election democracy, the institutional setting – the nomination process and the electoral system – seems to affect candidates' campaign styles to a greater extent than representational roles. Most candidates are party centred in their campaign style, while almost half the candidates believe that an elected representative should primarily represent the voters and not the party. However, when it comes to representational style, most candidates think MPs should vote with the party if the party hold a different opinion than the voters in the constituency. Consequently, and as might be expected based on the empirical support for the responsible party mandate model, when it comes to behaviour, party discipline seems to trump the candidates' representational focus. Consequently, the parties' institutional arrangements have a strong bearing on the candidates' behaviour between elections and constrain their conduct in parliament.

The question, then, is what consequences this finding has for the concept of between-election democracy. First, institutional arrangements have a bearing on both election and between-election behaviour. And second, while the focus between elections is mostly on the relationship between citizens and representatives, the findings in this chapter remind us that political parties are an essential part of the representational process both during and between elections.

References

Aardal, B. (2002) 'Electoral systems in Norway', in Grofman, B. and Lijphart, A. (eds) *The Evolution of Electoral and Party Systems in the Nordic Countries*, New York: Agathon Press.

Agranof, R. (ed.) (1972) *The New Style in Election Campaigns*, Boston: Holbrook Press.

Aylott, N. (2011) 'Parties and party systems in the North', in Bergman, T. and Strøm, K. (eds) *The Madison Turn: Political parties and parliamentary democracy in Nordic Europe,* Ann Arbor, MI: University of Michigan Press.

Bergman, T., Müller, W. and Strøm, K. (2000) 'Introduction: Parliamentary democracy and the chain of delegation', *European Journal of Political Research,* 37: 255–60.

Bergman, T. and Strøm, K. (eds) (2011) *The Madison Turn: Political parties and parliamentary democracy in Nordic Europe,* Ann Arbor, MI: University of Michigan Press.

Bille, L. (2001) 'Democratizing a democratic procedure: Myth or reality? Candidate selection in Western European parties 1960–1990', *Party Politics,* 7: 267–76.

Bowler, S. and Farrell, D. (1992) 'The study of election campaigning', in Bowler, S. and Farrell, D. (eds) *Electoral Strategies and Political Marketing,* London: Macmillan.

Brox, B. J. and Shaw, D. R (2006) 'Political parties, American campaigns, and effects on outcome', in Katz, R. S. and Crotty, W. (eds) *Handbook of Party Politics,* London: Sage.

Cross, W. (2008) 'Democratic norms and party candidate selection: Taking contextual factors into account', *Party Politics,* 14: 596–619.

Denver, D., Hands, G., Fisher, J. and MacAllister, I. (2003) 'Constituency campaigning in Britain 1992–2001: Centralisation and modernization', *Party Politics,* 9: 541–59.

Esaiasson, P. (2000) 'How members of parliament define their task', in Esaiasson, P. and Heidar, K. (eds), *Beyond Westminster and Congress: The Nordic experience,* Columbus: Ohio State University Press.

Esaiasson, P. and Heidar, K. (eds) (2000) *Beyond Westminster and Congress: The Nordic experience,* Columbus: Ohio State University Press.

Esaiasson, P. and Holmberg, S. (1996) *Representation from Above: Members of parliament and representative democracy in Sweden,* Aldershot: Dartmouth.

Eulau, H. and Karps, P. D. (1977) 'The puzzle of representation: Specifying components of responsiveness', *Legislative Studies Quarterly,* 2: 233–54.

Fearon, J. (1999) 'Electoral accountability and the control of politicians: Selecting good types versus sanctioning poor performance', in Manin, B., Przeworski, A. and Stokes, S. (eds) *Democracy, Accountability, and Representation,* Cambridge: Cambridge University Press.

Gallagher, M. and Marsh, M. (eds) (1988) *Candidate Selection in Comparative Perspective: The secret garden of politics*, London: Sage.

Hazan, R. Y. and Rahat, G. (2010) *Democracy within Parties: Candidate selection methods and their political consequences*, Oxford: Oxford University Press.

Herrnson, P. S. (2007) *Congressional Elections: Campaigning at home and in Washington*, Washington, DC: CQ Press.

Hofnung, M. (2005) 'Fat parties – lean candidates: Funding Israeli internal party contests', in Arian, A. and Shamir, M. (eds) *The Elections in Israel 2003*, New Brunswick, NJ: Transaction Publishers.

Katz, R. and Mair, P. (eds) (1992) *Party Organizations: A data handbook on party organizations in Western Democracies, 1960–90*, Newbury Park, California: Sage.

Kiewiet, A. and McCubbins, M. (1991) 'Representation or abdication? How citizens use institutions to help delegation succeed', *European Journal of Political Research*, 36: 291–307.

Lijphart, A. (1999) *Patterns of Democracy: Government forms and performance in thirty-six countries*, New Haven, CT: Yale University Press.

Manin, B. (1997) *The Principles of Representative Government*, Cambridge: Cambridge University Press.

Marsh, M. (2000) 'Candidate selection' in Rose, R. (ed.) *International Encyclopedia of Elections*, Washington DC: CQ Press.

Matthews, D. and Valen, H. (1999) *Parliamentary Representation: The case of the Norwegian Storting*, Columbus: Ohio State University Press.

Müller, W. C. (2000) 'Political parties in parliamentary democracies: Making delegation and accountability work', *European Journal of Political Research*, 37: 309–33.

Narud, H. M. (2008) 'Partienes nominasjoner. Hvem deltar? Og spiller det noen rolle?', *Tidsskrift for samfunnsforskning*, 49: 543–73.

— (2011) 'Ascent of the young, the smart and the professional: Norway's parliamentary elite in comparative perspective', *Comparative Sociology*, 10: 840–72.

Narud, H. M., Pedersen, M. and Valen, H. (eds) (2002) *Party Sovereignty and Citizen Control: Selecting candidates for parliamentary elections in Denmark, Finland, Iceland and Norway*, Odense: University Press of Southern Denmark.

Narud, H. M. and Valen, H. (2007) *Demokrati og ansvar. Politisk representasjon i et flerpartisystem*, Oslo: Damm and Søn.

Norris, P. (ed.) (1997) *Passages to Power*, Cambridge: Cambridge University Press.

Plasser, F. and Plasser, G. (2002) *Global Political Campaigning*, London: Praeger.

Rahat, G. (2008) 'Entering through the back door: Non-party actors in intra-party (s)electoral Politics', in Farrell, D. and Schmitt-Beck, R. (eds) *Non-Party Actors in Electoral Politics: The role of interest groups and independent citizens in contemporary election campaigns*, Baden-Baden: Nomos-Verlag.

Rahat, G. and Hazan, R. Y. (2001) 'Candidate selection methods: An analytical framework', *Party Politics*, 7: 297–322.

Ranney, A. (1981) 'Candidate selection', in Butler, D., Penniman, H. R. and Ranney, A. (eds), *Democracy at the Polls*, Washington DC: AEI Publications.

— (1983) *Channels of Power*, New York: Basic Books.

Schattschneider, E. E. (1942) *Party Government: American government in action*, New York: Rinehart and Co.

Skare, A. (1996) 'Kandidatutvelging – mer enn riktig kjønn fra rett sted. Politisk utvelging og politiske endringer i en brytningstid', *Tidsskrift for samfunnsforskning*, 37: 328–62.

Strøm, K. (1999) 'Voter sovereignity and parliamentary democracy', in Narud, H. M. and Aalberg, T. (eds), *Challenges to Representative Democracy: Parties, voters and public opinion*, Bergen: Fagbokforlaget.

— (2000) 'Den besværlige parlamentarismen', *Tidsskrift for samfunnsforskning*, 41: 620–38.

Strøm, K., Müller, W. and Bergman, T. (eds) (2003) *Delegation and Accountability in Parliamentary Democracies*, Oxford: Oxford University Press.

Swanson, D. L. and Mancini, P. (1996) *Politics, Media and Modern Democracy*, London: Praeger.

Thomassen, J. (1994) 'Empirical research into political representation: Failing democracy or failing models?' in Jennings, M. K. and Mann, T. (eds) *Elections at Home and Abroad*, Ann Arbor: University of Michigan Press.

Urbinati, N. and Warren, M. E. (2008) 'The concept of representation in contemporary democratic theory', *Annual Review of Political Science*, 11: 387–412.

Urwin, D. W. (1997) 'The Norwegian party system from the 1880s to the 1990s', in Svåsand, L. and Strøm, K. (eds) *Challenges to Political Parties: The case of Norway*, Ann Arbor: University of Michigan Press.

Valen, H. (1988) 'Norway: Decentralisation and group representation', in Gallagher, M. and Marsh, M. (eds) *Candidate Selection in Comparative Perspective*, London: Sage Publications.

— (1992) Valg og politik, 2nd edn, Oslo: NKS forlaget.

— (2003) 'Sentrum – periferi motsetningen: En saga blott?', in Aardal, B. (ed.) *Velgere i villrede*, Oslo: Damm and Søn.

Valen, H., Narud, H. M. and Skare, A. (2002) 'Norway: Party dominance and decentralized decision making', in Narud, H. M., Pedersen, M. and Valen, H. (eds) *Party Sovereignty and Citizen Control: Selecting candidates for parliamentary elections in Denmark, Finland, Iceland and Norway*, Odense: Odense University Press.

Valen, H. and Narud, H. M. (2007) 'The conditional party mandate: A model for the study of mass and elite opinion patterns', *European Journal of Political Research*, 46: 293–318.

Von Beyme, K. (1985) *Political Parties in Western Democracies*, New York: St. Martin's Press.

Wahlke, J., Eulau, H., Buchanan, W. and Ferguson, L. C. (1962) *The Legislative System*, New York: Wiley.

Wattenberg, M. (1991) *The Rise of Candidate Centered Politics*, Cambridge, MA: Harvard University Press.

Whiteley, P. and Seyd, P. (2003) 'How to win a landslide by really trying: The effects of local campaigning on voting in the 1997 British General Election', *Electoral Studies,* 22: 201–324.

Zittel, T. and Gschwend, T. (2008) 'Individualised constituency campaigns in mixed-member electoral systems: Candidates in the 2005 German elections', *West European Politics,* 31: 978–1003.

Chapter Six

Institutional Incentives for Participation in Elections and Between Elections

Henrik Serup Christensen

Although the electoral channel still constitutes a cornerstone of representative democracy, the interaction between citizens and their elected representatives between elections is also of importance for the proper functioning of the democratic system. This interaction can take different expressions but political participation constitutes a central channel of communication. Through different political activities, citizens make claims on their formal leaders who can then either yield to their demands or risk facing the consequences on Election Day.

A central question is: what are the factors that shape how active citizens are in approaching the elected representatives between elections and what forms of participation do they use in doing so. Within the study of political participation there is a shortage of empirical work that examines how institutional incentives shape the ways in which citizens become active politically beyond the vote (Norris 2007). This is surprising considering the popularity of institutional research within political science (Munck and Snyder 2007). Related research areas have long recognised the potential impact of the institutional structure. Within research on electoral participation the effect of central institutions such as the electoral system has long been recognised (Norris 2004; Franklin 2004). Moreover, within research on social movements the political opportunity structure approach contends that the structure of the state shapes mobilisation in social movements (Eisinger 1973; Kriesi *et al.* 1992; Koopmans *et al.* 1995; Kitschelt 1986; Meyer 2004). It therefore seems likely that institutional characteristics may help explain whether and how individuals participate politically.

In this chapter, theoretical insights from the literature on social movements are used to examine whether the institutional setting provides incentives at the individual level for three forms of political participation. *Electoral participation* is examined as a pivotal participatory activity within representative democracy. In addition, two forms of participation between elections are considered. *Institutionalised participation*, which includes activities in conjunction with the formal political system, and *non-institutionalised participation* covering more peripheral activities whereby citizens voice their concerns. By examining the institutional incentives for these political activities, it is possible to gain a comprehensive understanding of how the institutional framework shapes patterns of political participation in and between elections and, by extension, how the institutional structures shape the interaction between citizens and representatives.

Political institutions and political participation as communication between citizens and representatives

Throughout this volume we discuss recent theoretical contributions recognising that non-electoral forms of representation are important activities for expanding and deepening representative democracy (Urbinati and Warren 2008). Empirical work has also suggested that there may be substantial differences in what styles of representation citizens prefer, and thereby also in how citizens perceive their own roles in representative democracy (Bengtsson and Wass 2010). Mansbridge (2003) outlines more dynamic conceptualisations of the relationship between citizens and representatives that go beyond seeing citizens as voters holding representatives accountable in elections. The most important alternative for the present purposes is anticipatory representation, which emphasises that representatives anticipate the reactions of voters and focus on what they will approve in the next election. Accordingly, the communication between citizens and representatives between elections becomes a central concern (Mansbridge 2003).

In addition to the electoral mechanism that constitutes the cornerstone of the representative system, all democracies offer a number of formal channels for citizens to communicate their preferences to the elected representatives. This communication between citizens and representatives between elections complements the electoral mechanisms by allowing for richer communication between citizens and representatives (Verba and Nie 1972; Verba et al. 1978; Barnes and Kaase 1979). In this communicative process, political parties have traditionally occupied a central role since they became the main vehicle for channelling citizen demands into political decision-making (White and Ypi 2010; Mair 2006). Political activities such as contacting politicians, and working for or donating money to political parties are examples of political activities that make use of formal channels. These activities all occur in conjunction with the formal political system and communicate demands to the representatives according to principles defined by the political system.

However, the communicative process cannot be limited to the formal channels since political activists also use activities that are not formally connected to the political system in order to communicate their demands to representatives. These activities frequently challenge the elite and involve reactions to the current status quo (Barnes and Kaase 1979; Kitschelt 1993; Norris 2002). Examples include demonstrations and civil disobedience but also more benign activities such as signing a petition. Although initially conceived as a threat to the survival of the representative system (Crozier et al. 1975), these activities have become recognised as legitimate ways for citizens to channel their political demands to the elected representatives (Barnes and Kaase 1979). Norris (2002) even suggests that today it is not only the marginalised in society who make use of these activities, since they have become normalised acts used by large shares of the population. Nevertheless, important differences persist compared to the aforementioned activities since the newer activities are bottom-up activities where citizens themselves define the principles of operation, including the targets and issues at stake.

Different conceptualisations have been proposed to capture the developments in the modes of participation between elections (Barnes and Kaase 1979; Teorell *et al.* 2007). In addition to electoral participation, a basic distinction can be drawn between *institutionalised* and *non-institutionalised* participation that occurs between elections (Marien *et al.* 2010).[1] The former includes activities that occur in close vicinity to the political system whereas participants in the latter circumvent the formal political sphere, opting instead for alternative ways to influence political decisions (Marien *et al.* 2010). Although previous literature suggests that there may be substantial differences in the incentives for participation among activities (labelled here as non-institutionalised participation) (Bäck *et al.* 2011; Christensen 2011), this distinction calls attention to the most pertinent differences for the present purposes (more on this in the following section).

Many established democracies have experienced declining levels of voter turnout and participation in the institutionalised activities whereas participation in the non-institutionalised forms of participation has increased (Norris 2002; Dalton and Wattenberg 2004; Marien *et al.* 2010; Christensen 2011). This development has elicited different interpretations connected to the information richness that the activities allow for in the communication between citizens and representatives. A number of scholars fear that declining levels of voter turnout and participation in institutionalised participation constitute a threat to the proper functioning of democracy since the non-institutionalised activities do not generate information-rich communication between citizens and representatives (Putnam 2000; Mair 2006; Stoker 2006; White and Ypi 2010). Others see the developments as a positive sign of the arrival of a new citizen ideal (Bennett 1998; Rosanvallon 2008). By offering citizens additional possibilities for expressing their political preferences and holding decision makers accountable, the non-institutionalised activities enrich the interaction between citizens and representatives and thereby strengthen democracy (Rosanvallon 2008). Hence, the rise of non-institutionalised participation is not necessarily detrimental to the proper functioning of representative democracy. Nonetheless, these activities cannot completely replace traditional engagement since the non-institutionalised activities are, by definition episodic and issue oriented and can therefore not sustain an ongoing dialogue between citizens and representatives. The changes in the patterns of participation therefore create challenges for the proper functioning of representative democracy.

There is good reason to examine what factors affect how citizens express their political demands. One factor that has received scant attention in the literature on political participation is the institutional structure of the state and how it affects the choice to participate between elections (Norris 2007). The anticipatory view on representation suggested by Mansbridge (2003) implies a need to consider systemic elements and the extent to which these affect the process

---

1. The labels are unfortunate for the present purposes. It should therefore be emphasised that institutionalised participation does not, by definition, have a closer connection to the institutional variables that are considered as explanatory variables here.

of 'continuing representation'. The representative systems aim for institutional solutions that ensure both accountability and responsiveness, two desirable goals that can be difficult to achieve at the same time (Christensen 2011). The political institutions thereby occupy a central role by shaping connections between citizens and representatives between elections. Research on electoral participation has established that institutional aspects such as the electoral system have a profound impact on cross-national differences in turnout (Norris 2004; Franklin 2004). Nevertheless, studies of the institutional impact on political behaviour between elections have remained conspicuously absent in survey research on political participation. It may well be helpful to adapt insights from related research fields to gain an understanding of how the institutional structures influence the individual choice to participate between elections. One such field is research on social movements, where the impact of the institutional framework on mobilisation in new social movements and protesting has been examined within the *political opportunity structure approach* (POS).

The premise underlying POS is that protest outside the formal political system is closely connected to more conventional political activity (Meyer 2004). The social context affects the extent of mobilisation in social movements by making certain political strategies more attractive and efficacious than others. Although there is no agreement on the proper conceptualisation of the relevant opportunity structures within POS (Meyer 2004), many examine the importance of *institutional openness* for mobilisation (Kitschelt 1986; Kriesi *et al.* 1992; Koopmans *et al.* 1995). This central notion of institutional openness may be defined as 'the degree to which it incorporates or excludes citizen demands for influence on decisions' (Morales 2009). This characteristic is closely related to the *concentration of decision-making powers*, which has been a central concept in another influential branch of research on institutional effects (Lijphart 1999; Powell 2000; Kittilson and Schwindt-Bayer 2010). Concentrated decision-making powers shield the formal decision makers from outside influencing attempts, whereas the system is relatively open for outside interests when the decision-making powers are dispersed (Powell 2000). Hence, the concentration of decision-making powers is inversely related to institutional openness since dispersed decision-making powers promote institutional openness and *vice versa*.

Kitschelt (1993) claims that one of the few valid generalisations in the literature on social protest is that social movements arise when groups cannot work through the established channels to communicate claims into the political process. Hence, the effect of institutional openness differs for acts of participation depending on the relationship to the formal political system. POS has focused on participation inside and outside the political system, which corresponds to the distinction between institutionalised and non-institutionalised participation outlined above. According to this specification, the institutional structure can be expected to have different implications for these two forms of participation. Institutional openness entails the system offers citizens a number of formally sanctioned venues – or institutionalised activities – for communicating their grievances to the formal representatives. Accordingly, institutional openness can be expected to promote institutionalised participation sanctioned by the formal political system by making it easier for citizens to channel demands into formal political decision-making. Institutional openness should therefore have a positive effect on institutionalised participation. If this mode of participation enables a richer communication between citizens and representatives, institutional openness may be beneficial for the proper functioning of democracy between elections, even if it does not necessarily entail that institutionalised participation is a more effective way for citizens to achieve the desired outcome. Conversely, institutional closedness makes it difficult for citizens to transfer their demands into formal political decision-making and, according to POS, citizens therefore opt for non-institutionalised forms of participation to express their demands. If the critics are right in supposing that non-institutionalised participation provides less tangible information for the decision makers (White and Ypi 2010; Mair 2006), a less information rich dialogue between citizens and representatives takes place in democracies with closed institutional structures and the quality of democratic representation may suffer as a result.

However, there is good reason to assess the merits of these propositions empirically. Empirical studies within POS often rely on comparative studies of a small number of countries and have predominantly relied on country level evidence such as the occurrence of demonstrations (Kriesi *et al.* 1992; Koopmans *et al.* 1995; Giugni and Passy 2004). Some studies have examined the institutional impact at the individual level but these have focused on specific types of participation such as membership of political organisations (Morales 2009) or protest (Nam 2007; Dalton *et al.* 2010). Nevertheless, there is no comprehensive overview of how the institutional structure affects patterns of participation when examining several activities simultaneously. It is therefore worthwhile to examine whether the institutional structure provides the expected incentives at the individual level. The validity of these claims is examined in the empirical analysis.

Data, variables and methods

The research question under scrutiny is whether institutional openness provides incentives for involvement in three forms of participation in representative democracy:

- participation in electoral democracy by casting a vote.
- participation between elections through institutionalised participation.
- participation between elections through non-institutionalised participation.

Previous literature on electoral participation has found that turnout is higher in systems with proportional electoral systems, which suggests that institutional openness provides a positive incentive for electoral participation (Franklin 2004). For the two non-electoral forms of participation, the expectations derived from POS are that institutional openness provides a positive incentive for institutionalised participation and a negative incentive for non-institutionalised participation (Kriesi *et al.* 1992; Koopmans *et al.* 1995; Kitschelt 1986; Meyer 2004).

Data

The data comes from the first round of the European Social Survey (ESS) of 2002. This cross sectional data provides a snapshot of the relationships and makes it possible to probe whether institutional effects on individual behaviour exist. The number of respondents is 35,685,[2] and the study comprises eighteen established European democracies. The selection is restricted to established democracies since institutional effects can take time to materialise, meaning they may be obscured in younger democracies. The limited number of countries confers some limits on the complexity of the models examined in this study, since it makes it difficult to estimate the between group variation in multilevel analysis (Kreft and de Leeuw 1998). Consequently, the analyses are restricted to examining the direct impact of the individual institutions, leaving the ensuing question of how institutional openness interacts with individual level factors to further research. The relative homogeneity of the countries gives the study a 'most similar' systems design which makes it possible to disregard a number of rival explanations at the macrolevel (cf. Morales 2009).

Variables[3]

The dependent variables are the three forms of participation. Electoral participation is measured with a question asking whether the respondent voted in the last national election. Self-reporting is the only available measure for electoral participation, even if this is not a very reliable measure of the actual extent to which respondents voted or not (cf. Cassel 2003). Although it is not possible to determine the extent of wrongful answers at the individual level, the aggregated figures at the country level can be compared to official records of turnout to get an idea of the extent of the problem. Although some countries have a substantial deviation from the official figures, there is no evidence to suggest that there is a systematic bias in the measure used.[4] Hence, it should provide an adequate solution to measuring the extent of voter turnout.

The two other dependent variables probe involvement in institutionalised and non-institutionalised forms of participation. These two variables are measured with indexes composed of answers to questions where the respondents indicate whether they have performed the activity in question during the last twelve months. The index for institutionalised participation includes contacting politicians, working

---

2. Some are excluded due to missing data. For more on the ESS. Online. Available: http//:www. europeansocialsurvey.org (accessed 5 December 2011).

3. More information on coding and distributions for all variables is available in the Appendix.

4. The largest difference at the country level is for Luxembourg, where about 65 per cent of the respondents report to have voted but the official turnout was 86.5 per cent (all official figures are from the IDEA database on electoral turnout). In Belgium and Israel the reported turnout is also lower than the official one, whereas the respondents in the other countries tend to overestimate their involvement. The average deviation is about 10.7 percentage points.

for a political party, and donating money. These are all traditional activities that function within the formal political system. The index for non-institutionalised participation includes signing a petition, attending legal demonstrations, and participating in illegal protests. These activities all occur at arm's length from the formal political system. The conceptualisation of political participation used here restricts the activities examined to those that involve interaction between citizens and representatives in line with the work of Verba and his colleagues in the 1970s (Verba and Nie 1972; Verba et al. 1978). This restrictive notion of political participation excludes forms of involvement such as political consumerism (Micheletti 2003) since these are often aimed at other actors than the formal political decision makers.[5]

Due to the different data material, these operationalisations differ from Marien et al. (2010). Most importantly, 'donating money' is, in their conceptualisation, considered to be a non-institutionalised activity. However, the phrasing of the ESS question suggests that the money goes to a political organisation or group, and the item is therefore most appropriately considered as part of the institutionalised activities.[6] All three dependent variables are coded dichotomously so '1' indicates having performed at least one activity and '0' indicates no activity. Since the answers only indicate whether the respondent has performed each activity and not how often, any attempt to probe the extent of involvement is tentative at best (cf. Topf 1995). The analyses therefore disregard the question of intensity or how many activities the participants perform.

The central independent variables of the study are the institutional factors used to measure the institutional openness of the system. Regrettably, there is little agreement on what institutional factors are the most important ones (Meyer 2004). Here, the examination is confined to five central institutional variables that concern the horizontal and the vertical distribution of decision-making powers. The horizontal dimension includes four institutional linkages identified by the parliamentarian chain of governance (Olsen 1978)[7]: The effective electoral threshold, executive dominance, minister-mandarin relations, and the system of interest mediation. The vertical dimension concerns the extent of decentralisation, which has been a central concern in previous work (Kitschelt 1986; Morales 2009; Lijphart 1999). How each institutional aspect affects the institutional openness

---

5.   For this reason, the chapter refrains from comparisons of levels of participation since this would be futile when not considering the full variety of political expressions. For an examination of the institutional impact on political consumerism, *see* Christensen (2011).

6.   An exploratory factor analysis of the six items supports this theoretical distinction since it leads to two dimensions being extracted with the items loading strongest onto the suggested dimensions (results not shown). Two items, 'wear badges/campaign stickers' and 'work for other organisation' were excluded since it is unclear whether they are best understood as activities between elections or as campaign activities that form part of the electoral democracy.

7.   This chain posits an ideal of the workings of the political system in a parliamentary democracy. Even if realities do not correspond to this ideal, it can help pinpoint the key institutional linkages that determine the functioning of the system.

is ascertained by determining how it concentrates the formal decision-making powers since this shapes how shielded the formal decision makers are from outside influencing attempts (Lijphart 1999; *see also* Powell 2000).

The effective electoral threshold represents the link between citizens and their elected officials and signals how the constitutional design envisions the role of citizens (Powell 2000). The threshold is a calculated value that represents the ease with which political parties win representation in parliament. Since the greater the number of effective parties competing in elections, the greater the access points available to citizens and the fragmentation of the political elites, a low effective electoral threshold is associated with institutional openness.

Executive dominance concerns the link between parliaments and executives and a pertinent question to address here is the degree of decision-making powers concentrated in the hands of the executive *vis-à-vis* the parliament (Strom 1984; Siaroff 2003). Here, a relatively weak government is associated with institutional openness since it denotes power sharing between the parliament and the executive. The empirical measure is obtained from Siaroff (2003) where he examines the relationship between legislatures and executives.

The minister-mandarin linkage involves the interaction between the political and administrative parts at the top echelons of the state. An important question concerns the relationship between ministers and mandarins – politicians and top civil servants – since this issue has important consequences for the concentration of decision-making powers (Pollitt and Bouckaert 2004). Dahlström and Lapuente (2008) provide the empirical measure with a dichotomy distinguishing between separated and integrated minister/mandarin career paths for capturing this aspect. Institutional openness is associated with separated career paths since this disperses decision-making powers among political and administrative elites.

The system of interest mediation concerns the link between the state and civil society. A common distinction is made between corporatist and pluralist systems, but there is some controversy in the literature over the link between the system of interest mediation and institutional openness (Morales 2009). Corporatist arrangements may imply a lack of openness since new interests and demands are excluded from the decision making (Christiansen and Togeby 2006; Kitschelt 1986). On the other hand, corporatism introduces an element of power sharing since the government consults various interests before taking major decisions (Lane and Ersson 1997). Furthermore, corporatism entails an ideology of social partnership and the absence of a winner-take-all mentality (Katzenstein 1985). Accordingly, corporatism is associated with institutional openness for the present purposes since it disperses decision-making powers. Siaroff (1999) provides the measure used to gauge the extent of corporatism in his meta study of previous studies of corporatism.

The degree of political decentralisation is a major determinant in the structure of the political system (Kitschelt 1986; Morales 2009). An adequate measure to gauge this aspect is the proportion of local and regional spending in relation to total spending (Morales 2009). A greater share of costs incurred at lower levels of government implies institutional openness since this disperses decision-making

Table 6.1: Country scores for the institutional linkages (Coded 0–1 high openness)

Country	Effective threshold	Executive dominance	Minister/ mandarin	System of interest mediation	Fiscal decentrali- sation	Combined score of openness[□]
Austria	0.85	0.70	0.00	1.00	0.61	0.63
Belgium	0.75	0.70	0.00	0.44	0.23	0.42
Denmark	0.94	0.65	1.00	0.65	0.89	0.83
Finland	0.86	0.83	1.00	0.61	0.76	0.81
France	0.00*	0.35*	0.00	0.12	0.38	0.17
Germany	0.87	0.60	1.00	0.58	0.82	0.77
Greece	0.68	0.28*	0.00	0.00	0.09	0.19
Ireland	0.57	0.10	1.00	0.26	0.48	0.48
Israel	0.96	0.75	0.00	0.50	0.23	0.49
Italy	0.90*	0.80	0.00	0.15	0.44	0.35
Luxem.	0.87	0.55	0.00	0.50	0.30	0.44
Nether.	0.98	0.85	1.00	0.82	0.49	0.83
Norway	0.89	0.85	1.00	0.98	0.66	0.88
Portugal	0.83	0.53*	0.00	0.00	0.21	0.26
Spain	0.74	0.40	0.00	0.00	0.49*	0.29
Sweden	0.82	0.80	1.00	0.95	0.71	0.86
Switz.	0.77	0.95	0.00	0.59	1.00	0.66
UK	0.00	0.00	1.00	0.14	0.48	0.32
Mean	0.75	0.59	0.47	0.48	0.52	0.56

Sources: see Appendix.
* Major change during the period of scrutiny (*see* Christensen 2011), □ calculated by adding the five scores and dividing by five.

powers between several layers of government, whereas fiscal centralisation concentrates decision-making powers at state level.

Table 6.1 displays the scores on the five institutional parameters for the countries included in the study.

As can be seen, there is a clear dominance of systems with low thresholds due to the fact that most European countries have proportional electoral systems associated with low effective thresholds. This lack of variation implies that the results for this institutional aspect should be interpreted with caution.

In addition to the institutional variables, a number of individual level characteristics are included as control variables to verify that cross-country differences can actually be attributed to institutional effects. This concerns the central sociodemographic characteristics (age, gender and education) which have all been known to affect the propensity to be politically active (Marien *et al.* 2010). Measures for psychological political involvement and social attitudes are included since these also influence the likelihood of being politically active (Norris 2002). Finally, voluntary associational involvement has been argued to promote political participation (Putnam 2000; van Deth 2010). Since these function as control variables their impact will not be discussed in any greater detail.

Method of analysis

Multilevel logistics is the appropriate method of analysis since all dependent variables are dichotomous and the respondents are grouped by country (Snijders and Bosker 1999). The obtained coefficients of the variables indicate an increase or decrease in the logit of the odds ratio of the dependent variable (participate or not) when the independent variable increases its value by one unit. Also, because all variables are different, a coefficient indicates the change in effect of a variable when it changes from its minimum to its maximum value.

Since the emphasis is on examining the direct effect of the institutional structure on individual behaviour, the analytic approach deviates from the standard recommendation, suggesting starting at the individual level and working upwards to the contextual level (Hox 2002). The analysis begins by examining the relationship between the amalgamated institutional structure and participation in the three forms of citizen involvement under scrutiny. Following this, the links between the five institutional aspects and the participatory modes are examined to see what institutional linkages are more important for providing institutional incentives. Finally, it will be examined whether these persist when controlling for individual level characteristics.

Analysis

The first analysis examines whether the institutional structures provide the expected incentives for activity in the three forms of political involvement. Table 6.2 displays two models for each form of participation; empty models labelled M0 and bivariate multilevel regressions that explore the association between a combined index of institutional openness and the inclination for participation in M1.

The empty models decompose the variance to establish what proportion of the total variance is attributable to differences between countries and to see whether it is appropriate to use multilevel models. The intra class correlation coefficient (ICC) probes the share of total variability in participation that is explained by country differences. Although the scores are moderate, simulation studies suggest that even modest levels of ICC can make tests of significance in traditional linear models too liberal (Barcikowski 1981).

When including the measure of institutional openness in M1, the effect of institutional openness on participation appears to be limited. A significant relationship is only found for institutionalised participation between elections. The estimate as expected suggests that institutional openness promotes participation in institutionalised activities (Kriesi *et al.* 1992; Koopmans *et al.* 1995; Kitschelt

Table 6.2: Multilevel analysis of effect of institutional openness on electoral, institutionalised and non-institutionalised participation

	Electoral participation		Institutionalised participation		Non-institutionalised participation	
	M0	**M1**	**M0**	**M1**	**M0**	**M1**
	β (S.E.)	β (S.E.)	β (S.E.)	β (S.E.)	β (S.E.)	β (S.E.)
Fixed parameters						
intercept	1.15*** (0.11)	0.85** (0.28)	-1.20*** (0.08)	-1.58*** (0.17)	-0.85*** (0.11)	-1.24*** (0.30)
Institutional openness		0.56$^{n.s}$ (0.47)		0.68* (0.29)		0.71$^{n.s.}$ (0.50)
Random parameters						
$U_{0j} \sim N\,(0,\,\Omega u)\colon \Omega$	0.22** (0.07)	0.21** (0.07)	0.10** (0.03)	0.08** (0.03)	0.23** (0.08)	0.23** (0.08)
ICC	0.06	0.06	0.03	0.02	0.07	0.07
N countries	18	18	18	18	18	18
N respondents	35,204	35,204	35,408	35,408	35,276	35,276

Note: The estimates are from a multilevel logistic regression with standard errors in parenthesis. Since all variables are coded, the coefficients indicate an increase or decrease in the logit of the odds ratio (p/1-p) of the dependent variable (participate or not) when the independent variable changes from its minimum to its maximum value. Variables are coded 0–1. ICC estimated as $p = var\,(u_j)/(var\,(u_j) + \pi^2/3)$ (Snijders and Bosker 1999). **<0.01, ***<0.001, n.s. = not significant.

1986; Meyer 2004). However, there are no significant results for the two other forms of participation. In particular, there is no evidence that institutional openness affects non-institutionalised forms of participation adversely, as suggested by POS (Kriesi *et al.* 1992; Koopmans *et al.* 1995; Kitschelt 1986; Meyer 2004). Hence, institutional openness may be associated with a greater propensity for institutionalised participation between elections but the results are far from clear cut for political participation more generally.

This relationship between the amalgamated measure of institutional openness and participation leaves several questions unanswered, in particular because it does not make it possible to determine what institutional elements are more important in the process (Lane and Ersson 2000). Certain institutional characteristics – most notably the effective electoral threshold – may have a disproportionate effect when it comes to electoral participation (Powell 2000) whereas the system of interest mediation has been found to affect political behaviour between elections (Nam 2007; Morales 2009). Hence, there is good reason to examine separate rather than combined effects. This is done in Table 6.3.

Table 6.3: Multilevel analysis of effect of five institutional linkages on electoral, institutionalised and non-institutionalised participation

	Electoral participation	Institutionalised participation	Non-institutionalised participation
	M2	M2	M2
	β (S.E.)	β (S.E.)	β (S.E.)
Fixed parameters			
intercept	0.88** (0.34)	-1.31*** (0.19)	-0.82** (0.28)
Effective threshold	0.30$^{n.s.}$ (0.54)	-0.23$^{n.s.}$ (0.30)	-1.26** (0.44)
Executive dominance	0.18$^{n.s.}$ (0.77)	-0.39$^{n.s.}$ (0.43)	-0.06$^{n.s.}$ (0.63)
Minister-mandarin	0.41$^{n.s.}$ (0.29)	-0.09$^{n.s.}$ (0.16)	-0.24$^{n.s.}$ (0.24)
System of interest mediation	-0.02$^{n.s.}$ (0.51)	0.86** (0.28)	1.14** (0.41)
Fiscal decentralisation	-0.44$^{n.s.}$ (0.57)	0.29$^{n.s.}$ (0.32)	0.91^{v} (0.47)
Random parameters			
$U_{0j} \sim N (0, \Omega u): \Omega$	0.18** (0.06)	0.05** (0.02)	0.12** (0.04)
ICC	0.05	0.02	0.03
N countries	18	18	18
N respondents	35,204	35,408	35,276

Note: The estimates are from a multilevel logistic regression with standard errors in parenthesis. Since all variables are coded, the coefficients indicate an increase or decrease in the logit of the odds ratio (p/1-p) of the dependent variable (participate or not) when the independent variable changes from its minimum to its maximum value. Variables are coded 0–1. ICC estimated as $p = var (u_j)/(var (u_j) + \pi^2/3)$ (Snijders and Bosker 1999). ^{v} p<0.10, **<0.01, ***<0.001, n.s.= not significant.

The results suggest that significant results exist for participation between elections. Most notably, the system of interest mediation provides a positive incentive for participation in both institutionalised and non-institutionalised involvement. This is in line with expectations when it comes to institutionalised participation but for non-institutionalised participation it contradicts the expectation of a negative effect. Previous findings have also found this aspect to be of importance (Todosijević and Enyedi 2003; Morales 2009) but, as noted, there are diverging interpretations of why this is so. One explanation holds that corporatist systems are unresponsive to citizen demands and these therefore seek alternative outlets for their political interests (Kitschelt 1986). A different interpretation holds that corporatist systems endorse mobilisation by incorporating demands and interests from new political actors (Molina and Rhodes 2002). To settle which of these explanations can account for the observed differences is beyond the present purposes where it suffices to note that a significant linkage exists between them.

More significant effects are found for non-institutionalised participation. The negative incentive from executive dominance is in line with the theoretical expectations since it suggests that citizens do not engage in non-institutionalised participation when the parliament has relatively strong control over the government. Nam (2007) also finds that having weaker parliaments is associated with higher levels of protest since such parliaments reduce citizen control over the executive. The estimate for fiscal decentralisation is significant at a lenient 0.10 threshold. Although hardly conclusive, it is notable that this result runs counter to the theoretical expectations, since institutional openness in the form of decentralisation provides a positive incentive for non-institutionalised participation. State centralisation has previously been argued to promote protest (Kitschelt 1986) but this result suggests that the opposite is the case for non-institutionalised participation.

For electoral participation, the results replicate the findings for the combined measure of institutional openness, since none of the five institutional aspects provide a significant incentive for casting a vote. Although this result is hardly unexpected for most institutional elements, it is surprising that the effective electoral threshold is irrelevant since previous literature suggests that a proportional electoral system – associated with a low electoral threshold – provides positive incentives for electoral participation (Norris 2004; Franklin 2004). However, this may be caused by the lack of variation in the effective electoral threshold in a European context. The extent of participation is also likely to be particularly affected by other institutional aspects such as compulsory voting (Franklin 2004), and more nuanced measures of the electoral systems could also be employed (Franklin 2004; Norris 2004). Furthermore, since the voting measure relies on self-reporting, differences may be obfuscated, thereby reducing the explanatory powers of the institutional linkages.

However, the current models have two major deficiencies for identifying institutional effects. For one, they do not take into consideration that there may be differences in the distributions of individual level characteristics that help explain the differences. One of the main advantages of multilevel analyses is that it is possible to include variables at different levels of analysis simultaneously (Kreft and De Leeuw 1998; Snijders and Bosker 1999; Hox 2002). To ensure that the observed differences are actually due to institutional effects, it is necessary to control for these characteristics. Furthermore, multilevel analysis is less well suited for large models incorporating many different variables (Hox 2002). This problem becomes especially acute in the current case since the relatively low number of countries included in the study, combined with the limited variation in certain

Table 6.4: Multilevel analysis of effect of institutional linkages on electoral, institutionalised and non-institutionalised participation when controlling for individual level characteristics, parsimonious models

	Electoral participation	Institutionalised participation	Non-institutionalised participation
	M3	M3	M3
	β (S.E.)	β (S.E.)	β (S.E.)
Fixed parameters			
intercept	-2.87*** (0.30)	-2.94*** (0.15)	-0.48 n.s. (0.34)
Effective threshold	0.79 ᵞ (0.42)	n.s.	-1.06** (0.40)
Executive dominance	n.s.	n.s.	n.s.
Minister-mandarin	n.s.	n.s.	n.s.
System of interest mediation	-0.60 ᵞ (0.35)	-0.17 n.s. (0.22)	0.38 n.s. (0.40)
Fiscal decentralisation	n.s.	n.s.	0.35 n.s. (0.55)
Age	5.28*** (0.12)	0.24* (0.10)	-2.14*** (0.10)
Gender (1= male)	-0.18*** (0.04)	n.s.	-0.29*** (0.03)
Education	0.92*** (0.06)	0.22*** (0.05)	0.43*** (0.05)
Political interest	0.90*** (0.07)	0.99*** (0.07)	0.86*** (0.06)
Party identification (1 = yes)	0.57*** (0.04)	0.34*** (0.03)	0.29*** (0.03)
Political trust	0.46*** (0.09)	n.s.	-0.43*** (0.09)
Internal efficacy	0.21* (0.10)	1.83*** (0.08)	0.89*** (0.08)
External efficacy	0.18* (0.08)	0.33*** (0.07)	0.28*** (0.07)
Satisfaction w. democracy	n.s.	-0.45*** (0.07)	-0.32*** (0.07)
Social trust	n.s.	-0.25** (0.09)	0.58*** (0.09)
Ideology (1= right)	0.45*** (0.08)	-0.30*** (0.07)	-0.97*** (0.07)

(Cont'd.)

Table 6.4: (Cont'd.)

	Electoral participation	Institutionalised participation	Non-institutionalised participation
	M3	M3	M3
	β (S.E.)	β (S.E.)	β (S.E.)
Ideological extremism	0.18** (0.06)	0.25*** (0.05)	0.22*** (0.05)
Leisure association involvement	0.31*** (0.09)	1.06*** (0.07)	0.75*** (0.07)
Interest association involvement	1.40*** (0.11)	1.05*** (0.07)	0.77*** (0.07)
Random parameters			
$U_{0j} \sim N(0, \Omega u)$: Ω	0.18** (0.06)	0.09** (0.03)	0.16** (0.06)
ICC	0.05	0.03	0.05
Wald	3,530.97 (15df)***	2,951.12 (14df)***	2,438.22 (18df)***
N countries	17	17	17
N respondents	27,088	27,104	26,513

Note: The estimates are from a multilevel logistic regression with standard errors in parenthesis. Since all variables are coded, the coefficients indicate an increase or decrease in the logit of the odds ratio (p/1-p) of the dependent variable (participate or not) when the independent variable changes from its minimum to its maximum value. Variables coded 0–1. ICC estimated as p = var $(u_j)/(var(u_j) + \pi^2/3)$ (Snijders and Bosker 1999). ᵞ p<0.10, *p<0.05, **<0.01, ***<0.001, n.s. = not significant.

respects, may well lead to institutional effects being cancelled out when including several institutional variables. For this reason, Table 6.4 displays parsimonious models that control for individual level characteristics and only include significant variables. For the institutional variables, the included variables are those found to be significant in Table 6.3. Since no institutional variables had a significant effect on the propensity to vote, instead, this model includes the institutional variables with the greatest explanatory power.

Although the institutional impact diminishes considerably when controlling for individual level characteristics, some institutional effects continue to influence individual behaviour. The strongest effect is found for non-institutionalised participation, where the effective threshold continues to have a negative effect on participation, whereas the effects for the system of interest mediation and fiscal decentralisation vaporise when controlling for individual level characteristics. This indicates that citizens are less inclined to use non-institutionalised forms of participation when a low effective electoral threshold makes it easier to find a political party that reflects their opinions.

The implications of this are somewhat surprising for communication in representative democracy. Even if institutionalised participation is preferable to non-institutionalised participation since it improves the ongoing dialogue between citizens and representatives, non-institutionalised participation is preferable to citizens being passive since this eliminates the possibility of a dialogue taking place between elections. If institutional openness decreases non-institutionalised involvement but does not promote institutionalised participation, the overall effect may be negative for the communicative aspect of democracy between elections.

For electoral participation, two institutional aspects have significant estimates at a lenient 0.10 cut-off value, even when no effects were significant when examining all five institutional aspects simultaneously. Although these results are again far from conclusive evidence of an institutional effect, the results highlight the contradictory nature of any potential institutional effects. The effective threshold has a weak positive effect on turnout, meaning institutional openness promotes participation in elections, whereas the system of interest mediation provides a negative incentive for participation, meaning institutional openness is here associated with lower levels of turnout. This could reveal the lower salience of elections in these systems, since important political decisions are frequently decided in negotiations between elites rather than by a pure electoral majority.

For institutionalised participation there are no significant effects since the effect for the system of interest mediation becomes insignificant when controlling for individual level factors. The initial impacts found for the combined index of institutional openness and for the system of interest mediation thus turn out to be a mirage when controlling for the distribution of individual level characteristics. Contrary to the previous results, this suggests that institutional openness does not directly promote institutionalised participation.

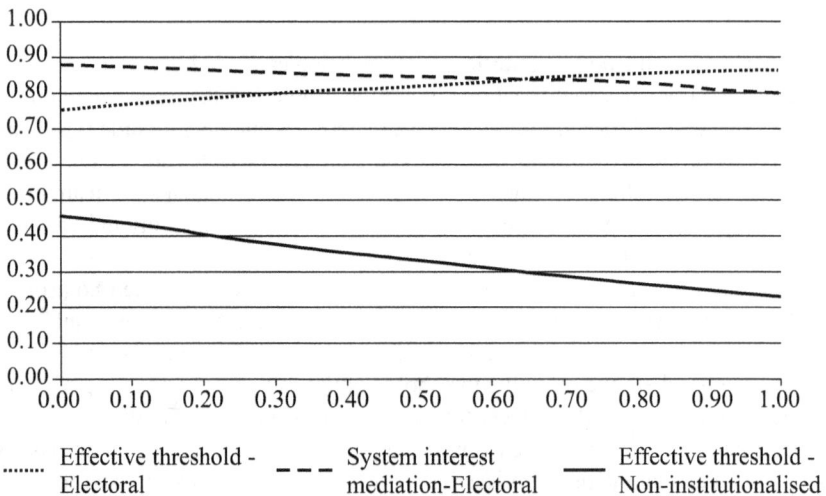

Figure 6.1: The predicted probability of participation

Figure 6.1 shows the developments in the predicted probabilities for participation as the significant institutional aspects increase their values from 0 to 1 while holding all other factors constant.

The figure clarifies the trade-off between electoral participation and non-institutionalised participation when it comes to the effective electoral threshold. As the threshold increases from 0 to 1, electoral participation increases from a value of approximately 0.75 to about 0.87, whereas non-institutional participation decreases from about 0.45 to 0.23. Electoral participation is, by definition, constitutive to representative democracies and non-institutionalised forms of participation do not in themselves provide the prerequisites for a fulfilling dialogue between elections. Nevertheless, they may be important ways for citizens to keep a check on the formal decision makers (Bennett 1998; Rosanvallon 2008). However, these results suggest that the institutional structures can make it difficult to achieve a varied assortment of political expressions in and between elections simultaneously.

Discussion of the results

The results obtained in these analyses are testimony to the difficulties involved in determining the link between political institutions and political participation.

First of all, the institutional incentives differed markedly for different forms of participation. For electoral participation, most findings suggested that the institutional impact on turnout was negligible. It would thus seem like the social movement theories have little to teach scholars interested in electoral behaviour when it comes to institutional impact. Although not surprising as such, this shows the importance of considering different institutional aspects for different purposes.

Institutional openness at the system level promoted participation in institutionalised activities at the core of the representative democracy. This implies that institutional openness could promote a better functioning democracy between elections, since these activities have been argued to be superior to the non-institutionalised alternatives for creating information-rich communication between elections and channelling citizen preferences to the decision makers (Stoker 2006; Mair 2006; White and Ypi 2010). Nevertheless, this effect evaporated when examining the effects of the separate institutional aspects and controlling for individual characteristics. It is therefore not possible to draw firm conclusions on this effect.

The most persistent impact was found for non-institutionalised participation, where a negative effect from the electoral threshold persisted even when controlling for other factors. As suggested by POS, institutional openness in this regard may diminish non-institutionalised participation.

The effect of institutional openness generally appears to be less straightforward than assumed by POS since such openness does not unequivocally promote institutionalised participation and thereby a richer dialogue between citizens and representatives. It is worth pointing out here that earlier contributions noted the complexities involved in the relationship between the institutional structure and political behaviour. Eisinger (1973) contends that the relationship between the institutional structure and the propensity for protest was curvilinear. Although such a curvilinear relationship cannot be rejected, the present findings entail further complexities since the effect of institutional openness differ for different institutional aspects. The findings suggest that there is a trade-off between a functioning electoral democracy measured by levels of turnout, and a vibrant democracy between elections in terms of a vigilant citizenry that keeps decision makers accountable through non-institutionalised activities. The necessity of institutional trade-offs has also been emphasised by Powell (2000) when it comes to the functioning of electoral democracy. This implies that institutional openness may have contradictory effects and is therefore not a cure-all for democratic ills.

Despite some notable findings, the impact of the institutional aspects faded when controlling for individual level characteristics. Hence, the impact of the institutional structure found for social movements (Meyer 2004) does not necessarily imply corresponding institutional incentives at the individual level. The institutional structures may help mobilise particular subgroups of citizens active in social movements, but they do not necessarily constitute a strong force in activating the general public. However, the political institutions may still interact with individual characteristics to promote participation, a proposition in line with the findings for electoral participation of Karp and Banducci (2007) (see also Marien and Christensen 2013). To resolve this issue it is necessary to examine cross level interactions, which requires including more countries in the analyses in order to be able to handle the additional complexity of the models.

These results leave several questions for future research to address. The source of data restricted the study to a European context, which circumscribed the variation in the institutions under scrutiny, in particular for the effective electoral threshold. Future studies should aim to include more countries with a richer institutional variation. It might also be advantageous to include institutional aspects other than the ones examined here since the limited effect may be due to this selection.

In addition, some conceptual issues may obfuscate the institutional effects. This study adopts a restrictive notion of political participation, limiting the activities included to those that clearly concern interaction between citizens and the formal representatives. Furthermore, although the distinction between institutionalised and non-institutionalised forms of participation is in line with the theoretical assumptions, it may be too unsophisticated to examine institutional incentives. Previous studies suggest that institutional incentives do exist, but they are stronger for civic engagement at a distance from the formal political system (Christensen 2011). However, even in this case the effect of institutional openness is fragmentary and filled with contradictions. Although the findings do not altogether dismiss the significance of the institutional context for individual behaviour, they suggest there is a need to reconsider how the institutional structures affect political participation and the interaction between citizens and representatives.

Appendix

Table A.6.1: Coding of variables and descriptive statistics

	Coding	n	Mean	s.d.
Dependent variables				
Electoral	Some people don't vote nowadays for one reason or another. Did you vote in the last [country] national election in [month/year]?, 0/1, 1=yes.	35,225	0.75	0.43
Institutionalised	There are different ways of trying to improve things in [country] or helping prevent things from going wrong. During the last twelve months, have you done any of the following? Index based on three activities (1) contacted a politician, government or local government official; (2) worked in a political party or action group; and (3) donated money to a political organisation or group. Coded 0/1, '1' performed at least one activity.	35,419	0.23	0.42
Non-institutionalised	There are different ways of trying to improve things in [country] or helping prevent things from going wrong. During the last 12 months, have you done any of the following? Index constructed based on three activities: (1) signed a petition; (2) taken part in a lawful public demonstration; and (3) participated in illegal protest activities. Coded 0/1, '1' performed at least one activity.	35,284	0.30	0.46
Independent variables				
Effective electoral threshold	1=lowest effective threshold. Source: Lundell and Karvonen (2008)	35,685	0.75	0.27
Executive dominance	1=lowest executive dominance. Sources: Siaroff (2003); Powell (2000); Lijphart (1999)	35,685	0.59	0.27
Minister-Mandarin relations	Dichotomous 0/1, 1=separated. Source: Dahlström and Lapuente (2008); Arian *et al.* (2002) for Israel; Schedler (1997) for Switzerland	35,685	0.47	0.50
System of interest mediation	1= highest degree of corporatism. Source: Siaroff (1999)	35,685	0.48	0.33

(Cont'd.)

Table A.6.1 Cont'd.

	Coding	n	Mean	s.d.
Fiscal decentralisation	1 = highest degree of fiscal decentralisation. Source: World Bank. Online. Available: http://www1.worldbank.org/publicsector/decentralization/fiscalindicators.htm. (accessed 5 December 2011)	35,685	0.52	0.25
Age	1 = highest age	35,380	0.42	0.17
Gender	0/1, 1= male	35,640	0.47	0.50
Education	5 categories, 1 = highest educational level	35,423	0.47	0.34
Political interest	4 categories, 1 = highest political interest	35,564	0.48	0.30
Party identification	0/1, 1 = party identification	34,864	0.54	0.50
Internal efficacy	Index created from 3 questions on internal efficacy, each 5 categories, coded, 1 = high internal political efficacy	34,107	0.46	0.22
External efficacy	5 categories, 1 = high external political efficacy	34,574	0.43	0.23
Political Trust	Index created from two items (Trust parliament and Trust politicians), coded, 1= highest trust	35,006	0.35	0.27
Satisfaction democracy	0–10, coded, 1= highest level of satisfaction	34,227	0.56	0.24
Social trust	Index based on 3 questions on social trust, coded, 1= highest social trust	35,199	0.53	0.20
Ideology	0–10, with 10 right wing, coded, 1 = right wing	31,571	0.51	0.22
Ideological extremism	Calculated distance from middle on ideology index, coded, 1 = extreme	31,571	0.31	0.30
Leisure associations	Index measuring level of involvement in 1) religious or church organisation; 2) cultural or hobby activities; 3) sports club or club for outdoor activities; 4) social club, etc. Coded, 1 highest involvement	33,645	0.17	0.22
Interest associations	Index measuring level of involvement in: 1) trade unions; 2) business/professional/farmers' organisation; 3) consumer or automobile organisation; 4) organisation for science/education/teachers and parents. Coded, 1 highest involvement	33,645	0.15	0.21

References

Arian, A., Nachmias, D. and Amir, R. (2002) *Executive Governance in Israel*, Gordonsville: Palgrave Macmillan.

Bäck, H., Teorell, J. and Westholm, A. (2011) 'Explaining modes of participation: A dynamic test of alternative rational choice models', *Scandinavian Political Studies*, 34: 74–97.

Barcikowski, R. S. (1981) 'Statistical power with group mean as the unit of analysis', *Journal of Educational Statistics*, 6: 267–85.

Barnes, S. and Kaase, M. (1979) *Political Action: Mass participation in five Western democracies*, Beverly Hills: Sage Publications.

Bengtsson, Å. and Wass, H. (2010) 'Styles of political representation: What do voters expect?', *Journal of Elections, Public Opinion and Parties,* 20: 55–81.

Bennett, W. L. (1998) 'The uncivic culture: Communication, identity, and the rise of lifestyle politics', *P. S.: Political Science and Politics*, 31: 41–61.

Cassel, C. S. (2003) 'Overreporting and electoral participation research', *American Politics Research,* 31: 81–92.

Christensen, H. S. (2011) *Political Participation Beyond the Vote – How the institutional context shapes patterns of political participation in 18 Western European democracies*, Turku: Åbo Akademi University Press.

Christiansen, P. M. and Togeby, L. (2006) 'Power and democracy in Denmark: Still a viable democracy', *Scandinavian Political Studies,* 29: 1–24.

Crozier, M., Huntington, S. P. and Watanuki, J. (1975) *The Crisis of Democracy: Report on the Governability of Democracies to the Trilateral Commission*, New York: New York University Press.

Dahlström, C. and Lapuente, V. (2008) 'New public management as a trust problem: Explaining cross-country differences in the adoption of performance-related pay in the public sector', *QoG Working Paper Series*, 2008(7). Online. Available at: http://www.pol.gu.se/digitalAssets/1314/1314624_new-public-management-as-a-trust-problem.pdf (accessed 29 November 2010).

Dalton, R. J., Van Sickle, A. and Weldon, S. (2010) 'The individual–institutional nexus of protest behaviour', *British Journal of Political Science,* 40: 51–73.

Dalton, R. J. and Wattenberg, M. P. (eds) (2000) *Parties without Partisans: Political change in advanced industrial democracies*, Oxford: Oxford University Press.

Eisinger, P. (1973) 'The conditions of protest behaviour in American cities', *American Political Science Review,* 81: 11–28.

Franklin, M. N. (2004) *Voter Turnout and the Dynamics of Electoral Competition in Established Democracies Since 1945*, New York: Cambridge University Press.

Giugni, M. and Passy, F. (2004) 'Migrant mobilisation between political institutions and citizenship regimes: A comparison of France and Switzerland', *European Journal of Political Research,* 43: 51–82.

Hox, J. (2002) *Multilevel Analysis: Techniques and Applications*, Mahwah: Lawrence Erlbaum Associates.

Karp, J. A. and Banducci, S. A. (2007) 'Political efficacy and participation in twenty-seven democracies: How electoral systems shape political behaviour', *British Journal of Political Science,* 37: 1–24.

Katzenstein, P. J. (1985) *Small States in World Markets: Industrial policy in Europe*, Ithaca, N.Y.: Cornell University Press.

Kitschelt, H. P. (1986) 'Political opportunity structure and political protest: Anti-nuclear movements in four democracies', *British Journal of Political Science,* 16: 57–85.

— (1993) 'Social movements, political parties, and democratic theory', *Annals of the American Academy of Political and Social Science,* 528: 13–29.

Kittilson, M. C. and Schwindt-Bayer, L. (2010) 'Engaging citizens: The role of power-sharing institutions', *Journal of Politics,* 72: 990–1002.

Koopmans, R., Kriesi, H. P., Duyvendak, J. W. and Giugni, M. G. (1995) *New Social Movements in Western Europe: A comparative analysis*, Minneapolis: University of Minnesota Press.

Kreft, I. and de Leeuw, J. (1998) *Introducing Multilevel Modelling*, London: Sage.

Kriesi, H. P., Koopmans, R., Duyvendak, J. W. and Giugni, M. G. (1992) 'New social movements and political opportunities in Western Europe', *European Journal of Political Research,* 22: 219–44.

Lane, J. E. and Ersson, S. (1997) 'The institutions of konkordanz and corporatism: How closely are they connected?', *Swiss Political Science Review,* 3: 5–29.

— (2000) *The New Institutional Politics: Performance and outcomes*, London and New York: Routledge.

Lijphart, A. (1999) *Patterns of Democracy: Government forms and performance in thirty-six countries*, New Haven: Yale University Press.

Lundell, K. and Karvonen, L. (2008) *A Comparative Data Set on Political Institutions*, Åbo Akademi University: Department of Political Science and Administration.

Mair, P. (2006) 'Ruling the void? The hollowing of Western democracy', *New Left Review,* 42: 25–51.

Mansbridge, J. (2003) 'Rethinking representation', *American Political Science Review,* 97: 515–528.

Marien, S. and Christensen, H. S. (2013) 'Trust and Openness: Prerequisites for democratic engagement?', in Demetriou, K. N. (ed.) *Democracy in Transition: Political participation in the European Union*, New York: Springer: 109–134.

Marien, S., Hooghe, M. and Quintelier, E. (2010) 'Inequalities in non-institutionalised forms of political participation: A multilevel analysis of 25 countries', *Political Studies,* 58: 187–213.

Meyer, D. S. (2004) 'Protest and Political Opportunities', *Annual Review of Sociology,* 30: 125–45.

Micheletti, M. (2003) *Political Virtue and Shopping: Individuals, consumerism, and collective action,* New York: Palgrave.

Molina, O. and Rhodes, M. (2002) 'Corporatism: The past, present, and future of a concept', *Annual Review of Political Science,* 5: 305–31.

Morales, L. (2009) *Joining Political Organisations: Institutions, mobilisation and participation in Western democracies,* Colchester: ECPR Press.

Munck, G. L. and Snyder, R. (2007) 'Debating the direction of comparative politics: An analysis of leading journals', *Comparative Political Studies,* 40: 5–31.

Nam, T. (2007) 'Rough days in democracies: Comparing protests in democracies', *European Journal of Political Research,* 46: 97–120.

Norris, P. (2002) *Democratic Phoenix: Reinventing political activism,* Cambridge: Cambridge University Press.

— (2004) *Electoral Engineering: Voting rules and political behavior,* Cambridge: Cambridge University Press.

— (2007) 'Political activism: New challenges, new opportunities', in Boix, C. and Stokes, S. C. (eds) *Oxford Handbook of Comparative Politics,* Oxford: Oxford University Press: pp. 628–650.

Olsen, J. P. (1978) 'Folkestyre, byråkrati og korporativisme – skisse av et organisasjonsteoretisk perspektiv', in Olsen J. P. (ed.) *Politisk organisering,* Oslo: Universitetsforlaget, pp. 13–114.

Pollitt, C. and Bouckaert, G. (2004) *Public Management Reform: A comparative analysis,* Oxford: Oxford University Press.

Powell, G. B., Jr (2000) *Elections as Instruments of Democracy: Majoritarian and proportional visions,* New Haven: Yale University Press.

Putnam, R. D. (2000) *Bowling Alone: The collapse and revival of American community,* New York: Simon and Schuster.

Rosanvallon, P. (2008) *Counter-Democracy: Politics in the age of distrust',* Cambridge: Cambridge University Press.

Schedler, K. (1997) 'The state of public management reforms in Switzerland', in Kickert, W. (ed.) *Public Management and Administrative Reform in Western Europe,* Cheltenham and Northampton: Edward Elgar, pp. 121–140.

Siaroff, A. (1999) 'Corporatism in 24 industrial democracies: Meaning and measurement', *European Journal of Political Research,* 36: 175–205.

— (2003) 'Varieties of parliamentarism in the advanced industrial democracies', *International Political Science Review,* 24: 445–64.

Snijders, T. and Bosker, R. (1999) *Multilevel Analysis: An introduction to basic and advanced multilevel modelling,* London: Sage.

Stoker, G. (2006) *Why Politics Matters,* London: Palgrave Macmillan.

Strom, K. (1984) 'Minority governments in parliamentary democracies: The rationality of nonwinning cabinet solutions', *Comparative Political Studies,* 17: 199–227.

Teorell, J., Torcal, M. and Montero, J. R. (2007) 'Political participation: Mapping the terrain', in van Deth, J., Montero, J. R. and Westholm, A. (eds) *Citizenship and Involvement in European Democracies: A comparative analysis*, London and New York: Routledge, pp. 334–57.

Todosijević, B. and Enyedi, Z. (2003) 'Structure versus culture again: Corporatism and the "new politics" in 16 Western European countries', *European Journal of Political Research,* 42: 629–42.

Topf, R. (1995) 'Beyond Electoral Participation', in Klingemann, H.-D. and Fuchs, D. (eds) *Citizens and the State*, Oxford: Oxford University Press, pp. 52–91.

Urbinati, N. and Warren, M. (2008) 'The concept of representation in contemporary democratic theory', *Annual Review of Political Science,* 11: 387–412.

van Deth, J. W. (2010) 'Schools and schoolyards: The associational impact on political engagement', in Maloney, W. A. and van Deth, J. W. (eds) *Civil Society and Activism in Europe: Contextualizing engagement and political orientations*, London and New York: Routledge, pp. 77-99.

Verba, S. and Nie, N. H. (1972) *Participation in America: Social equality and political democracy*, New York: Harper and Row.

Verba, S., Nie, N. H. and Kim, J. O. (1978) *Participation and Political Equality: A seven-nation comparison.* Cambridge, MA: Cambridge University Press.

White, J. and Ypi, L. (2010) 'Rethinking the modern prince: Partisanship and the Democratic Ethos', *Political Studies,* 58: 809–28.

Chapter Seven

Political Parties in the Streets: The Development and Timing of Party-Sponsored Protests in Western Europe

Swen Hutter

> Hundreds of thousands of French people took part in demonstrations across the country on Saturday to protest against government plans to reform the 35-hour work week. Organized by an alliance of trade unions and backed by the opposition Socialist Party (PS), more than half a million people took part in marches in 100 towns and cities – with 90,000 joining the largest demonstration in Paris (Agence France Presse, 05/02/2005).

This short news item illustrates the research object of the present chapter, i.e. political parties' involvement in protest events in the streets. In other words, the chapter takes the main collective actors engaged in electoral competition but focuses on their involvement in a major form of non-electoral mobilisation. More specifically, the chapter concentrates on the development and the timing of protests sponsored by political parties in four West European countries: Britain, France, Germany, and the Netherlands. Sponsorship is broadly defined and means that political parties (co-)organise, take part in and/or call for the participation in a protest event (Rucht 1998). By adopting a BED perspective, I am especially interested in whether the development and timing of party-sponsored protests reflect electoral incentives: are political parties' protest actions between elections coloured by their participation in elections?

To answer my research question, I proceed in two steps. The first step focuses on the long-term development of party-sponsored protests in the four countries, while the second step looks more closely at the timing of such activities between elections. In both steps, the guiding hypothesis assumes that party-sponsored protests are shaped by incentives created by the parties' involvement in electoral politics. At first, I examine the *differentiation hypothesis* proposed by Herbert Kitschelt. Kitschelt (2003) has argued that 'politicians in the early twenty-first century face a much more complicated and challenging task of representation and interest intermediation than ever before.' Therefore, political organisations tend to specialise and we witness a transformation from 'competitive politics among a few omnibus "party department" stores to more complex competitive landscapes populated by multiple political "boutiques"' (Kitschelt 2003). In short, according to the differentiation hypothesis, political parties should focus increasingly on electoral competition and leave the protest arena to single-issue groups with less institutionalised access options. Thus, in the long run, electoral incentives should drive political parties to be less involved in contentious forms of political mobilisation.

In the second step, I zoom in on the more short- to mid-term timing of parties' activities in the streets between elections. More precisely, I ask whether the timing of protests supported by parties is systematically related to the electoral cycle (*between-election hypothesis*). Again, the proposed mechanism linking protest and electoral politics is that parties sponsor protest events mainly due to incentives provided by their participation in elections. Here, I follow other research that assumes electoral cycle effects on parties' and citizens' behaviour (e.g. Alesina *et al.* 1993; Drazen 2001; Franzese 2002; Katsimi and Sarantides 2012; Nadeau and Blais 1993; Nordhaus 1975; Reif and Schmitt 1980; Schmitt 2005; Stimson 1976; Tufte 1975; Kölln and Aarts, this volume). While there are good reasons to expect that party-sponsored protests peak shortly before Election Day, others argue that (opposition) parties should mainly opt to protest in the middle of the electoral cycle when the next elections are still far off (e.g. Kriesi 2011; McAdam and Tarrow 2010; 2013; Vadlamannati 2008).

The chapter is structured as follows. In Section Two, I distinguish the two main arenas of mass mobilisation in contemporary democracies: the electoral arena and the protest arena. This distinction is taken up when I present the two guiding hypotheses in more detail (*see* Section Three). Thereafter, Section Four introduces the protest event data used to trace the development and timing of parties' protest activities. Section Five is devoted to the empirical findings, while Section Six concludes the chapter with a short summary and suggestions for future research.

A tale of two separated arenas

Following Ferree *et al.* (2002), an arena is the place where one can observe those who are actively engaged in political contestation. The mere bystanders, who observe what happens, and the backstage area, where the ones trying to become involved in the arena prepare themselves, are not included. However, I do not delineate arenas on the basis of the issues being discussed, but by the modal form of how ordinary people become involved in the struggle that takes place in the different arenas (*see* Flam 1994; Kriesi 1993). More specifically, I introduce five crucial differences between the two arenas that are most heavily characterised by the direct participation of citizens: the electoral arena and the protest arena (for a summary, *see* Table 7.1).[1]

---

1.   Discussing arenas is very much in line with other classifications that try to capture modes of political interest intermediation by distinguishing political parties, interest groups and social movements as main types of intermediary mobilising agents (e.g. Rucht 1996), organisations (e.g. Burstein 1998), or modes of political mobilisation (e.g. Kitschelt 2003). However, the arena concept shifts the attention from the collective political actors to a broader focus on the forms of mobilisation and participation, respectively.

Table 7.1: Conceptual differences of the protest arena and the electoral arena

	Protest arena	Electoral arena
Modal form of participation	Participation in protest events	Participation in elections
Degree of institutionalisation	Low	High
Degree of issue linkage	Low	High
Main organisations	SMOs	Political parties
Main sites of mobilisation	'Street' and mass media	Legislature and mass media

The centre and pivotal point of the two arenas is the *modal form of political participation*: protest *vs* vote. Taking part in protest events or elections is the main way for ordinary people to enter these two arenas. Mobilising this active participation is one of the core competencies and resources of the collective actors involved in the two arenas. The concept of 'protest politics' underscores this dual role.

> [Protest politics] usually denotes the deliberate and public use of protest by groups or organisations (but rarely individuals) that seek to influence a political decision or process, which they perceive as having negative consequences for themselves, another group or society as a whole (Rucht 2007).

However, to define what counts as a protest event is no easy task. Following the ground-breaking work of Tilly (1976, 1995, 2008), one can trace the development of a modern 'repertoire of contention' in the course of the eighteenth and nineteenth centuries. Although this repertoire is far from stable and self-contained, it limits what counts as a protest event. These forms range from demonstrations or occupations of public sites via boycotts and blockades all the way to riots that involve violence against property or individuals, to list only a few of the most common examples. In contrast to protest politics, the modal participation form of the electoral arena (i.e. the act of participation in elections) can be more easily defined. It consists of a formal expression of a preference for a candidate who seeks a public office.

The crucial role of the modal participation form goes hand in hand with other characteristics differentiating the arenas, among others, the *degree of institutionalisation* and the *degree of issue linkage*. Both aspects can be traced from the individuals' and the political systems' perspectives. In line with the former, one can distinguish different modes of participation according to the variations in volume, initiative, resources, and skills required for effective participation as well as in reference to the degree of cooperation with others (e.g. Dalton 2006; Verba *et al.* 1995). Voting varies little in volume and requires little individual initiative, resources or skills, as well as involving almost any cooperation among individual participants. By contrast, protest varies more in volume and requires a higher amount of initiative, individual skills and cooperation.

From a macro perspective, one can distinguish similar features referring to timing, participants, collective competitors, and impact (e.g. Goldstone 2003; Kitschelt 2001, 2003). In the case of elections, these aspects are very much predetermined and regulated. Think of the 'electoral cycle,' which refers to a rather fixed period of time. The people entitled to participate, the competitors, the rules of the competition, and the way of aggregating individual preferences into collective outcomes (e.g. parliamentary seats) are very much predetermined in the electoral arena. Protest politics is far more episodic and less predictable. The term 'protest cycle' seems like a world apart from its sibling in the electoral arena. However, its less institutionalised character not only includes the question of whether and when protest happens, but also who takes part and who is mobilised by whom – not to speak of the impact of protest (*see* Gava *et al.,* this volume).

Furthermore, Verba *et al.* (1995) stress that an individual voter is not able to convey a high amount of information to political authorities (*see also* Dalton 2006). By contrast, protesting allows one to communicate quite specific claims to the authorities. Even though it is quite easy to understand what protesters want, their specific claims are most often not linked to other concerns. The arena of electoral politics, by contrast, is far more characterised by a linkage and an ordering of different issues into broad 'ideological packages' (Kitschelt 2001). On the supply side, the main competitors in the electoral arena present programmes that cover and link different issues. On the demand side, the voters are forced to choose between these alternative packages.

The next distinction refers to the main *organisations* that dominate the arenas. Protest politics is regarded as the core competence and resource of social movement organisations (SMOs) that are distinguished from other formal organisations because they mobilise their constituencies for protests and do so with political goals in mind (Kriesi 1996; McCarthy and Zald 1977). SMOs are regarded as challengers, i.e. as actors who do not have regular access to the decision-making process via more established channels and, therefore, need to organise protest events to draw attention to their claims and to reinforce the positions of established allies. The electoral arena, by contrast, is the main terrain for political parties. Parties are the main organisations that people form to compete for electoral office. In Schattschneider's (1960 [1942]) realist view, a 'political party is first of all an organised attempt to get power. Power is here defined as control of the government'. Parties are also more involved in the business of issue linkage, in contrast to the more issue-specific SMOs (Kitschelt 2001, 2003).

The modal form of participation and its main actors are related to yet another difference: the *main site of political mobilisation* (Kitschelt and Rehm 2008). Protest politics relies on 'the streets' as the major site for citizens to express their claims. Following Snow *et al.* (2004), the term 'street' should be understood in a literal and metaphorical sense. Hence, it covers the whole array of protest tactics. It is even more important to stress that, by means of staging protest events, actors strive for public attention, which is their main instrument for putting pressure on authorities. That is why the mass media holds a key position with respect to the protest arena. In this spirit, Gamson and Wolfsfeld (1993) even state that an event 'with no media coverage at all is a nonevent'. Nowadays, the electoral arena is also unthinkable without the presence of the mass media (Manin 1995), a fact that is most obvious during election campaigns. Thus, election campaigns and protest events might be understood as the most condensed images of the two arenas in the mass media. At the same time, the electoral arena is not as closely tied to the mass media. The individual act of voting takes place in the polling booth, and the main organisations of electoral politics (political parties) have a firm standing in the legislative branches as another main mobilisation site.

So far, I have presented a story of two neatly separated arenas that can be differentiated along several dimensions. While such conceptual differences help to structure our thinking about modes of political mobilisation, Goldstone (2003) rightly insists that we should not forget that the activities taking place there are 'different but parallel approaches to influencing political outcomes, often drawing on the same actors, targeting the same bodies, and seeking the same goals.' While most authors acknowledge this and highlight that such distinctions are just analytically instructive, these distinctions still structure most contemporary research and lead to lively but often separate research fields. Usually, party and electoral research is very focused on the electoral arena, while the study of protest is left to social movement scholars (but *see* Goldstone 2003; Hutter and Kriesi 2013; McAdam and Tarrow 2010).

This chapter starts a conversation between party and social movement research by tracing protest events in the streets that are supported by political parties. Thus, the analysis carried out here takes the pivotal actors of electoral politics and focuses on their activities in the protest arena. Following the BED perspective proposed in the present volume, I am interested in whether electoral incentives structure the protest activities of political parties in the long and short run. The following section elaborates on the two hypotheses that guide my exploratory analyses: the differentiation hypothesis and the between-election hypothesis.

Hypotheses on the development of party-sponsored protests

As stated before, both hypotheses presume that the development of party-sponsored protests is shaped by electoral incentives, i.e. incentives created by the parties' involvement in electoral politics. Thus, both build on a similar mechanism that links electoral politics with protest politics. More precisely, political parties are seen as strategically timing their involvement in protest activities in view of their involvement in electoral competition. To cut a long story short, the differentiation hypothesis argues that, in the long run, we observe an increasing division of labour among collective political actors because of institutional and functional exigencies provided by the different political arenas. Therefore, political parties are expected to become less involved in protest events over time, and we should observe an increasing correspondence between sites of mobilisation and types of mobilising actors more generally. The between-election hypothesis, by contrast, focuses on the mid- to short-term timing of parties' activities in the streets. Again, the timing is expected to follow incentives closely linked to the electoral arena. More precisely, the rhythm of party-sponsored protests is expected to closely mirror the relative timing of elections. The following paragraphs present the two hypotheses in more detail.

The differentiation hypothesis

Herbert Kitschelt (2003) has argued that we have witnessed an increasing differentiation in the patterns of interest mobilisation since the end of the 'Golden Age' of Western capitalism. According to his argument, the post-war period was characterised by fused political arenas, while the various arenas have become increasingly differentiated since the 1970s. 'The progressive differentiation of modes of collective interest mobilisation and growing separation of political entrepreneurs in movements, interest groups, and parties from each other is the big story of the last third of the twentieth century in European democracies' (Kitschelt 2003). In a theoretical *tour de force*, he explains this development by internal learning processes among political entrepreneurs and their followers that were fuelled by economic, social, and political-institutional changes.

Regarding the learning processes, Kitschelt focuses on two key challenges faced by political entrepreneurs: problems of collective action and social choice, respectively. In contrast to movements and interest groups, political parties are seen as the actors that have invested the most in solving both types of problems. As argued in Section Two, this is caused by the fact that parties frame their stakes as long-term, durable, and encompassing programmes. To realise such programmes, political entrepreneurs need to invest in an infrastructure that allows communicating with potential adherents and disbursing selective incentives for solving collective action problems (Olson 1965). Furthermore, parties need to invest in techniques of collective preference alignment (e.g. formal rules for aggregating individual preferences into organisational purposes). Such techniques help to overcome social choice problems, 'namely, the instability and paralysis of a collectivity with many activists that results from the heterogeneity of individual preferences'. In the long run, political actors that have invested a lot in solving both problems 'are likely to enter the arena of elections for representative office based on territorial representation'.

When it comes to the external conditions, Kitschelt (2003) regards such diverse developments as the revolution of information technology, the up-skilling of the labour force, the increasing openness of national economies, the intensifying of physical and social mobility, as well as the internal politics of the welfare state as catalysts behind the breakdown of traditionally fused patterns of interest intermediation. Most importantly, he argues that all these transformations have led to the decline of mass parties and party-centred networks that were central to the associationally interlocked systems of interest intermediation in European democracies until the 1970s (Kitschelt 2003).

Let me illustrate this argument by focusing on the impact of international economic openness. By exposing formerly protected sectors to competition, globalisation is expected to lead to rising income inequalities and to create new social divisions (most importantly, it is expected to create tensions between formerly sheltered sectors and highly competitive and export-oriented ones) (e.g. Alderson and Nielsen 2002; Mayda and Rodrik 2005; Schwartz 2001; Walter 2010). This is expected to 'lead to a sectoral cleavage which cuts across the traditional class cleavage and tends to give rise to cross-class coalitions' (Kriesi *et al.* 2008). When it comes to the traditionally fused systems of interest intermediation, Kitschelt (2003) argues that these new divides and coalitions weaken traditional patterns of 'highly centralist, corporatist interest intermediation around encompassing economic interest groups and their party affiliates'.

What does the differentiation hypothesis tell us about parties' protest politics? Overall, these processes are expected to result in a strict division of labour among political parties, interest groups and social movements. Having invested differently in solving problems of collective action and social choice, political actors are more or less well adapted to compete in the different arenas. Thus, Kitschelt argues,

> Parties focus increasingly on electoral competition, at the expense of interest group representation or social movement protest actions [...]. Social movements, finally, concentrate on public actions outside institutionalised arenas of bargaining to affect public opinion and political elites through the media. (Kitschelt 2003)

Thus, the differentiation hypothesis predicts that parties become less involved in protest events over time since, in times of complex political markets, organisations need to specialise and we see an increasing correspondence between sites of mobilisation and types of mobilising actors. To come back to the shopping metaphor, the huge 'department stores' disappear and are replaced by more specialised 'boutiques'.

The between-election hypothesis

While the differentiation hypothesis focuses on the broad transformations that have occurred during the last decades, the between-election hypothesis focuses on the timing of party-sponsored protests over a far shorter period of time, i.e. the period between two (national) elections.

The electoral cycle concept is often used in political science and refers to the relative timing of elections. The notion of 'electoral cycle effects' assumes that the behaviour of politicians and citizens shows some systematic variation over the electoral cycle. For example, authors have examined whether economic policies follow cyclical patterns. Here, the main assumption is that office-seeking politicians use economic policies just before the election to increase their re-election chances (e.g. Alesina *et al.* 1993; Katsimi and Sarantides 2012; Nordhaus 1975; for reviews, *see* Drazen 2001; Franzese 2002). Similarly, many have observed post-election changes in citizens' attitudes on a variety of subjects (e.g. evaluations of winning candidates, government popularity or more diffuse support measures) (e.g. Clarke and Acock 1989; Nadeau and Blais 1993; Kölln and Arts, this volume).

A lively debate on electoral cycle effects has also taken place in the literature on 'second-order elections' (either on the sub- or supranational level) (e.g. Koepke and Ringe 2006; Reif and Schmitt 1980; Schmitt 2005; Stimson 1976; Tufte 1975). Again, the authors expect that the results of a second-order election depend on the stage at which it takes place during the national electoral cycle. For example, government parties are expected to lose the most in the middle of the electoral cycle, while small opposition parties are expected to win the most at that time. Although the empirical results are mixed and the mechanisms behind electoral cycle effects are not always clear, it remains a powerful idea both that politicians strategically plan their activities and that citizens behave differently depending on the relative timing of elections.

As argued in Section Two, the timing of electoral politics is very much predetermined, whereas protest politics is far more episodic and one cannot identify clear-cut and recurrent patterns. Thus, at first sight, we should not expect that the rhythm of protest politics closely mirrors the electoral cycle. However, the literature provides at least two contrasting arguments on the general linkage between elections and protest mobilisation.

Some authors argue that elections provide opportunities and threats that provoke protest mobilisation since there is so much at stake on Election Day (e.g. Andrews 1997; McAdam and Tarrow 2010). Thus, movement groups are expected to proactively mobilise in the run-up to the elections in order to advance their interests. Furthermore, since election campaigns increase political awareness and knowledge in general (e.g. Andersen et al. 2005), they might also increase participation in protest events. This suggests a close temporal clustering of protests around elections. Unfortunately, this hypothesis has rarely been tested in a quantitative way (for an illustrative case study, see McAdam and Tarrow 2013). In a rare example, Vadlamannati (2008) finds that scheduled elections are associated with an increase in riots in the Indian states.

Alternatively, authors have argued that if elections and protests are seen as parallel ways to influence political decisions, then protests are less likely around elections since elections already provide an important 'mechanism through which political change can occur' (Piven and Cloward 1977; see also Kriesi 2011). Thus, we would expect protests to be more common in the middle of an electoral cycle when the next elections are still far away and the protest arena provides an alternative opportunity for voicing discontent in the absence of available options in the electoral arena.

In view of these general arguments, I formulate two, more specific, hypotheses on parties' activities in the streets and the electoral cycle. Following the first line of reasoning, I expect that party-sponsored protests are more likely just before Election Day. Political parties are expected to strategically plan their protest activities with the elections in mind. Thus, they use protest events for their campaigns since protests are a way to gain media attention, as well as to show mobilising capacity and responsiveness to (new) societal demands. Alternatively, one could expect that political parties' involvements in protest events is most likely to occur in the middle of the electoral cycle. On the one hand, (opposition) parties might want to influence political decisions by using public protests since they still have to wait for too long to get a chance through the electoral channel. On the other hand, political parties in general might want to show their close linkage and responsiveness to citizens' demands by supporting protest events between elections.

Design and methods

In this chapter, I am mainly interested in general trends and not in the differences across the four countries under scrutiny, i.e. Britain, France, Germany, and the Netherlands. Western Europe is chosen because it is where the differentiation of political interest intermediation is expected to be most pronounced (Kitschelt 2003). Methodologically, the chapter is based on protest event analysis (PEA), a form of quantitative content analysis of mostly media sources, to assess the changes in the protest arena. The aim of PEA is to retrieve and describe protest events in such a manner as to allow for cross-sectional and longitudinal analyses (Koopmans and Rucht 2002). Compared to survey data, protest event analysis is better suited to measuring actual protest mobilisation as well as many additional features of protest events (e.g. the goal of an event). Most importantly for the present purpose, it allows us to trace the organisations that support or take part in protest events.

More precisely, two different datasets are used. On the one hand, I rely on an updated version of the data used by Kriesi *et al.* (1995) to study new social movements (*see also* Kriesi *et al.* 2012). This allows me to cover protest events in the four countries from 1975 to 2005.[2] On the other hand, I rely on the so-called Prodat data collected by Rucht and colleagues that covers protests in Germany from 1950 to 2002 (e.g. Rucht 2001, 2003). Ideally, we would have data going as far back in time in the other countries as well. Unfortunately, the Rucht *et al.* data for Germany is an exceptional case in that respect.[3]

The Kriesi *et al.* data comes from one quality national newspaper per country, and the Monday editions were consulted. The newspapers are *The Guardian* (Britain), *Le Monde* (France), *Frankfurter Rundschau* (Germany), and *NRC Handelsblad* (Netherlands). The choice of Monday editions was dictated not only by the necessity to reduce the work of collecting a large number of events over a long period of time, but also because the Monday edition reports on events during the weekend. Since protests tend to be concentrated on the weekend, the dataset includes a high proportion of all protest events occurring during the period under study. All events noted in the Monday edition were coded, including those

2. The original dataset also covers protest events in Austria and Switzerland for the same period. Due to the small overall number of protest events for Austria and missing information on organisations for the 1990s in Switzerland, I excluded the two countries from the following analyses.

3. Another rare example is the data of Doug McAdam, John McCarthy, Susan Olzak, and Sarah Soule on the US case (1950–1995). Online. Available at: http://www.stanford.edu/group/collec-tiveaction/cgi-bin/drupal/) (accessed 3 August 2012). Furthermore, Kriesi *et al.* (1981) collected data on 'political activation events' in Switzerland for the period 1945 to 1978.

occurring one week before or after the publication date. That is why around 25 per cent of all coded events occurred during weekdays.[4] Prodat is based on a very similar strategy of data collection. However, it differs in some important ways since it covers two quality newspapers (*Frankfurter Rundschau* and *Süddeutsche Zeitung*) but only the national sections. Furthermore, Prodat is based on a more extensive sampling strategy. Rucht *et al.* sampled all Monday editions (but coded only protests taking place during the weekend) and all editions of every fourth complete week (but coded only the events one day before the publication day).[5]

Overall, Kriesi *et al.'s* strategy resulted in a dataset of 14,497 protest events in the four countries from 1975 to 2005 that involved approximately 108 million participants.[6] There is considerable variation by country in the number of events coded: 5,346 events in West Germany; 5,107 in France; 2,063 in Great Britain; and 1,981 in the Netherlands. The recoded Prodat dataset covers 8,875 events in Germany from 1950 to 2002 that involved around 63 million participants.

In general, the data contains information on the formal organisations that sponsor an event. Sponsorship means that the organisations mobilise for,

---

4.   PEA in general, and Kriesi *et al.'s* sampling strategy more specifically, has been the object of critique in the literature. While this is not the place for a detailed summary and empirical assessment of this discussion (e.g. Earl *et al.* 2004; Koopmans and Rucht 2002), I want to stress three points that, in combination, highlight the strength of the current strategy of data collection. First, it can be shown that the Monday strategy yields valid and reliable data for the analyses carried out here. For example, Barranco and Wisler (1999) found that about half of the public demonstrations in Swiss cities took place either on Saturdays or Sundays, and tests with continuous time data conducted by Koopmans (1995, 1998) and Hutter (forthcoming) for Germany, as well as by Giugni (2004) for the United States, found similar patterns. In general, the results show that the national ebbs and flows of protest mobilisation are traced accurately with the sampling strategy. Second, some distortions can be empirically assessed and used in interpreting the results. As Earl *et al.* (2004) sum up in the literature on the comparison of newspaper with other data sources (mainly police archives), three sets of factors predict whether news media covers an event or not: (a) event characteristics (e.g. size, violence); (b) news agency characteristics (e.g. political or local orientation of the newspaper); and (c) issue characteristics (e.g. media attention cycles). As Rucht and Neidhardt (1998) state, 'In the case of very large events, as in cases of violent demonstrations leading to significant damage to property and/or injuries, we can expect a total coverage even when using only one national newspaper'. Furthermore, the studies show that these factors are very similar across countries (e.g. McCarthy *et al.* 2008). Third, it is most important for the present argument that the biases are consistent over time. Although some authors find inconsistent patterns across short periods of a week or a month (e.g. Myers and Schaefer Caniglia 2004; Swank 2000), most studies show that results tend to be stable, especially within individual newspapers, and over longer periods of time (e.g. Barranco and Wisler 1999; McCarthy *et al.* 1996; McCarthy *et al.* 2008).

5.   Moreover, Prodat includes strikes and other action forms (e.g. internal protest meetings, resolutions, and litigations) that are not covered by the Kriesi *et al.* data. However, for the analyses carried out in this chapter, I dropped these action forms (do-files available upon request).

6.   As the present research focuses on long-term trends and the national level, all events taking place on East German and Northern Irish soil were excluded for the following analysis. Where numbers of participants are missing, they have been replaced by the national median of the number of participants for a given type of event (e.g. a demonstration) in that country. Following the strategy of Kriesi *et al.* (1995), events with more than one million participants are coded as involving 999,998 participants (N = 13).

organise, or take part in the event. As Rucht notes (1998), '[t]hose serving as sponsors of protest almost always also participate, so that these roles can only rarely be separated when information is derived from newspapers'. Thus, the present analysis is based on a broad understanding of sponsorship and does not differentiate between various forms and degrees of supporting activities. At the same time, note that if party representatives were only reported as sharing the concerns of the protestors, this was not coded as sponsorship of a protest event. In contrast to Neidhardt and Rucht (2001), I do not restrict the analysis to events that are *exclusively* sponsored by political parties because parties often join forces with other types of organisations (especially SMOs) in the protest arena.

In the following section, three indicators are used to assess the extent of party-sponsored events. The first indicator is the relative share of events that are (co-)sponsored by a political party as a percentage of all coded protest events. The second indicator is the absolute number of party-sponsored events, and the third indicator is the absolute number of participants involved in these events. Thus, the first indicator shows how important parties are within the 'whole' protest arena of a country, and the other two focus only on the (changing) numbers of events and participants that are (co-)sponsored by political parties. Usually, participation rates (standardised by population figures) and the relative share of events are used for comparative research. The absolute number of events, by contrast, depends very much on the size of the country as well as the number of 'important cities'. Thus, it is less easy to standardise this measure.

Empirical findings

To begin with, I look at the extent and the long-term development of party-sponsored protests in the four countries. This should allow testing of Kitschelt's differentiation hypothesis. For that purpose, Table 7.2 shows the overall number of people involved as well as the absolute number and relative share of events supported by at least one political party. In absolute terms, the two datasets cover 2,082 party-sponsored protest events. While 9.0 per cent of all German events coded for the years 1950 to 2002 by Rucht *et al.* saw political parties in the streets, the average share is 7.7 per cent for the four countries covered by the Kriesi *et al.* data.

Table 7.2 also highlights that a substantial number of participants have taken part in these events. While it is absolutely true that political parties by no means dominate the protest arena, the figures still indicate that the neat analytical connection between types of actors and sites of mobilisation becomes blurred in reality (Section Two; *see also* Rucht 1998). Thus, the protest activities that political parties offer are a relevant topic for empirical research. At the same time, the three indicators highlight pronounced cross-national differences. From 1975 to 2005, political parties in Germany and France were far more present in the protest arena than their Dutch and British counterparts.

Let us come to the main interest of this chapter, i.e. to the question of whether, over time, political parties are less often found in the streets, as suggested by

Table 7.2: The long-term development of protests sponsored by political parties

	Germany 1950–2002	Germany 1975–2005	France 1975–2005	Netherlands 1975–2005	Britain 1975–2005
(a) Number of participants	224,000	146,000	113,000	53,000	18,000
(b) Number of events	800	618	458	82	124
(c) Share of events	9.0%	11.6%	9.0%	4.2%	6.0%
Linear trends over years?					
(a)	**0.31****	-0.09	**0.31***	-0.19	-0.06
(b)	**0.59*****	-0.09	0.22	-0.02	**-0.78*****
(c)	0.18	0.04	0.18	**0.30***	**-0.72*****
Decade with lowest/highest value?					
(a)	**1950s**/1980s	**1970s**/1980s	**1970s/2000s**	2000s/1980s	2000s/1980s
(b)	**1950s**/1980s	**1970s**/1980s	**1970s**/1990s	1980s/1990s	1990s/**1970s**
(c)	1960s/1970s	**1970s**/1980s	**1970s**/1990s	1980s/2000s	2000s/**1970s**
(N=all protest events)	(8,875)	(5,342)	(5,106)	(1,973)	(2,063)

*** $p<0.001$, ** $p<0.01$, * $p<0.05$
Sources: Prodat and own data
Note: The three indicators used are (a) the number of participants reported for party-sponsored protest events; (b) the absolute number of party-sponsored events; as well as (c) the relative share of party-sponsored events as a percentage of all coded protest events. To compare the participation figures cross-nationally, the number of participants was divided by the number of inhabitants in the middle of the respective research period. To measure trends in the development of party-sponsored protests, I report correlation coefficients based on yearly figures for the three indicators as well as the decades with the lowest and highest values, respectively. Significant correlation coefficients as well as the first and last decade covered by the datasets are shown in bold.

Kitschelt (2003). Since we know from studying the general development of protest politics that protests tend to occur in waves (e.g. Koopmans 1993, 2004; Tarrow 1989, 1998), I present two simple measures indicating whether there are some general trends behind these waves. On the one hand, I calculated yearly figures for all three indicators and report whether we observe some underlying linear trend over time by means of correlation coefficients. On the other hand, I report the decades that saw the most and the least party-sponsored activities in the protest arena. Thus, the results will confirm Kitschelt's differentiation hypothesis (a) if we observe significant and negative correlations coefficients; and (b) if the first and the last decade covered by the datasets are also the ones with the highest and lowest presence of parties in the protest arena, respectively.

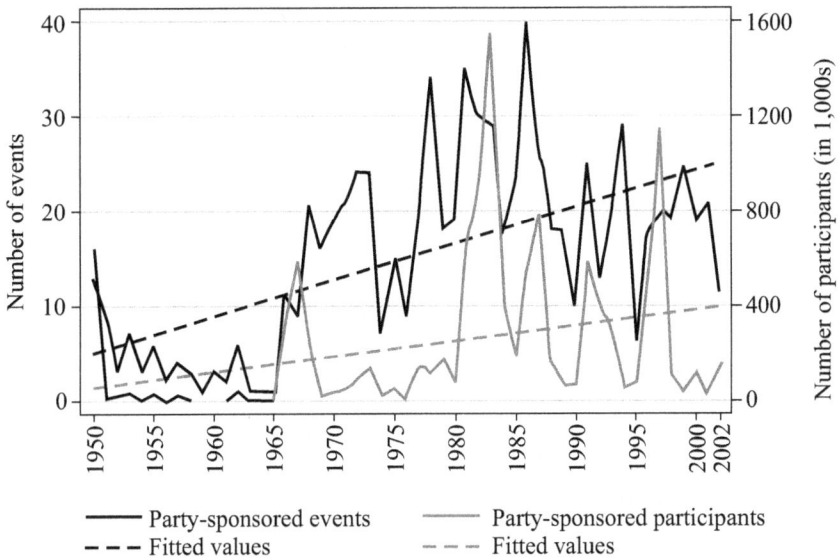

Figure 7.1: The long-term development of party-sponsored protests in Germany, 1950–2002

Most measures in Table 7.2 do not support the differentiation hypothesis. Based on the data at hand, we do not find that political parties are leaving the protest arena over time. Most importantly, the long-term German data suggests an opposite pattern. In terms of the absolute number of both participants and events, political parties are more often found in the streets in Germany. This is indicated by the significant linear trends as well as by the fact that the 1950s were the period that saw the lowest number of all decades under scrutiny (for a graphical representation, *see* Figure 7.1).[7] Similarly, the four-country data indicates, more often than not, an increasing rather than a decreasing trend. Great Britain is the only country where political parties have withdrawn from the protest arena. In Great Britain, the number of party-sponsored events, as well as their share in terms of all reported protests, have declined significantly over the thirty-one-year period. France is the main countering example. There, the participation figures have risen significantly over time, and all three measures indicate that the 1970s saw the least active parties in the protest arena, while political parties were far more likely to sponsor protests in France in the 1990s and early 2000s.

One could object that Kitschelt's differentiation hypothesis is, above all, a story about established mainstream parties. Therefore, Table 7.3 presents the results for the Social Democrats only. The analysis focuses on the family of Social

---

7.   One could object that Germany is a special case due to the legacy of the Second World War. However, tests with data for Switzerland covering the period from 1945 to 1978 show similar trends (results available from the author).

Democratic parties because this is the prime example when people talk about mass parties and party-centred networks that were central to the associationally interlocked systems of interest intermediation (Bartolini 2000). On the one hand, the results for the Social Democrats are very similar to the ones for all parties (*see* Table 7.3). Most importantly, the long-term trends in Germany contradict the differentiation hypothesis by indicating that the Social Democrats are more, not less, likely to take to the streets over time. On the other hand, the even lower absolute and relative figures highlight that protests by mainstream parties of the left are a relatively rare phenomenon these days. Furthermore, the data from Britain and the Netherlands indicates that protests became even rarer from the mid-1970s to the mid-2000s. Thus, while the trend lines do not really support Kitschelt's prediction, the low levels certainly highlight that mainstream political parties rarely take it to the streets in Europe.

Having found that party-sponsored protest activities do not follow a clearly decreasing trend when we look at the long-term development during the last decades, let us now turn to the question of whether the short- and mid-term trends in the parties' protest activities mirror the electoral cycle. As argued in Section Three, one can formulate at least two hypotheses on how the extent of party-sponsored protests depends on the stages of the electoral cycle.

The results presented in Table 7.4 assess the first expectation that parties are most involved in protest events shortly before Election Day. To make this assessment, I distinguish between those events that take place during national election campaigns and those that take place during the rest of the legislative period. The election campaign is simply defined as the three-month period before the next national parliamentary election takes place (*see also* Kriesi *et al.* 2008). Again, I look at same three dependent variables as before. The relative share of party-sponsored events as a percentage of all coded events is easy to compare across the two time periods. To compare the absolute number of events and participants reported during election campaigns and beyond, I calculate monthly averages (N=372 per country).

Overall, the results in Table 7.4 do not support the hypothesis that political parties strategically enter the protest arena shortly before elections take place. Apart from the higher share of party-sponsored protests in Germany during election campaigns, none of the differences is statistically significant. Furthermore, the average number of participants even indicates that party-sponsored events attract more participants during periods outside the national election campaigns. While this measure is highly shaped by a few very large protests, the absolute and relative numbers of party-sponsored events underscore that there seems to be no systematic trend between the timing of elections and parties' involvement in protest events.

Do we find more support for the idea that parties' protest activities are coloured by their participation in elections when we look at the development across the whole electoral cycle? To answer this question and to see whether we observe some significant mid-term effects, I focus on all electoral cycles that were completely covered by the Kriesi *et al.* data. I do not consider legislative periods that lasted

Table 7.3: The long-term development of protests sponsored by Social Democratic parties

	Germany 1950–2002	Germany 1975–2005	France 1975–2005	Netherlands 1975–2005	Britain 1975–2005
(a) Number of participants	135,000	82,000	55,000	51,000	16,000
(b) Number of events	263	258	166	27	30
(c) Share of events	3.0%	4.8%	3.3%	1.4%	1.5%
Linear trends over years?					
(a)	**0.31****	-0.19	**0.36****	-0.17	-0.10
(b)	**0.36*****	-0.19	0.11	**-0.40****	**-0.53*****
(c)	0.05	-0.18	0.06	-0.27	**-0.41****
Decade with lowest/highest value?					
(a)	**1950s/1980s**	**1970s/1980s**	**1970s/2000s**	**2000s/1980s**	**1970s/1980s**
(b)	**1950s/1980s**	**1970s/1980s**	1980s/1990s	**2000s/1970s**	**2000s/1980s**
(c)	1960s/1980s	**1970s/1980s**	1980s/1990	**2000s/1970s**	1990s/1980s
(N=all protest events)	(8,875)	(5,342)	(5,106)	(1,973)	(2,063)

*** *p*<0.001, ** *p*<0.01, * *p*<0.05
Sources: Prodat and own data
Note: For the indicators, *see* Table 7.2.

less than three years and/or with less than ten party-sponsored protest events. In the end, the analyses are based on six full electoral cycles in Germany, five in France, as well as three in Britain and the Netherlands, respectively. To get closer to the electoral cycle effects, each period has been divided into ten sub-periods or stages. I then calculate the share of events/participants reported during each sub-period as a percentage of all party-sponsored participants/events reported during the whole legislative period. Thus, 100 per cent refer to all party-sponsored events and participants during a given electoral cycle.

Again, Figure 7.2 does not reveal any uniform trends in party-sponsored protests over the electoral cycle. By contrast, the differences over time vary markedly across countries. For example, the German figures show a rather steady development based on the share of party-sponsored events, while we see some post-election effects when we look at the share of participants involved in party-sponsored protests. The share of participants is significantly higher shortly after the national elections than at all other stages of the electoral cycle. The French participation rates, by contrast, do not significantly differ across the different sub-periods of the electoral cycle. In France, one finds only that the share of party-sponsored events is significantly higher both in the middle of the electoral period and at the end as compared to the post-election months. The British and Dutch figures fluctuate more strongly over the electoral cycle. However, these results are based on three electoral cycles. Therefore, we find only significant effects as regards the peaks in the share of participants in the Netherlands during the fourth stage and in Britain during the second stage of the electoral cycle.

Finally, I focus on the question of whether political parties are more likely to sponsor a protest event taking place at a certain stage of the electoral cycle when controlling for the most important other characteristics of a given event. To do so, I change the strategy of data analysis by performing logistic regressions and using single protest events as my cases (for similar strategies, *see* Soule and Davenport 2009; van Dyke *et al.* 2004; Walker *et al.* 2008). More specifically, the models include two independent variables related to the timing of the event: (a) has the event taken place during the election campaign or not?; (b) has the event taken place in the middle of the electoral cycle or not (stages four to six were coded as 1)? Regarding other characteristics of a protest event, I include information on the involvement of other formal organisations, the action form, number of participants, and the goal of the event.

However, the between-election hypothesis is not supported when controlling for other protest characteristics. As can be seen in Table 7.5, only the French political parties tend to be more likely to support protest events that take place both during the election campaign and in the middle of the electoral cycle. In all other countries, we only find significant effects of the other event characteristics on party sponsorship. In most countries, political parties are most likely to support moderate protest events with both a high number of participants and co-sponsorship by other formal organisations. Thus, it seems more likely that it is the event itself that leads political parties to enter the protest arena rather than the relative timing of elections.

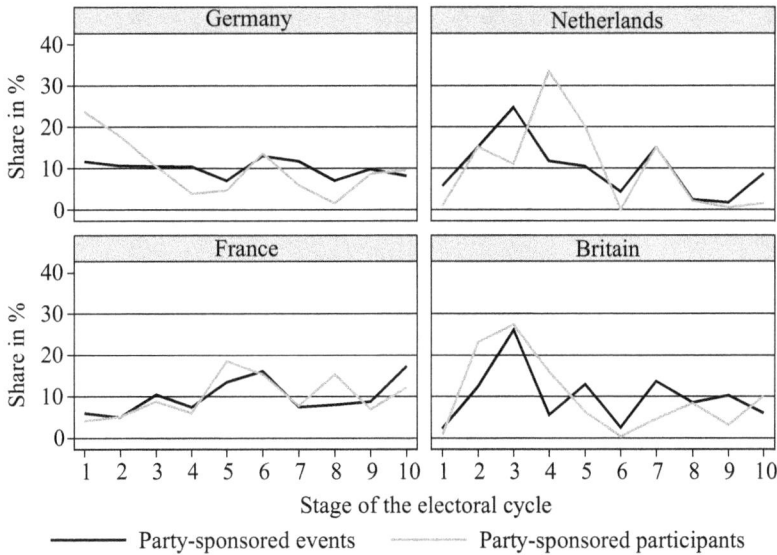

Figure 7.2: The distribution of party-sponsored protests over the electoral cycle, 1975–2005

Note: The values indicate the relative share of party-sponsored protest events/participants during a certain sub-period (as a percentage) of all party-sponsored protest events/participants reported during a given electoral cycle. Thus, 100 per cent refers to all party-sponsored protest events/participants per electoral cycle.

Table 7.4: Party-sponsored protests during election campaigns, 1975–2005

	Germany		France		Netherlands		Britain	
During election campaign?	Yes	No	Yes	No	Yes	No	Yes	No
(a) Average number of participants (per month)	3,760	27,168	13,552	18,022	106	2,280	159	2,934
(b) Average number of events (per month)	1.79	1.65	1.52	1.21	0.24	0.22	0.33	0.31
(c) Share of all protest events	**15.8%**	**11.3%**	10.7%	8.9%	4.8%	4.1%	6.2%	6.0%

Sources: Prodat and own data

Note: The absolute number of party-sponsored participants and events was calculated per month (N=372). The share of party-sponsored protests (as a percentage) of all coded events is based on the overall number of events during the three months before Election Day and beyond. A list of all legislative periods covered by the Kriesi *et al.* data can be found in the Appendix. I performed two-group mean comparison tests to see whether the differences are statistically significant. Significant differences are shown in bold.

Table 7.5: The impact of electoral cycle and event characteristics on party sponsorship, 1975–2005

	Germany	France	Netherlands	Britain
Election campaign (yes=1)	0.18	0.46*	0.07	-0.08
Middle of electoral cycle (yes=1)	0.04	0.50***	-0.07	-0.39
Event characteristics				
Supported by:				
an established interest organisation	1.42***	1.73***	1.51***	0.05
a social movement organisation	0.97***	0.85***	-0.04	-0.76**
Moderate action form (yes=1)	0.64***	1.52***	0.64**	1.38***
Number of participants (1 to 5)	0.21***	0.10*	-0.05	0.41***
Issue area				
Cultural liberalism=ref.				
Immigration	-0.22	-0.19	-1.01	-1.80*
Environment	0.75***	0.74***	1.81***	2.49***
Cultural (others)	0.22	-0.47**	0.96*	0.98*
Welfare	-2.27***	-2.37***	1.08*	0.30
Economic (others)	-1.17***	-1.98***	-1.98**	1.00**
Others	-1.18***	-1.52***	-0.37	0.54
Constant	-3.88***	-4.41***	-4.01***	-5.56***
N	4,297	3,778	1,542	1,694
Pseudo-R^2	0.15	0.27	0.16	0.20

*** $p<0.001$, ** $p<0.01$, * $p<0.05$; logistic regression, unstandardised coefficients
Source: Own data
Note: Logistic regression analysis (1=party-supported protest event). The number of participants has been classified into five groups: <100=1; 101–1,000=2; 1,001–5,000=3; 5,001–10,000=4; >10,000=5; the issue categories are explained in detail in Hutter (2012).

Conclusion

This chapter presented the first systematic results on a neglected topic: the development and timing of protest events that are sponsored by political parties. In other words, the chapter looked at the involvement of the main actors of electoral politics in a major form of non-electoral mobilisation. This shed light on parties' activities between elections and helped bridge disciplinary divides (*see* McAdam and Tarrow 2010). By adopting an BED perspective, the chapter focused on as to whether the development and timing of party-sponsored protests is driven by electoral incentives. On the one hand, I discussed Kitschelt's (2003) differentiation hypothesis that, in the long run, political parties are less likely to take part in protest politics. On the other hand, I focused on the question of whether the more mid- to short-term timing of party-sponsored protests shows electoral cycle effects (between-election hypothesis).

To sum up, the results do not support the idea that political parties' activities in the streets are mainly coloured by their participation in elections. Although the overall share and number of party-sponsored protests is considerably low, the results indicate mainly no or increasing trends over time. Comparing the four West European countries under scrutiny, Britain is the only case where Kitschelt's prediction seems to hold in the time period covered by the present study. Furthermore, the empirical findings suggest that political parties are *not* more likely to protest either during election campaigns or in the middle of the electoral cycle when the next elections are still far away. Again, only the French picture tends to support this view, while the developments in the other three countries do not support this close connection between the timing of party-sponsored protests and elections. That is, the rhythms of party-sponsored protests seem to depend far more on the dynamics within the protest arena itself.

While the empirical findings disconfirm the far-reaching claim that parties' protest activities only take place in the shadow of elections, this chapter was clearly just a first look at a more complex question. Further research is needed that elaborates the striking cross-national differences and tries to integrate more information on the types of protests supported by political parties. Furthermore, we should study more closely how the activities in the streets vary across political parties. For example, how do ideological orientations (e.g. left *vs* right or radical *vs* moderate), government status, or niche characteristics affect a party's protest activities? Moreover, the quantitative aggregate analysis carried out here should be supplemented by more fine-grained and qualitative case studies. There is a lot more to be explored when it comes to parties' activities in the streets of Western Europe and beyond.

References

Alderson, A. S. and Nielsen, F. (2002) 'Globalization and the great U-turn: Income inequality trends in 16 OECD countries', *American Journal of Sociology*, 107: 1244–99.

Alesina, A., Cohen, G. D. and Roubini, N. (1993) 'Electoral business cycles in industrial democracies', *European Journal of Political Economy*, 9: 1–23.

Andersen, R., Tilley, J. and Heath, A. F. (2005) 'Political knowledge and enlightened preferences: Party choice through the electoral cycle', *British Journal of Political Science*, 35: 285–302.

Andrews, K. T. (1997) 'The impacts of social movements on the political process: The civil rights movement and black electoral politics in Mississippi', *American Sociological Review*, 62: 800–19.

Barranco, J. and Wisler, D. (1999) 'Validity and systematicity of newspaper data in event analysis', *European Sociological Review*, 15: 301–22.

Bartolini, S. (2000) *The Political Mobilization of the European Left, 1860–1980: The class cleavage*, Cambridge: Cambridge University Press.

Burstein, P. (1998) 'Interest organizations, political parties, and the study of democratic politics', in Costain, A. and McFarland, A. (eds) *Social Movements and American Political Institutions*, Lanham, MD: Rowman and Littlefield, pp. 39–56.

Clarke, H. D. and Acock, A. C. (1989) 'National elections and political attitudes: The case of political efficacy', *British Journal of Political Science*, 19: 551–62.

Dalton, R. J. (2006) *Citizen Politics: Public opinion and political parties in advanced industrial democracies,* Washington: CQ Press.

Drazen, A. (2001) 'The political business cycle after 25 years', *NBER Macroeconomics Annual*, 15: 75–138.

Earl, J., Martin, A., McCarthy, J. D. and Soule, S. A. (2004) 'The use of newspaper data in the study of collective action', *Annual Review of Sociology*, 30: 65–80.

Ferree, M. M., Gamson, W. A., Gerhards, J. and Rucht, D. (2002) *Shaping Abortion Discourse: Democracy and the public sphere in Germany and the United States*, Cambridge: Cambridge University Press.

Flam, H. (1994) 'A theoretical framework for the study of encounters between states and anti-nuclear movements', in Flam, H. (ed.) *States and Anti-Nuclear Movements*, Edinburgh: Edinburgh University Press, 9–26.

Franzese, R. J. (2002) 'Electoral and partisan cycles in economic policies and outcomes', *Annual Review of Political Science*, 5: 369–421.

Gamson, W. A. and Wolfsfeld, G. (1993) 'Movements and media as interacting systems', *Annals of the American Academy of Political Science*, 528: 14–125.

Giugni, M. (2004) *Social Protest and Policy Change: Ecology, antinuclear, and peace movements in comparative perspective*, Lanham: Rowman and Littlefield Publishers.

Goldstone, J. A. (2003) 'Bridging institutionalized and noninstitutionalized politics', in Goldstone, J. A. (ed.) *States, Parties, and Social Movements*, Cambridge: Cambridge University Press, 1–24.

Hutter, S. (forthcoming) *Protesting Culture and Economics in Western Europe: New cleavages in left and right politics*, Minneapolis: University of Minnesota Press.

— (2012) 'Restructuring protest politics: The terrain of cultural winners', in Kriesi, H., Grande, E., Dolezal, M., Helbling, M., Hutter, S., Hoeglinger, D. and Wüest, B. (eds) *Political Conflict in Western Europe*, Cambridge: Cambridge University Press.

Hutter, S. and Kriesi, H. (2013) 'Movements of the left and movements of the right reconsidered', in van Stekelenburg, J., Roggeband, C. M. and Klandermans, B. (eds) *The Changing Dynamics of Contention*, Minneapolis: University of Minnesota Press.

Katsimi, M. and Sarantides, V. (2012) 'Do elections affect the composition of fiscal policy in developed, established democracies?', *Public Choice*, 151: 325–62.

Kitschelt, H. (2001) 'Parties and political intermediation', in Nash, K. and Scott, A. (eds) *The Blackwell Companion to Political Sociology*, Oxford: Blackwell, pp. 149–63.

— (2003) 'Landscapes of political interest intermediation: Social movements, interest groups, and parties in the early twenty-first century', in Ibarra, P. (ed.) *Social Movements and Democracy*, New York: Palgrave Macmillan, pp. 81–103.

Kitschelt, H. and Rehm, P. (2008) 'Political participation', in Caramani, D. (ed.) *Comparative Politics*, Oxford: Oxford University Press, pp. 445–72.

Koepke, J. R. and Ringe, N. (2006) 'The second-order election model in an enlarged Europe', *European Union Politics*, 7: 321–46.

Koopmans, R. (1993) 'The dynamics of protest waves: West Germany, 1965–1989', *American Sociological Review*, 58: 637–58.

— (1995) 'Appendix: The newspaper data', in Kriesi, H., Koopmans, R., Duyvendak, J. W. and Giugni, M. (eds) *New Social Movements in Western Europe: A comparative analysis*, Minneapolis: University of Minnesota Press, pp. 253–73.

— (1998) 'The use of protest event data in comparative research: Cross-national comparability, sampling methods and robustness', in Rucht, D., Koopmans, R. and Neidhardt, F. (eds) *Acts of Dissent: New developments in the study of protest*, Berlin: Edition Sigma, pp. 90–110.

— (2004) 'Protest in time and space: The evolution of waves of contention', in Snow, D. A., Soule, S. A. and Kriesi, H. (eds) *The Blackwell Companion to Social Movements*, Oxford: Blackwell Publishing, pp. 19–46.

Koopmans, R. and Rucht, D. (2002) 'Protest event analysis', in Klandermans, B. and Staggenborg, S. (eds) *Methods of Social Movement Research*, Minneapolis: University of Minnesota Press, pp. 231–259.

Kriesi, H. (1993) *Political Mobilization and Social Change: The Dutch case in comparative perspective*, Aldershot: Avebury.

— (1996) 'The organizational structure of new social movements in a political context', in McAdam, D., McCarthy, J. D. and Zald, M. N. (eds), *Comparative Perspectives on Social Movements: Political opportunities, mobilizing structures, and cultural framings*, Cambridge: Cambridge University Press, pp. 152–84.

— (2011) 'The political consequences of the financial and economic crisis in Europe: electoral punishment and popular protest', Paper prepared for presentation at the 'Popular Reactions to the Great Recession' conference, at Nuffield College, Oxford, June 2011.

Kriesi, H., Grande, E., Lachat, R., Dolezal, M., Bornschier, S. and Frey, T. (2008) *West European Politics in the Age of Globalization*, Cambridge: Cambridge University Press.

Kriesi, H., Grande, E., Dolezal, M., Helbling, M., Hoeglinger, D., Hutter, S. and Wüest, B. (2012) *Political Conflict in Western Europe*, Cambridge: Cambridge University Press.

Kriesi, H., Koopmans, R., Duyvendak, J. W. and Giugni, M. (1995) *New Social Movements in Western Europe: A comparative analysis*, Minneapolis: University of Minnesota Press.

Kriesi, H., Levy, R., Ganguillet, G. and Zwicky, H. (eds) (1981) *Politische Aktivierung in der Schweiz, 1945–1978*, Diessenhofen: Rüegger.

McAdam, D. and Tarrow, S. (2010) 'Ballots and barricades: On the reciprocal relationship between elections and social movements', *Perspectives on Politics,* 8: 529–42.

— (2013) 'Social movements and elections: Toward a broader understanding of the political context of contention', in van Stekelenburg, J., Roggeband, C. M. and Klandermans, B. (eds) *The Changing Dynamics of Contention*, Minneapolis: University of Minnesota Press,

McCarthy, J. D., McPhail, C. and Smith, J. (1996) 'Images of protest: Dimensions of selection bias in media coverage of Washington demonstrations, 1982 and 1991', *American Sociological Review,* 61: 478–99.

McCarthy, J. D., Titarenko, L., McPhail, C., Rafail, P. S. and Augustyn, B. (2008) 'Assessing stability in the patterns of selection bias in newspaper coverage of protest during the transition from communism in Belarus', *Mobilization,* 13: 127–46.

McCarthy, J. D. and Zald, M. N. (1977) 'Resource mobilisation and social movements: A partial theory', *American Journal of Sociology,* 82: 1212–41.

Manin, B. (1995) *Principes du Gouvernement Représentatif*, Paris: Flammarion.

Mayda, A. M. and Rodrik, D. (2005) 'Why are some people (and countries) more protectionist than others?', *European Economic Review,* 49: 1393–1430.

Myers, D. J. and Schaefer Caniglia, B. (2004) 'All the rioting that's fit to print: Selection effects in national newspaper coverage of civil disorders, 1968–1969', *American Sociological Review,* 69: 519–43.

Nadeau, R. and Blais, A. (1993) 'Accepting the election outcome: The effect of participation on losers' consent', *British Journal of Political Science,* 23: 553–63.

Neidhardt, F. and Rucht, D. (2001) 'Protestgeschichte der Bundesrepublik Deutschland 1950–1994: Ereignisse, themen, akteure', in Rucht, D. (ed.) *Protest in der Bundesrepublik. Strukturen und entwicklungen,* Frankfurt/ New York: Campus, pp. 27–70.

Nordhaus, W. D. (1975) 'The political business cycle', *The Review of Economic Studies,* 42: 169–90.

Olson, M. (1965) *The Logic of Collective Action: Public goods and the theory of groups,* Cambridge MA: Harvard University Press.

Piven, F. F. and Cloward, R. A. (1977) *Poor People's Movements: Why they succeed, how they fail,* New York: Vintage Books.

Reif, K. and Schmitt, H. (1980) 'Nine second-order national elections: A conceptual framework for the analysis of European election results', *European Journal of Political Research,* 8: 3–44.

Rucht, D. (1996) 'The impact of national contexts on social movement structures: A cross-movement and cross-national comparison', in McAdam, D., McCarthy, J. D. and Zald, M. N. (eds) *Comparative Perspectives on Social Movements: Political opportunities, mobilizing structures, and cultural framings,* Cambridge: Cambridge University Press, pp. 185–204.

— (1998) 'The structure and culture of collective protest in Germany since 1950', in Meyer, D. S. and Tarrow, S. (eds) *The Social Movement Society: Contentious politics for a new century,* Lanham: Rowman and Littlefield Publishers, pp. 29–57.

— (ed.) (2001) *Protest in der Bundesrepublik Deutschland. Strukturen und entwicklungen,* Frankfurt: Campus Verlag.

— (2003) 'The changing role of political protest movements', *West European Politics,* 26: 153–76.

— (2007) 'The spread of protest politics', in Dalton, R. J. and Klingemann, H. D. (eds) *The Oxford Handbook of Political Behavior,* Oxford: Oxford University Press, pp. 708–23.

Rucht, D. and Neidhardt, F. (1998) 'Methodological issues in collecting protest event data: Units of analysis, sources and sampling, coding problems', in Rucht, D., Koopmans, R. and Neidhardt, F. (eds) *Acts of Dissent: New developments in the study of protest,* Berlin: Edition Sigma, 65–89.

Schattschneider, E. E. (1960 [1942]) *Party Government,* Holt, Rinehart and Winston: New York.

Schmitt, H. (2005) 'The European Parliament elections of June 2004: Still second-order?', *West European Politics,* 28: 650–79.

Schwartz, H. (2001) 'Round up the usual suspects!: Globalization, domestic politics, and welfare state change', in Pierson, P. (ed.) *The New Politics of the Welfare State,* Oxford: Oxford University Press, pp. 17–44.

Snow, D. A., Soule, S. A. and Kriesi, H. (2004) 'Mapping the terrain', in Snow, D. A., Soule, S. A. and Kriesi, H. (eds) *The Blackwell Companion to Social Movements*, Oxford: Blackwell Publishing, pp. 3–16.

Soule, S. A. and Davenport, C. (2009) 'Velvet glove, iron fist, or even hand? Protest policing in the United States, 1960–1990', *Mobilization*, 14: 1–22.

Stimson, J. A. (1976) 'Public support for American presidents', *Public Opinion Quarterly*, 40:1–21.

Swank, E. (2000) 'In newspapers we trust? Assessing the credibility of news sources that cover protest campaigns', *Research in Social Movements, Conflict and Change,* 22:27–52.

Tarrow, S. (1998) *Power in Movement: Social movements and contentious politics*, Cambridge: Cambridge University Press.

— (1989) *Democracy and Disorder: Protest and politics in Italy 1965–1974*, Oxford: Oxford University Press.

Tilly, C. (1976) 'Major forms of collective action in Western Europe, 1500–1975', *Theory and Society*, 3: 365–76.

— (1995) *Popular Contention in Great Britain, 1758–1834*, Cambridge, MA: Harvard University Press.

— (2008) *Contentious Performances*, Cambridge: Cambridge University Press.

Tufte, E. R. (1975) 'Determinants of the outcomes of midterm congressional elections', *American Political Science Review,* 69: 812–26.

Vadlamannati, K. C. (2008) 'Does timing of elections instigate riots? A subnational study of 16 Indian states, 1958–2004', *William Davidson Institute Working Papers*, p. 939.

van Dyke, N., Soule, S. A. and Taylor, V. A. (2004) 'The targets of social movements: Beyond a focus on the state', *Research in Social Movements, Conflicts and Change*, 25: 27–51.

Verba, S., Schlozman, K. L. and Brady, H. E. (1995) *Voice and Equality: Civic voluntarism in American politics*, Cambridge: Harvard University Press.

Walker, E. T., Martin, A. W. and McCarthy, J. D. (2008) 'Confronting the state, the corporation, and the academy: The influence of institutional targets on social movement repertoire', *American Journal of Sociology,* 114: 35–76.

Walter, S. (2010) 'Globalization and the welfare state: Testing the microfoundations of the compensation hypothesis', *International Studies Quarterly,* 54: 403–26.

Chapter Eight

Signalling Through Voting Intention Polls Between Elections

Ann-Kristin Kölln and Kees Aarts

Two of the tasks required of citizens of modern democracies are authorising representatives and holding them accountable. Both can be seen as acts of signalling political preferences, defined as utterances of positive or negative feelings in response to someone's previous behaviour. Elections provide a major occasion or instrument for signalling in representative democracies (Manin *et al.* 1999) but between-election time equally offers opportunities to signal preferences, albeit through less formal routes.

In the periods between elections, non-electoral forms of political participation provide obvious means for sending messages to those who are in power. Non-electoral political participation covers a wide range of activities, from signing a petition to political violence. These forms of participation have been at the core of much research since the 1960s, emphasizing various aspects including the cumulative nature of participation (e.g. Milbrath and Goel 1977), its multidimensionality (Verba *et al.* 1978), the distinction between conventional and unconventional forms (Barnes and Kaase 1979) and the rise of new forms of participation (Stolle *et al.* 2005).

Besides non-electoral political participation, citizens have another potentially powerful instrument for signalling satisfaction or discontent. This instrument is opinion polls. Political opinion polls have, since they started in the days of George Gallup, developed from information providers on vote intentions in election campaigns into a means of continuously charting, tracking and evaluating public preferences on a variety of topics. Unlike other non-electoral forms of political participation, polls are supposedly representative of the entire population, just like voting. To what extent signalling through polls can be shown to be a deliberate form of political participation and a response mechanism to representatives' prior behaviour between elections is the central question this contribution seeks to investigate.

More precisely, in this chapter we address the extent to which intended vote choices between parliamentary elections can be understood as expressions of signalling discontent with the political parties in power. To do so, we focus on the case of the Netherlands, 2006–2010. The Netherlands is a good choice for answering the research question as it employs an electoral system of extreme proportional representation at parliamentary elections, with one nationwide district of 150 seats and a very low threshold of 0.67 per cent of the valid vote. The implication is that local (constituency related) and strategic (party-size related) considerations play a smaller role in Dutch elections than elsewhere, and vote intentions can therefore be better compared with reported voting behaviour (Cox and Shugart 1996; *see also* Irwin and van Holsteyn 2012).

Focusing on the single case of the Netherlands has the obvious advantage that the data allow for an in-depth study. Especially during such an economically and politically turbulent time as 2006 to 2010, an in-depth study is interesting. An equally obvious drawback is that in a single case study it is relatively hard to distinguish between non-systematic, idiosyncratic factors on the one hand, and, on the other, the signal provided by the electorate. Drawing this distinction is the major challenge this paper faces and for this purpose panel data will be utilised. Panel data have the advantage of tracking individual choices, their underlying motivations, and their respective changes over time, making effects attributable to causes. High quality panel data remedy some of the negative side effects that a case study typically yields. Overall, the chapter argues that vote intentions expressed through polls mark an additional response mechanism of (dis)satisfaction for the interaction between citizens and representatives.

We proceed as follows. First, the theoretical background of signalling vote intentions between elections is further outlined. This discussion results in the formulation of some empirical hypotheses. After introducing the case of the Netherlands 2006–2010, and the operationalisations and data to be used, we present the main results of our analyses.

Political representation as interactions through exchanging signals

Democratic theory acknowledges the importance of elections as pillars of the proper working of liberal democracies. They are the most formal component of political representation, connecting citizens with representatives through a mandate. Elections are cyclical and have a forward- and backward-looking role (Alonso *et al.* 2011). The main difference between these two roles lies with which time perspective is emphasised in the electoral cycle – the previous election versus the upcoming election. From the viewpoint of a citizen between two elections, forward-looking *promissory representation* puts the previous election at time point T1 in the centre of attention. Backward-looking *anticipatory representation* focuses on the next election at T2 instead (Mansbridge 2003).[1] Between elections[2]

---

1. Without making a sharp distinction in terms, Manin (1997) attaches a higher democratic value to the part played by the backward-looking vision and thus by accountability. He concludes that it is the retrospective role of elections that makes them democratic. This is because *ex-post* judgments over policies expressed through a formal vote put power into citizens' hands and grants them sovereign power. By contrast, the *ex-ante* vision of elections is less democratic since those who are authorized to govern can still betray the governed by not following the authorisation.

2. Mansbridge (2003) refers to between-election time as time T2. This, however, does not sufficiently take into account the fundamental difference in duration between elections, on the one hand, and between-election time, on the other. Elections are understood as a single event covering several hours of a day whereas between-election time usually spans several years. Hence, in order to avoid confusion we are using the term 'between-election time' whenever we refer to the time period between two elections.

T1	voter	*Authorisation* ──────────────▶ representative
Between-election	voter	*Follow Authorisation and Responsiveness* ◀────────────── representative
T2	voter	*Accountability* ──────────────▶ representative

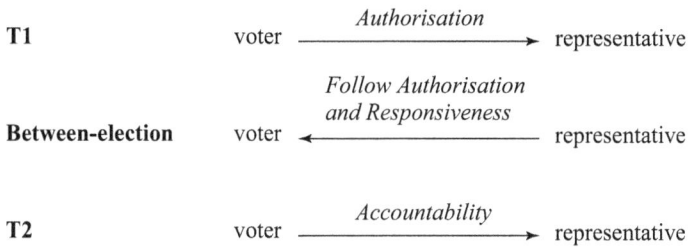

Figure 8.1: Triad of communication between voters and representatives in the course of an electoral cycle

normative theories of representative democracy demand, above all, responsiveness, defined as a representative's obligation to react or 'be responsive to the needs and claims of his constituents' (Pitkin 1967: 57). These separate interactions between voters and representatives[3] across an electoral cycle accumulate to a triad of communication as displayed in Figure 8.1.

The triad of communication as found between voters and representatives is in fact a distinct characteristic of any kind of social interaction between actors (Mead 1934; Turner 1988). According to the interactionist George Mead (1934), in a two-actor interaction in which each actor moves freely in space, actor A gestures and thereby sends a signal, x. Actor B becomes aware of the signal and responds by altering her movement, thereby sending out her own signal, y. Now, A receives signal y and responds by changing her behaviour again. It is easy to see that the theory of social interaction and specifically the triad of communication correspond largely to the interaction between voters and representatives, each responding to the other's previous behaviour with a separate signal.

A major flaw in the translation from the abstract interactionist model to the relationship between voters and representatives concerns the time line. Formally, the interaction between voters and representatives can be described as threefold with multiple repetitions, where T1 and T2 refer to two individual events and the between-election period as a third sequence in between. While theorists of social interaction and democracy usually depict the interaction as involving these three sequences, it should be emphasised that two of these sequences are merged into the single act of voting. On Election Day, voters are asked to both authorise representatives and hold them accountable (Pitkin 1967).[4] Thus, T1 and T2 are aspects of one and the same event. For voters it means that they are assigned a highly difficult task: signalling two opinions in a single act.

The coinciding signals do not impede the viability of the interactionist and democratic model of the relationship between representatives and voters.

3. 'Representative' here refers to both the elected or appointed person and the political party (as a collective representative). The potentially important distinction between the two is disregarded for the purpose of this study.

4. This does not hold, obviously, for the very first election to take place.

However, when studying voting behaviour we need to be aware that the single vote can be the result of two different evaluations in the voter's mind, or a mix of both. Notwithstanding this difficulty, voting is still a means to signal political preferences. Elections represent the main occasion for citizens to interact with representatives and to signal them their preferences. The vote provides a major link between citizens' political preferences and the composition of their political representatives.

Classic democratic theory is torn as to whether or not a vote should be the only signal citizens are supposed to send. According to the elitist theory of democracy, citizens should be silent in the period between elections, not sending any additional signal. As Schumpeter (1943: 295) famously argued, voters 'must understand that, once they have elected an individual, political action is his business and not theirs.' By contrast, Mill defended an egalitarian-liberal view of democracy. To him, political interaction is not simply an event represented by Election Day, it is an 'uninterrupted back-and-forth movement' (Urbinati 2002: 74) between voters and representatives in which elections are followed by communication between the two groups of actors involved. This participatory conception of democracy gives additional meaning to between-election time for citizens. It points to the possibilities of non-electoral political participation, as argued above. Voters are not just the receiving end of the interaction but also responsive (and sometimes instigative) between elections. For the interaction model this means that between-election time not only comprises a single interaction initiated by representatives (as displayed in Figure 8.1) but multiple tos and fros, with citizens also sending signals back. In an egalitarian-liberal vision of democracy, voters communicate with representatives, be it at- or between-election time.

Distinguishing at-election from between-election signals

For signalling political opinions between elections, citizens obviously cannot use the same tools as on Election Day, namely their ballot sheet. Instead, they have other tools at their disposal which are capable of sending signals to representatives. For example, protesting, signing petitions, or personally contacting representatives are all alternative, supplementary tools for signalling political opinions. While these forms of communication differ a lot in the scope of their efficacy they all belong to the group of between-election signals. All types of signals have in common that they are (at least partly) aimed at influencing public policies. The distinction between at- and between-election signals is important, for a comparison shows that they differ in at least six characteristics as displayed in Table 8.1.

Firstly, consider the most obvious characteristic – that of time span. While the at-election signal of voting only covers a single day in most countries, between-election signals of protesting or signing petitions can easily spread over several days or weeks. Political participation through consumer activism may even last for years.

Secondly and equally apparent, the modes of participation differ across these two groups of signals. Voting is institutionally granted (at times, even compulsory)

Table 8.1: Participation by voting and non-electoral participation distinguished by key characteristics

Characteristic	Participation by voting	Non-electoral participation
Means	Voting	Partisan activism, protesting, signing petitions, personally contacting, etcetera
Time span	One day	Variable
Mode of participation	By strict protocols	Variable, from conventional to unconventional
Depth of information	Low	Low to high
Scope of information	Broad	Narrow to broad
Impact	Small but certain	Potentially large but uncertain
Level of representativeness	High	Unknown (usually)

and is usually a highly regulated means of participation. By contrast, between-election signals comprise modes of participation that vary from activism in political parties to unconventional or protest activities (Barnes and Kaase 1979).

Thirdly, electoral and non-electoral forms of participation can be distinguished in terms of the depth of information they produce. A vote is relatively information-poor and only expresses a preference amongst predetermined alternatives (Urbinati and Warren 2008). Between-election signals, by comparison, can be information-rich. They are sometimes a result of a selection from predetermined alternatives, as in the case of regulated citizen participation in collective decision making. However, most commonly they present preferences suggested by the initiators themselves. Take, for instance, the between-election signal of protesting. Usually, citizens protest for or against a specific issue. The signal they send is rich in information and displays a preference that is not necessarily predetermined by a representative; it is on the citizens' own account.

Fourthly, related to the depth of information is the scope of information. Voting is a signal that is broad in its scope because it signals a preference for a range of issues or an entire programme. In contrast to this, between-election signals are usually (but not necessarily) narrower.

Fifthly, at- and between-election signals differ according to the impact they yield. In the case of between-election signals, citizens do not know in advance whether their signal will have an impact, let alone be heard. The potential impact can, however, be very large. By contrast, the individual vote has a small but fixed and predictable impact in mass elections.

Lastly, another difference lies with the level of representativeness. Between-election signals usually suffer from unknown levels of representativeness. When thousands of citizens protest, say, against nuclear energy, it is unclear whether this group is representative of the millions of citizens that chose to stay at home. Protests usually only represent the opinions of one particular group but it is unclear whether these beliefs also hold for the general population. Even though holding elections does not guarantee representativeness, the chances of reaching a higher level of representativeness are much greater in comparison to protesting, for example.

Signalling through polls as non-electoral political participation

Signalling through polls can be regarded as one kind of non-electoral participation. When participation in polls is compared with other forms of non-electoral participation, several similarities and dissimilarities result, as displayed in Table 8.2.

In contrast to other forms of non-electoral political participation, polls usually take place over a short period of time and individual participation in a poll never takes more than a single day – comparable with voting in an election. Also, participation in a poll is highly regulated by (survey) protocols. Similarities with the characteristics of voting are further found in the depth and scope of information. The depth of information provided through polls is usually low, but the scope of information is broad.

Generally speaking, the expected impact of polls is not essentially different from that of other types of non-electoral participation. But there is more to say on this account. Polls may have not only direct effects on political decision-making, but also indirect ones, via the formation of political opinions. The best known instance of such indirect effects is the bandwagon effect. Bandwagon effects have been assumed to exist even before the first Gallup polls were publicised (Irwin 2006). It should, however, be noted that the empirical evidence for simple, straightforward bandwagon effects is feeble. The psychological mechanism is more complex, according to Irwin (2006: 12): 'there is evidence that voters react cognitively to the polls. [...] [V]oters formulate expectations concerning the outcome of the election and what the consequences of the expected outcome will be'. In that way polls may have indirect effects on political decision-making.

Finally, opinion polls are generally representative of a target population, as long as the poll is based on adequate sampling methods. In that case, polling can be

Table 8.2: Non-electoral participation and polling distinguished by key characteristics

Characteristic	Non-electoral participation	Polling
Time span	Variable	One day
Mode of participation	Variable, from conventional to unconventional	By strict protocol
Depth of information	Low to high	Usually low
Scope of information	Narrow to broad	Usually broad
Impact	Potentially large but uncertain	Potentially large but uncertain
Level of representativeness	Unknown (usually)	Usually high

seen as a good additional, informal means of communication with representatives (Chappell 1990; Geys and Vermeir 2008; Manin *et al.* 1999; Mansbridge 2003). Compared to a vote, a poll might lack the certainty of immediate consequences[5] but it does have the potential of achieving high levels of representativeness. It is this feature that makes it a good tool for sending representative response signals to those in power during between-election time.

The distinctions in signalling are important, but equally important is the recognition that polls and elections are both means of signalling (dis)satisfaction to representatives, means that are compatible with theories of representative democracy (Geys and Vermeir 2008). The notion of anticipatory representation fits with the idea of citizens sending signals through polls. Anticipatory representation holds that representatives want to gauge public preferences in order to please voters in the next election. Hence, representatives pay close attention to surveys and changes in public opinion while in office (Goodhart and Bhansali 1970; Mansbridge 2003). Rational anticipation tells them that high levels of popularity at between-election times, expressed as high levels of vote intention, are a good proxy for doing well on Election Day itself.[6] Hence, representatives try to do well in opinion polls, or at the very least they like it if they do so.

In essence, the signals communicated through polls represent a more continuous yet informal measure and feedback system for representatives' performance between elections (Jennings 2009). Some even argue that polls as supplements to votes are needed to provide adequate communication between citizens and representatives (Urbinati and Warren 2008).[7] Despite its lower overall impact compared to vote choice, sending signals by expressing vote intentions is a powerful tool for citizens to create 'dynamic representation' (Stimson *et al.* 1995). In sum, between-election signalling incorporated into the anticipatory vision of representation can mean a representative has opportunities to gauge informal signals and be responsive to them in order to influence the outcomes of future, formal signals.

From a representative's perspective this provides her with at least two kinds of signals to receive: an electoral vote every few years and expressed vote intentions as a more continuous yet informal way of voicing preferences. Both represent one perspective, namely the citizens', that facilitates an interplay and constant feedback to a representative's prior behaviour. They can both be considered as replies fuelled by citizens' perceived responsiveness to representatives' actions. Unlike the objective facet of responsiveness (e.g. a measure of congruence between policy and mass public opinion), the subjective version of perceived responsiveness

---

5.   Instead of having any immediate electoral consequences, polling has political consequences which should not be neglected, as shown, for example, by Geys and Vermeir (2008).

6.   *See* Stimson *et al.* (1995: 545).

7.   Urbinati and Warren (2008: 402) criticise votes for being an insufficient communication tool between citizens and representatives. In order to gauge citizen preferences or long-term interests, additional means are required than just a vote every four to five years. They argue that 'votes in themselves are information-poor'.

concerns the extent to which citizens feel responded to, or are satisfied with, government policies (Denters and Geurts 1993; Lane 1959). Do citizens actually feel that their signal was sufficiently responded to (Miller and Listhaug 1990)? Crucially, even if citizens *feel* represented it is arguably secondary whether or not they actually *are* represented by objective standards, for 'perceptions *are reality* to the voters' (Dalton *et al.* 2011: 27) [emphasis added]. This means that perceived responsiveness should be linked to citizens' decision making and, ultimately, vote choice. Hence, it is on the basis of citizens' perceived responsiveness that new citizen signalling takes place: either in terms of vote choice or, more immediately, vote intention (Fox and Phillips 2003). Previous research acknowledges the influence polling has on representatives and their behaviour but has not yet established the extent to which vote intentions actually display a response signal to representatives' actions between elections or, similarly, to vote choice on Election Day.

Hypotheses

So far we have argued that political representation is an interaction between at least two types of actors, citizens and representatives, each responding to the other's actions by sending a signal. We also distinguished between different groups of citizen signals crucial for political representation: at-election and between-election signals, and among the latter, polling signals and other forms of non-electoral participation. We showed that they differ in several key characteristics making them very different in nature. Polling, as one of the between-election citizen signals, however, appeared to be similar to voting in a couple of important features. Specifically, it appeared to be similarly shaped in terms of the depth and scope of information and in its level of representativeness. Additionally and possibly more importantly, it is a signal which should be (and is being) perceived by representatives, as previous research suggests.

Knowing that the vote matters most to representatives, an additional signal that is similar in its level of representativeness and scope of information (like vote intention) represents a supplementary tool for citizen feedback to representatives' performance with similar power. It fills between-election time with meaningful interaction, just as an egalitarian-liberal vision of democracy demands. If both signals – vote choice and vote intention – are responses to representatives' actions, it prompts the question of the extent to which they differ as a response mechanism.

In order to answer this question we test the following hypotheses based on the theoretical framework presented above. Our strategy is to first compare at-election and between-election signals separately, investigating their stability over time as response signals. In a second step we investigate both signals simultaneously, comparing the extent to which they reflect response mechanisms fuelled by citizens' perceived responsiveness.

Firstly, we consider at-election signals as response mechanisms and test their stability over time. Our expectation is that party choice stability over two elections is connected to a retrospective evaluation of government performance. Based on that we formulate our hypothesis as follows:

H1   Citizens, whose retrospective evaluation of government performance is positive, are more likely to be stable in their vote choice for a governing party over two elections, compared to citizens whose retrospective evaluation of government performance is negative.

Secondly, we study between-election signals as a response mechanism. Likewise, we expect here that satisfaction and the level of responsiveness are reflected in the signals citizens send.

H2   Citizens whose satisfaction with government policies changes between elections are more likely to change their vote intention accordingly.

The Netherlands 2006–2010

Signals are only detectable when, with measurement instruments given, they are more powerful than the surrounding noise. The hypotheses derived from our theoretical perspective can only be tested when the theoretical perspective is not blurred beforehand by political incidents or completely different developments in the data to be analysed. Non-systematic factors can be expected to cancel each other out when a large number of cases is studied simultaneously but, when a single case is studied, non-systematic factors deserve special attention. Therefore we provide a brief overview of the main political developments in the Netherlands in the period studied (2006–10).

Dutch politics in the first decade of the twenty-first century were uncharacteristically eventful and volatile. New parties successfully challenged the established parties, and no coalition government (thus far) completed its term. The early elections of 22 November 2006 (called in June after the progressive-liberal Democrats 66 (D66) had left the coalition with the Christian Democrats (CDA) and Conservative Liberals (VVD)) resulted in a new coalition of the CDA, the orthodox-Calvinist Christian Union (CU), and the Labour Party (PvdA). Jan-Peter Balkenende (CDA) continued as Prime Minister.

The new coalition started in February 2007 but decided to devote its first 100 days to a tour of the country, aimed at developing ideas for government policies. This tour, and the Government's apparent lack of decisiveness, resulted in decreasing poll results for the coalition partners. Meanwhile, former VVD minister Rita Verdonk was expelled from her party after repeated clashes with VVD leader Mark Rutte, and, in 2007, started her own political party, Trots op Nederland (Proud of the Netherlands (TON)), which received much support in the polls.

The financial crisis that developed over the course of 2008 changed the political scenery in the Netherlands, at least for a time. The quick and firm measures taken by the Government to save the (large) Dutch financial sector led to a recovery of the polling results for the social-democratic PvdA, led by Finance Minister Wouter Bos. But the crisis also put an end to many of the coalition's plans, and the remainder of the Government's term was dominated by discussions about necessary cutbacks in the Government budget. Late in 2009, the coalition formed a group of civil servants who were to prepare scenarios for cutbacks in all policy fields. While this group was still deliberating, a government crisis unfolded over the issue of the continuation of Dutch military participation in the ISAF mission in Afghanistan. The PvdA ministers left the Government in February 2010, and a caretaker government of the CDA and CU prepared for election on 9 June 2010.

The 2010 elections were a crushing defeat for the CDA. For the first time in more than a century, the liberals became the largest party – but with just 20 per cent of the vote. The PvdA finished second, with one seat less. Geert Wilders' Freedom Party (PVV) rose to become the country's third party with more than 15 per cent of the vote.

After a difficult cabinet formation, a government was formed consisting of VVD and CDA ministers, led by Prime Minister Mark Rutte and supported in parliament by Wilders' PVV.

Measures and data

For testing our hypotheses we use panel data that have been collected as part of the LISS project (Longitudinal Internet Studies for the Social Sciences). It is a web-based panel derived from a probability sample of households drawn from the population register by Statistics Netherlands. For our data, interview waves were conducted in December 2007, 2008, 2009, and 2010. The 2007 and 2010 waves also include recall questions about the 2006 (22 November) and 2010 (09 June) general elections. It is a dynamic panel in which 3,361 respondents participated in all four waves. The panel is maintained by CentERData and freely available.[8] Table 8.3 presents the panel wave characteristics. The panel data include measures of vote choice, vote intention, and evaluations of government performance in all four waves. The at-election signal of vote choice is measured through recalled vote choice.[9] The question asked is: 'For which party did you vote in the parliamentary elections of 22 November 2006?'.[10] The between-election signal of vote intentions is measured by asking respondents: 'If parliamentary elections were held today, for which party would you vote?'.[11] In both questions respondents are presented with a list of political parties, plus opt-out alternatives such as 'prefer not to say' or 'I don't know'. The hypothetical vote intention question includes two further options pertaining to those individuals who either would not vote or would not be eligible.

The explanatory variable of perceived responsiveness is slightly more complicated. It pertains to an individuals' subjective feeling of how well government

---

8. Refer to http://www.lissdata.nl for more information and for the data and documentation (accessed 27 July 2013).

9. We are aware that by using the item of recalled vote choice we are jeopardising the reliability of one of our dependent variables. However, the recall question in the survey panel we used proves to be extremely accurate, reproducing the election result of 2006 precisely, one year later.

10. The original Dutch wording is 'Op welke partij hebt u bij de laatste Tweede Kamer verkiezingen op 22 November 2006 gestemd?'.

11. The original Dutch wording here is the following: 'Als er vandaag verkiezingen voor de Tweede Kamer zouden zijn, wat zou u dan stemmen?'.

Table 8.3: Panel wave characteristics

	Wave 1	Wave 2	Wave 3	Wave 4
Period	December 2007, March 2008[8]	December 2008, January 2009[9]	December 2009, January-February 2010	December 2010, January 2011
Gross n	8,204	8,289	9,398	7,328
Net n	6,811	6,037	6,386	5,394
Wave response	83.0	72.8	68.0	73.6
Panel	3,361	3,361	3,361	3,361

deals with their demands. This feeling can be said to be reflected and summarised in government satisfaction. Once an individual feels that government policies meet her demands, satisfaction with government will rise. Hence, government satisfaction appears to be a good proxy for an individual's perception of the responsiveness of representatives. For testing the at- and between-election response signal we use the item of satisfaction with current government policies. It asks respondents: 'How satisfied or dissatisfied are you, generally speaking, with what the government has done lately?'[14], measured on a five-point scale where '1' and '5' mean 'very dissatisfied' and 'very satisfied', respectively.

Results

Firstly, we considered purely the at-election signal and its stability over time. For that we compared recalled vote choice in the 2006 and 2010 elections. Table 8.4 represents the movement of respondents' recalled vote choices over two elections. Around 25 per cent of the respondents showed a stable opposition party preference in their recalled vote choice, in comparison to a slightly higher 29.4 per cent of people who expressed stable support for the governing parties in their recalled vote choice. Further, it can be seen that a considerable number also switched in their vote choice from one election to the next. In fact, almost 16 per cent of respondents moved from a previous choice for a government party to an opposition party in 2010, compared to only 4.2 per cent of respondents who travelled the opposite way. This underlines the decreased popularity of the three coalition partners, CDA, PvdA and CU, over the four-year period, and the ensuing changes in voting behaviour.

---

12. Non-respondents of December 2007 were re-invited to fill out the module in March 2008. A total of 323 people complied; in the analyses these people are not distinguished from the December 2007 respondents.

13. Three questions, omitted in December and January, have been asked in the February 2009 questionnaire. These questions include vote intention.

14. In the Dutch questionnaire it says: 'Hoe tevreden of ontevreden bent u in het algemeen met wat de regering in de afgelopen tijd heeft gedaan?'.

Table 8.4: Reported voting behaviour, 2006 and 2010 (percentages of total number of respondents)

2010	2006				
	Opposition party	**Government party**	**Did not vote**	**Won't say/ don't know**	**Total**
Opposition party	24.8	15.7	4.0	2.2	1,227
Government party	4.2	29.4	1.1	1.0	936
Did not vote	2.4	3.2	7.5	0.5	358
Won't say/don't know	1.2	1.2	0.6	1.2	109
Total	858	1,298	346	128	2,630

Table 8.5: (Recalled) vote change and satisfaction with government policies

		Satisfaction with government policies in 2009			
		Very dissatisfied	**Dissatisfied**	**Neither (dis) satisfied**	**Very satisfied**
Voting behaviour in 2006 and 2010	Opposition, stable	56.2	42.7	26.6	15.8
	Government, stable	9.5	21.9	37.6	59.0
	From opposition to government	1.9	6.1	5.6	3.4
	From government to opposition	19.0	21.2	19.1	16.8
	Nonvoter, stable	13.3	8.1	11.1	5.0
	N =	105	590	1,033	417

With these descriptives over time in mind, we moved on to testing our first hypothesis. Here we were interested in the extent to which the combination of vote choices over two elections reflected a response signal to how well the government was doing in the period in between. The results are shown in Table 8.5 and generally support our hypothesis. Voting behaviour was indeed closely related to people's satisfaction with government policies: if people were satisfied with government policies they voted for a governing party again. Fifty-nine per cent of those respondents who were (very) satisfied showed a stable government party choice. We also found support in the other direction: if people showed dissatisfaction with government policy they were also likely to stay with their previous vote choice of an opposition party. Even more so, 21.2 per cent of dissatisfied respondents and 19 per cent of (very) dissatisfied respondents switched their vote choice from a previously governing party to an opposition party. The results indicate quite strongly that (recalled) vote choice acts as a response signal to how well the governing party has been doing during their term in office.

Table 8.6: Satisfaction with government policies 2007–2009

	2007	2008	2009
Very dissatisfied	6.1	2.7	4.8
Dissatisfied	33.4	16.9	27.9
Neither (dis)satisfied	47.7	49.0	49.7
(Very) satisfied	12.9	31.4	17.6
N =	3,361	3,361	3,361

The most interesting test of our approach to polls as a means for signalling between-election evaluations of political parties focuses on the period between elections. We focus on the between-election signals at three time points between the 2006 and 2010 elections: December 2007, 2008 and 2009. First, we only consider respondents' satisfaction with government policies over the term of office. We find (Table 8.6) considerable variation as to how satisfied respondents were with government policies between 2007 and 2009. What emerges immediately is that just under half of the respondents in each wave expressed a somewhat neutral opinion about government performance. In each wave the largest group of people was neither satisfied nor dissatisfied with the policies the government had issued. While in 2007 and 2009 the second largest group was made of respondents who were dissatisfied with government policy, an equally large group (around 30 per cent) reported high levels of perceived responsiveness in December 2008. This is rather unusual but can probably be explained by the swift actions the Dutch Government took when the financial crisis peaked in the Netherlands.

The results depicted in the table thus suggest that respondents did indeed react to policy changes. Hence, surveys gauging people's perceived responsiveness or satisfaction with government policy reveal between-election responses to the government's performances. We do not yet know the extent to which respondents also translate these opinions into an actual response signal.

The results so far display at- and between-election signals separately. In what follows we present results on combined analyses. Firstly, we only consider the actual signals of vote choice and vote intention and their stability over time. Markov chain models have been estimated to capture the shape of over-time variation.

A Markov chain models a response variable (in our case, a preference for a governing party) in discrete time (in our case, intervals of approximately one year) as a stochastic process given the past realisations of this response variable (previous preferences for a governing party). The model may just include the preference of one year before (a first-order Markov chain), but it may also be the case that information about the preferences of earlier years is needed to obtain a satisfactory estimate of the present preference (higher-order Markov chains). Since we use a dichotomous response variable, loglinear Markov chain models have been estimated (Agresti 1990).

Table 8.7: Loglinear Markov chain models of reported vote/vote intention for government party

	First order	Second order	Third order	Fourth order
Gov06*Gov07	3.37	2.58	2.28	2.13
Gov07*Gov08	3.14	1.40	1.39	1.52
Gov08*Gov09	3.50	1.90	1.92	2.03
Gov09*Gov10	2.80	1.88	1.49	1.37
Gov06*Gov08		1.58	1.24	1.06
Gov07*Gov09		2.19	1.41	1.58
Gov08*Gov10		1.42	1.04	0.80
Gov06*Gov09			1.16	0.80
Gov07 *Gov10			1.07	0.62
Gov06*Gov10				1.20
Likelihood ratio	764.01	213.96	108.42	24.79
Df	22	19	17	16
P =	0.000	0.000	0.000	0.074

Note: Entries denote conditional log odds ratios; n = 2,435

If the signals would simply echo one another, with only non-systematic variation, a simple first-order Markov chain would be sufficient to describe over-time variation. The first column of Table 8.7, which depicts the results of a first-order Markov chain, shows that this is not the case. A model in which the present preference for a governing party depends only on the preference one year earlier does not fit the data at all, as the goodness-of-fit test shows. In fact, as the second, third and fourth columns of Table 8.7 show, no Markov chain model of any order adequately fits the development of vote choice and vote intention over time. The only model that comes near to an acceptable fit with the data is the fourth-order Markov chain, in which every intention depends on *all* previously uttered intentions. The conclusion must be that for an adequate description of between-election signalling, other factors should be included in the model. An obvious other factor, to which we now turn, is the respondent's satisfaction with government policies.

Our second hypothesis states that citizens whose satisfaction with government policies changes between elections are more likely to change their vote intention accordingly. For a test of this hypothesis we follow Goodman (1973) and conduct a modified path analysis to estimate the effects that satisfaction with government policies has on voting for any of the government parties.

Path analysis is a method for analysing the causal relationships among a set of interval variables, based on their correlations. Modified path analysis adapts this method to categorical variables. As we are using dichotomised variables, the

Government party 06	3.23	Government party 07	3.13	Government party 08	3.44	Government party 09	2.70	Government party 10

1.51   0.35   0.82   1.35   .30

Satisfaction 07	1.98	Satisfaction 08	1.98	Satisfaction 09

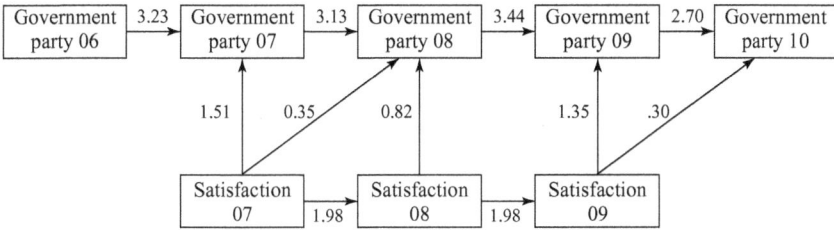

Figure 8.2: Modified path analysis of vote (intention) for government party and satisfaction with government policies, 2006–2010

Note: Entries are logit estimates; variables have been dichotomised.

modified path analysis entails a series of simple, recursive path analyses using logit analysis, which can be combined to produce a joint model. The complete model is depicted in Figure 8.2; the partial logit models underlying the model are summarised below, with corresponding goodness-of-fit statistics. Some of the partial models are saturated; this means that a goodness-of-fit test is not possible as there are no degrees of freedom in the model.

(1) Gov07 = Gov07 + Gov07*Gov 06 + Gov07*Sat07. LR = 0.422, df = 1 (p = 0.516)

(2) Sat08 = Sat08 + Sat08*Sat07. (saturated model)

(3) Gov08 = Gov08 + Gov08*Gov07 + Gov08*Sat07 + Gov08*Sat08. LR = 2.863, df = 4 (p = 0.581)

(4) Sat09 = Sat09 + Sat09*Sat08. (saturated model)

(5) Gov09 = Gov09 + Gov09*Gov08 + Gov09*Sat08 + Gov09*Sat09. LR = 5.592, df = 4 (p = 0.232)

(6) Gov10 = Gov10 + Gov10*Sat09 + Gov10*Gov09. LR = 0.255, df = 1 (p = 0.613)

It appears that by introducing satisfaction with government policies as a variable, changes in vote intentions (for government or opposition parties) can be explained very well. All models that permit a test show a very good fit.[15] From the logic of modified path analysis, it follows that the model as a whole fits the data as well. This is the model depicted in Figure 8.2.

Our second hypothesis is also supported by the data. If we take our logic of signalling between elections further, the next step would be to try to replace people's general satisfaction with what the government has recently done with more substantive explanations. Although a full analysis is beyond the scope of the present chapter, an example may clarify how signals can be interpreted.

---

15. The overall goodness-of-fit is approximately equal to the sum of the partial measures: LR = 9.132, df = 10 (p > 0.500).

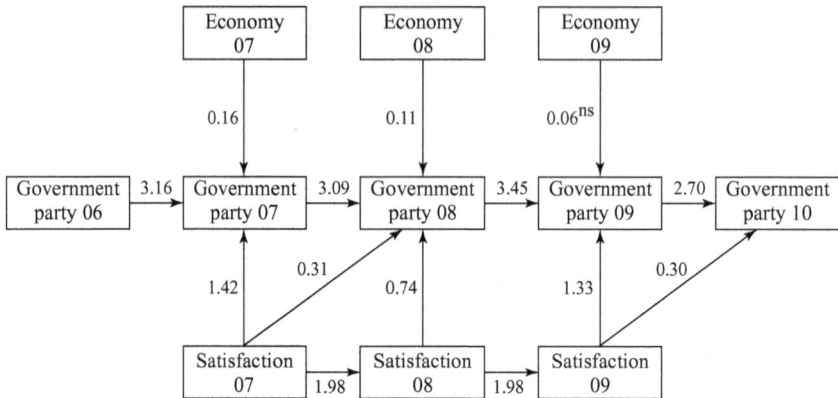

Figure 8.3: Logistic regression analyses of vote (intention) for government party, satisfaction with government policies, and satisfaction with the functioning of the economy 2006–2010

Note: Entries are logistic regression coefficients; ns= not significant at $p<0.05$

The financial crisis that started in 2008 is without any doubt among the most important events affecting Dutch politics in the 2006–2010 period. (Dis)satisfaction with government policies, and preference for a government party, are expected to result at least to some extent from people's evaluation of the economic situation, even though, according to most observers, the state of the economy cannot be unambiguously attributed to the government policies of a small country. A first impression of how satisfaction with the economy affects the model depicted in Figure 8.2, is presented in Figure 8.3. In Figure 8.3, additional variables have been introduced in the model, measuring how satisfied (on a 0–10 scale) respondents were with the way in which the economy was functioning in the Netherlands, in 2007, 2008 and 2009. Overall, we observe a decrease in average satisfaction with the economy from 6.18 in 2007, to 5.46 in 2008, followed by a small recovery to 5.68 in 2009. Figure 8.3 shows only the statistically significant effects of a series of logistic regression analyses.[16]

Satisfaction with the functioning of the economy in the Netherlands affects the preference for a government party in 2007 and 2008, but not in 2009. In 2007 and 2008, adding this new variable hardly affects the independent impact of satisfaction with government policies on electoral preference. In 2009, the preference for a government party can be adequately explained by previous preference and policy satisfaction one year earlier. While satisfaction with the functioning of the economy does sometimes have an impact on electoral preference, this variable does not in any way replace the satisfaction with what the government has done lately.

---

16. For Figure 8.3, logistic regression was used rather than the log-frequency model of Figure 8.2 because the model now contains covariates (satisfaction with the economy, 0–10 scale) that cannot be adequately analysed in a log-frequency model.

Conclusion and discussion

This chapter set out to investigate the extent to which polling can be seen as a deliberate response signal to representatives' performance. We argued that polling can be seen as a form of non-electoral political participation that deserves to be studied in its own right as it can be distinguished from both voting and other forms of non-electoral participation. We conducted a basic analysis of between-election signalling through polls by analysing individual changes in a survey panel over a complete parliamentary term in the Netherlands and found some interesting results. The analysis has shown that at the individual level (changes in) political preferences for or against government parties cannot simply be regarded as a kind of autoregressive process. External factors are needed to model these between-election developments. Based on theoretical considerations about the concept of responsiveness we took into account the obvious external factor of satisfaction with current government policies. And indeed, we found that satisfaction with government policies adequately explains changes in vote intentions between elections. Vote intention can thus be seen as a means of communication, or indeed participation, that voters have at their disposal to signal satisfaction and dissatisfaction. Vote intention as a citizen signal displays a response mechanism to representatives' performance in tasks.

With this finding this study contributes to existing literature in several ways. Firstly, it adds to the literature on the influence of polling on political decision-making. We were able to show that the citizen-representative interaction is a constant back-and-forth process, each responding to the other's previous action, rather than just a one-way communication from either representatives to citizens or the other way around. Secondly, our findings also link with the literature on political representation for the period between elections because the results of our data indicate that between-election time provides representatives and citizens with several opportunities for communication, complying with an egalitarian-liberal view of democracy. Lastly, our findings also tell a story about Dutch politics during the first phase of the economic crisis. Citizens in the Netherlands appear to have responded directly to the Government. Moreover, the results of our analyses indicate that citizens in the Netherlands were rather satisfied with the Government's initial actions to face the economic crisis, albeit only over a short period.

The main limitation of this chapter is the use of panel data (with one-year intervals) as a proxy for polls data. It may be argued that the respondents in a large and long-running panel survey like the LISS panel are fully aware that the views and opinions that they express will not make the headlines in tomorrow's newspapers. The analytical strategy used here therefore needs to be corroborated with data from actual polls. The panel-data used in this paper, because of their quality, nevertheless represent a good choice for a first test of our hypothesis. Finally, comparative data is also needed from other countries and time periods. The period under study here, 2006–2010, was anything but normal, with the economic crisis clearly and vastly influencing Dutch representatives' and citizens' decision making alike. Additionally, future research should look at more comprehensive models of between-election signalling through polls, incorporating other potential explanations such as, for example, specific policy preferences.

References

Agresti, A. (1990) *Categorical Data Analysis*, New York: John Wiley and Sons.

Alonso, S., Keane, J. and Merkel, W. (2011) 'Editors' introduction', in Alonso, S., Keane, J. and Merkel, W. (eds) *The Future of Representative Democracy*, Cambridge: Cambridge University Press.

Barnes, S. H. and Kaase, M. (1979) *Political Action: Mass participation in five Western democracies*, Beverly Hills, CA: Sage.

Chappell, H. W. (1990) 'Economic performance, voting, and political support: A unified approach', *The Review of Economics and Statistics*, 72: 313–20.

Cox, G. W. and Shugart, M. S. (1996) 'Strategic voting under proportional representation', *Journal of Law, Economics and Organization*, 12: 299–324.

Dalton, R. J., Farrell, D. M. and Mcallister, I. (2011) 'The dynamics of political representation,' in Rosema, M., Denters, B. and Aarts, K. (eds) *How Democracy Works: Political representation and policy congruence in modern societies*, Amsterdam: Pallas Publications.

Denters, B. and Geurts, P. (1993) 'Aspects of political alienation: An exploration of their differential origins and effects', *Acta Politica*, 4: 445–69.

Fox, G. and Phillips, E. N. (2003) 'Interrelationship between presidential approval, presidential votes and macroeconomic performance, 1948–2000', *Journal of Macroeconomics*, 25: 411–24.

Geys, B. and Vermeir, J. (2008) 'The political cost of taxation: New evidence from German popularity ratings', *Electoral Studies*, 27: 633–48.

Goodhart, C. A. E. and Bhansali, R. J. (1970) 'Political Economy', *Political Studies*, 8: 43–106.

Goodman, L. A. (1973) 'The analysis of multidimensional contingency tables when some variables are posterior to others: A modified path analysis approach', *Biometrica*, 60: 179–92.

Irwin, G. A. (2006) *Bandwagon without a band: Farewell address*, Leiden University.

Irwin, G. A. and van Holsteyn, J. J. M. (2012) 'Strategic electoral considerations under proportional representation', *Electoral Studies*, 31: 184–91.

Jennings, W. (2009) 'The public thermostat, political responsiveness and error-correction: Border control and asylum in Britain, 1994–2007', *British Journal of Political Science*, 39: 847–70.

Lane, R. E. (1959) *Political Life: Why and how people get involved in politics*, Chicago: Markham.

Manin, B. (1997) *The Principles of Representative Government*, Cambridge: Cambridge University Press.

Manin, B., Przeworski, A. and Stokes, S. C. (1999) 'Introduction', in Przewoeski, A., Stokes, S. C. and Manin, B. (eds) *Democracy, Accountability, and Representation*, Cambridge: Cambridge University Press.

Mansbridge, J. (2003) 'Rethinking representation', *American Political Science Review*, 97: 515–28.

Mead, G. H. (1934) *Mind, Self, and Society*, Chicago: University of Chicago Press.

Milbrath, L.W. and Goel, M. L. (1977) *Political Participation: How and why do people get involved in politics?*, 2nd edn, New York: McGraw-Hill.

Miller, A. H. and Listhaug, O. (1990) 'Political parties and confidence in government: A comparison of Norway, Sweden and the United States', *British Journal of Political Science, 29:* 357–86.

Pitkin, H. F. (1967) *The Concept of Representation*, Berkeley: University of California Press.

Schumpeter, J. (1943) *Capitalism, Socialism and Democracy*, London: George Allen and Unwin.

Stimson, J. A., Mackuen, M. B. and Erikson, R. S. (1995) 'Dynamic representation', *American Political Science Review, 89:* 543–65.

Stolle, D., Hooghe, M. and Micheletti, M. (2005). 'Politics in the supermarket: Political consumerism as a form of political participation', *International Political Science Review, 26:* 245–269.

Turner, J. H. (1988) *A Theory of Social Interaction*, Stanford, CA: Stanford University Press.

Urbinati, N. (2002) *Mill on Democracy: From the Athenian polis to representative government*, Chicago: University of Chicago Press.

Urbinati, N. and Warren, M. E. (2008) 'The concept of representation in contemporary democratic theory', *Annual Review of Political Science,* 11: 387–412.

Verba, S., Nie, N. H. and Kim, J.-O. (1978) *Participation and political equality: A seven-nation comparison.* Cambridge: Cambridge University Press.

Chapter Nine

'We Need to Decide!': A Mixed Method Approach to Responsiveness and Equal Treatment

Liz Richardson

One core idea under discussion in this volume is that representation outside of the electoral moment is a dynamic relationship involving a variety of interactions that may take place between representatives and represented. The mechanism associated with representation between elections is responsiveness. Responsiveness demands the existence of a dynamic two-way relationship, underpinned by communication and mutual influence, with information exchange as a critical element, and the involvement of a broad range of interest advocacy and lobby groups. What happens if these relationships do not exist, or operate at a sub-optimal level?

This chapter looks at the practice of two central values in between-election democracy: equality and responsiveness. One ideal-type of democratic representation expects representatives to be responsive to constituents, through communication of choices made and, where necessary, mutual adjustment of preferences. This is underpinned by equality of treatment of interest groups in a pluralist system. The literature described in this volume (e.g. Pitkin 1967; Alonso *et al.* 2011; Mansbridge 2003; Page and Shapiro 1992; Stimson *et al.* 1995; Wlezien 1995) argues that policy responsiveness could be, or should be, high. Other chapters in this book discuss understandings of the direction of responsiveness (cf. also Eulau and Karps 1977), and critique the different normative claims. But there are also serious questions over the extent to which responsiveness is an empirical reality. It is also still unclear whether politicians are equally responsive to people and groups with lower resources (Gilens 2005; Bartels 2008; Enns and Wlezien 2011). It is recognised that there are significant gaps between ideals and reality in existing representative practices, and relationships between representatives and the represented. While there are studies of general attitudes and behaviours of both citizens and politicians, there is a gap in the literature on how processes of responsiveness take place in detail, and in the everyday context of real-life politics.

How do representatives go about being responsive? Do they favour groups and interests which 'shout the loudest' or are better resourced? Are all voices listened to equally or not? What do representatives choose to respond to when faced with competing demands, not all of which they can prioritise? How do representatives themselves understand the process of responding to the represented, and what are their own justifications and explanations of their choices?

A case has been made for the value of examining empirical examples within the framework of between-election democracy. Here a mixed methods approach is used to explore these two democratic values as they operate in the test-bed of real politics. First we explore the literature on the role of communication and lobby groups in democratic representative relationships, before presenting evidence on gaps in these ideal-type relationships in practice, using British local government as an example. Using evidence from a field experiment, we explore the issue of equality of treatment in representation by looking at how representatives respond to representations from lobby groups that are both more and less professionalised. This was a randomised controlled trial of politicians in local government in England. Next, we turn to a sister field experiment which looked at responsiveness to interest groups in a wider context of other demands being made on them as political representatives. Finally, we present qualitative data to learn from politicians themselves how they reason when choosing between demands.

The role of lobby groups in representative relationships, and the English context

The introductory chapter sets out a framework for an empirical analysis which highlights that representation between elections is a dynamic process of continuous and two-way interactions between representatives and the represented. In this chapter, the focus is on the responsiveness of representatives to a broad range of interest, advocacy, and lobby groups within a pluralist and (ideally) equal system. Some functional limitations of electoral representation are: information deficits, shifting definitions of constituencies, increased segmentation of interests or issues, and a proliferation of claims and claimants (Urbinati and Warren 2008). A consequence is that the 'practices of democratic representation increasingly go beyond electoral venues, a phenomenon that testifies to the expansion and pluralisation of spaces of political judgment in today's democracies' (Urbinati and Warren 2008). The insensitivities of electoral procedures to information mean that:

> Elected representatives are left to rely on other means (polls, advice, focus groups, letters, petitions, and the like) to guess what voters intend them to represent [...] insofar as electoral representation works, it does so in conjunction with a rich fabric of representative claimants and advocacy within society (Urbinati and Warren 2008).

Interest, advocacy and lobby groups function as 'surrogate representatives... [that] claim to represent constituencies within public discourse and within collective decision-making bodies' (Disch 2011). Interest groups 'have the potential to compensate for electoral inflexibilities – providing high levels of targeted, information-rich representation' (Disch 2011).

The literature suggests that in the dialogue between representatives and the represented, representatives should prioritise lobbying by groups which can make formal or informal claims to represent a wider constituency (Mansbridge 2003).

As outlined in the introduction to this volume, within a pluralist system there are questions about the extent to which government is equally responsive to the expressed opinions of all groups of citizens, or whether citizens of resources are more often listened to. What is also implied is that pluralism requires equality in responsiveness to a range of claimants, but also that claimants with additional resources to provide information-rich communications should be privileged.

If representation and responsiveness is predicated on the existence of a relationship between citizen advocates and representatives, what if these interactions do not exist, or operate at a sub-optimal level? In the UK, data from relationships between citizens and elected representatives in local government are instructive. British local government has responsibility for a wide range of policy decisions affecting the principal services of education, social services, the environment, regulation, and the local economy, and it may devise policies in the local interest.

Local councillors have policy-making responsibilities in local government, are usually organised by political party groups, and undertake a variety of roles from community representative to executive decision-maker. Councillors, also known as local elected members, represent electoral units called wards which range in population size from between around 3,000 to 20,000. The majority of wards have three councillors, although in some cases there are fewer than three members per ward. Local councillors are typically selected to stand as candidates by the local branches of their political parties. The UK does not have a strong tradition of independent candidates.

Since 2000, power has been concentrated in an executive, a mayor, or a cabinet (Gains *et al.* 2005). Nevertheless, councillors are still involved with policy through their contacts with the party group and their involvement with scrutiny committees. The history of central-local relations in British local government has seen a high degree of centralisation, particularly in comparison to neighbouring European countries (Durose *et al.* 2011). In spite of centralisation, local government maintains its autonomy to decide local policies (Boyne 1985; Atkinson and Wilks-Heeg 2000), and there remains scope for local discretion and democratic responsiveness in local government. British local governments have a large degree of discretion to follow budgets and make new policies, and a long tradition of interest group participation in local government, identified in the community power studies of the 1970s (e.g. Newton 1976; Dearlove 1973), has been rediscovered in subsequent years (Stoker and Wilson 1991; Maloney *et al.* 2000).

However, in the setting of British local government, the picture is of many gaps in relationships and interactions. Local political representatives are important to the public and seen as influential: in 2000, research showed that 66 per cent thought councillors were in charge of public services in their local area, and 65 per cent considered them to have the most influence on issues affecting their local area (LGA 2008). Despite this, in 2002, when asked, 26 per cent said they knew nothing at all about their local members; 65 per cent had never met any of their local councillors; and 61 per cent said they did not know the name of their local councillor (LGA 2008).

The British public do not feel that channels for both unidirectional and mutual communication or deliberation, or spaces for the 'interlocking sites of opinion formation and decision making' (Disch 2011), or, indeed, two-way information flows are fully functional. For example, the 1998 British Social Attitudes survey Local Government Module (Chivite-Matthews and Teal 2001) showed that 88 per cent said 'local councils would make better decisions if they made more effort to find out what local people want', and only 7 per cent felt 'local councillors should just get on and make the important decisions themselves. After all, that's what we elected them for'. Ten years on, a 2008 survey of public perceptions (DCLG 2008) showed that 38 per cent did not feel councillors were representative of their communities, 59 per cent did not believe that councillors adequately reflected their views, 62 per cent did not feel that they were given an adequate say in how local council services are run, and 92 per cent believed that councils could be more accountable. Moreover, citizens believe local politicians to be out of touch. For example, in 2004 (DCLG 2007) only 7 per cent of councillors thought they were out of touch with the public, compared to 43 per cent of the public who thought this was the case. The study showed that 69 per cent of councillors believed they made decisions in touch with local views, whereas only 19 per cent of the public agreed.

Studies (for example, *see* Newton *et al.* 2010) have examined why citizens do or do not feel they have influence over the decisions made by politically-led institutions of local government. One study showed that 34 per cent of the variance of feelings of external efficacy, or influence, was explained by whether people felt that local public services acted on the concerns of local people (Newton *et al.* 2010). Residents judged that local public institutions were responsive in several different ways, focused on communication and information channels: if they listened and heard what residents had to say; if they fed back on the outcomes of decisions; and if they made decisions people felt the majority agreed with.

In terms of the need for equal treatment within a pluralist system, citizens felt that local councillors' behaviour had deteriorated between 2007 and 2009, and that local councillors were self-interested, disrespectful and did not treat people equally (Standards for England 2009). Between 2007 and 2009, there was a rise of 4 per cent (from 28 to 32 per cent) in people saying all or most councillors use their political power for their own personal gain, and a fall in the percentage of people saying that councillors work in the interests of the neighbourhood, with 29 per cent in 2009 saying only a few or none do so (Standards for England 2009).

Equality of treatment in representation

The first field experiment used a randomised controlled trial to test equality of treatment by local representatives to a less- and more-professionalised lobbying letter (for a more detailed account, *see* Richardson and John 2012). The method of the randomised controlled trial relies on randomising subjects into treatment and control groups or between treatment groups when a control is not possible or desirable. Random allocation, provided the sample size is large enough, means it is possible to make the inference that an intervention has an impact from observing differences between the groups. In studies of responsiveness, the method can help researchers make a connection between the selection of the lobbying tactic and the observation of the policy outcome. Observational studies cannot correct for selection and endogeneity so, for example, they cannot rule out the lobbyist selecting a legislator who is positively disposed to their case and not selecting those who are hostile. By randomising the allocation of lobbying tactics to legislators in a randomised controlled trial, it is possible to make an inference as to the outcome. There are few examples of field experiments in studies of lobbying.

The lobbying letters were written by citizen interest groups which were recruited in eight local authority areas to campaign on a matter of importance to them. These groups sent lobbying letters to randomly selected local councillors in their areas. The researchers investigated each groups' previous experience of organising community projects to ensure that they: would be credible to decision makers; had a relevant membership base; and, if successful in the lobby, would be able to fulfil their part of the bargain. We decided not to work with a number of groups after making initial contact because they did not meet these criteria. Our lobby was of hard-pressed legislators by under-resourced groups, therefore the experiment needed to be genuine, as well as following ethical guidelines and principles. The groups were fully aware of the aims and methods of the project and were willing to write different kinds of letters on our behalf. The intervention met ethical guidelines, especially as the recipients of the letters were public figures who would receive these kinds of letters as part of their job.[1] There was no deception involved as each lobby was a real issue the local group wished to follow in any case.

Methods for the letter-writing experiment

The intervention was carried out in eight English local authorities from November 2008 to the end of June 2009. We selected the authorities on the basis of the availability of a comparable and willing interest group to do the intervention, and actively recruited groups in different places in order to get variations in political control and location. The interest groups that were involved in the experiment included faith organisations, refugee/new migrant organisations, organisations working with black and ethnic minority groups, participatory arts organisations, disability/carers' networks and youth groups.

There were a total of 496 locally elected councillors in the eight local authorities. To generate the sample, we randomly selected half of them, which yielded a sample size of 248. These local politicians were then randomly allocated into two treatment groups by a university employee from outside the research team. Each councillor received one letter from the local association working with

---

1. The project received ethical approval from Manchester University's Senate Committee on the Ethics of Research on Human Beings on 20 November 2008.

the researchers. The letters followed a standard and consistent structure for both treatments. Treatment one was designed to be the less-professionalised treatment, based on the literature on lobbying. For example, the request being made by the 'lobbyist' was unclear, and there were no details establishing the credibility of the group, which has been shown to be a factor in effective lobbying (Druckman 2001; Gerber and Lupia 1992). Treatment two was designed to be the more professionalised treatment, for example, a clear lobbying request, and details of the groups' memberships and previous work to establish credibility of their claims to a wider constituency. Treatment two also provided private information and a summary of public information for the local representative, again, factors seen in the literature as critical to successful lobbying outcomes, and things valued by local politicians and therefore more likely to generate a response (Potters and van Winden 1992; Hansen 1991; Hall and Deardorff 2006; Mahoney 2007). Independent blind coding of the letters confirmed that they had adequately operationalised the treatment designs of the less- and more-professionalised formats.

Findings

Whether a local representative responded by telephone, letter or e-mail was used in the analysis as a standardised outcome variable. Overall, the response rate from the councillors was 18.5 per cent. This included one line acknowledgements, refusals to help, denials of competence on the issue, as well as some more helpful responses. This research was designed to test whether different approaches to lobbying affected responses; the low response rate was a side finding from the original project. There was no statistically significant difference in the response rates between the less- and more-professionalised lobbying letters. Nor was test of difference of means statistically significant (t = 0.99, p = 0.16).

The number of responses is only one outcome. The quality of the responses is also critical as fewer but constructive and supportive responses from appropriate decision makers may be of more benefit to the interest groups than a larger number of non-committal or unhelpful answers from politicians not in a position to assist. A coding framework was designed that allowed for a series of different types of response from the same individual in order to establish if a response was backed up by other (seemingly) helpful actions or comments, or whether they were just empty phrases.

Responses were blind coded by two independent researchers and grouped using factor analysis. Regression analysis showed that the more-professionalised letter had a statistically significant effect on local politicians passing on the request to someone they felt was more able to deal with the issue. These representatives pro-actively referred the lobbyist on to someone else who had the power and authority to sort out the problem, including named relevant fellow councillors and/or public officials, usually with a covering note asking colleagues to respond to the interest group on their behalf. Other factors, such as offers of face-to-face discussion and direct help, denial of responsibility or rejection of the lobby, were not statistically significantly different between the less- and more-professionalised letters.

Empirical data from this experiment suggests that there was little evidence that a more professionalised approach affected the level of response and, for most factors, the nature of the response. Citizen interest groups exhibiting signs of being better resourced, or better able to argue their case were not responded to in a significantly different way from groups which exhibited non-professionalised lobbying behaviour. Except for politicians passing on letters to someone better able to help, the groups were treated equally. If lobbyists' resources or level of professionalism are not the deciding factors in responsiveness, then how are representatives making choices between competing demands? The low level of response overall in the field experiment also indicated that the idea from political theory that political representatives 'usually initiate and welcome' (Mansbridge 2003) interactions with the represented might be misplaced, at least in this case. If this is valid, what other demands on representatives might be being prioritised over relationships with these organised interest groups in democratic representation? What level of priority were councillors according to these sorts of lobbies? Was the null result between the more- and less-professionalised letters attributable to the low numbers in the first experiment? Given the weakness of experimental methods in generating transferable findings (external validity), would the result be replicable in other circumstances?

Responsiveness to competing demands: What politicians prioritise

Part of what it means to be responsive is for representatives to prioritise different demands made on them. The unanswered questions from the first field experiment promoted the researchers to conduct a second, sister field simulation experiment. This was designed to test empirically the overall level of responsiveness to the citizen interest group letters when compared to a series of competing demands. It also replicated the more- and less-professionalised design to see if the original experimental findings would be replicated. It was inspired by a study by Chin *et al.* (2000).

Methods for the prioritisation experiment

The idea of the prioritisation experiment was to simulate a moment in a typically busy councillor's day, when faced with how to respond to a full in-tray in between meetings, paid work and family life. It was carried out in nine different field settings, with a total of 109 councillors from over twenty different authorities, between October 2009 and July 2010. All of the settings were regular meetings or sessions that councillors normally participated in. Councillors were asked to prioritise and rank a set of ten different hypothetical requests in the field simulation exercise. Following completion of the prioritisation exercise, there was a group discussion to explore these issues directly with local councillors. The representatives were told that they were participating in a project about increased workloads for councillors.

Each participant received a pack containing three of the lobbying letters from the citizen interest groups, and seven other requests. Councillors were randomised into two groups: one group received a pack with three less-professionalised lobbying letters; the other group received a pack with three more-professionalised lobbying letters. The three lobbying letters were ones taken directly from the original letter writing experiment. All participants were given the same seven distracter tasks, which represented typical competing demands on representatives. The tasks were broadly in four categories: individual unorganised interests (a letter from an individual constituent); organised groups (a meeting request from the politician's political group for the distracter tasks, and the lobby group letters for the experimental treatment); civil servant requests (from paid staff in the local government organisation); and local visibility requests (from local civil society and faith organisations to attend local social events). The policy area or topic for all seven distracter tasks was designed to include all three subjects in the treatment letters, so choices between the distracter tasks and the lobbying letters would not need to be based on topic content. So, the experiment was testing a) whether the result between the more- and less-professionalised letters would be replicated; and b) where the lobbying requests ranked in the context of competing requests.

Findings

Table 9.1 shows the overall scores, average scores, and rankings for the ten requests and for the three lobbying letters combined compared to the seven distracter tasks, and rankings for the different categories of request.

Including both the more- and less-professionalised letters together, and combining the scores for all three treatment letters, the lobbying requests from organised citizen interest groups ranked fifth out of the eight individual requests, or third out of five categories of request (separating out organised groups into the distracter task and the treatment letters).

The top ranking priority overall for councillors was the letter from the individual constituent in the category of individual unorganised interests. The second priority was a meeting of their own political group in the category of organised groups (distracter tasks). Civil servant requests ranked third out of four categories. An internal request from an officer for contacts to help with an equalities and diversity workshop, and an internal request to attend a meeting on tackling crime both ranked higher than the refugee group's letters and dance group's letters. The bottom ranking category was local visibility requests, with a notice about a church fundraising lunch the lowest ranked individual request, and a community fun day ranked eighth overall.

Table 9.2 shows the differences in average scores and rankings between councillors who received the less-professionalised letters pack, and those who received the more-professionalised letters pack.

The constituent letters in the categories of unorganised individual interests and political group meeting (organised groups – distracter task) remain the top two priorities. Overall, the more-professionalised lobby letters rank slightly higher than the less-professionalised letters (third out of five categories compared to joint third for civil servant requests), but the difference is not statistically significant. Within the category of civil servant requests, the equalities and diversity workshop and the strategy meeting remain in fourth and fifth places, respectively. Within the category of organised groups for the treatment letters, in the information-rich letter group, the refugee group's lobby moves up one rank from sixth to fifth place, and the dance group's lobby moves up one rank from ninth to eighth place.

Table 9.3 shows a comparison of the sum of the ranks, using the Wilcoxon rank-sum test, which is also known as the Mann-Whitney two-sample statistic. The dance group seems to have been affected by the information-rich letter as it had a higher rank, which is statistically significant at $p. < 0.1$, which would be significant at $p. < 0.5$ for a one tailed test, which is appropriate in this context. Even if the 10 per cent test is taken to be the bar, this is acceptable with a small sample size. The other two were not statistically significant: there was no difference between treatment and control.

Representatives' explanations of their choices in responsiveness: How politicians prioritise

The prioritisation experiment showed what politicians chose to respond to, but not why. How do representatives understand this process of responsiveness, and explain their choices? Following the prioritisation exercise, a group discussion was held to explore their decisions. Questions posed were: what did you rank highest, and lowest? Why was this? What factors did you consider when making these choices? Did the following matter: the source of the request; the nature of the request; the way the request was put or framed; the salience or relevance of the topic to your constituency. How much correspondence do you receive in a typical week, and where is the bulk of it from? What proportion of the requests are of importance to your role? In the course of the discussion, councillors touched on some of the core issues in this chapter regarding the nature of the representative relationship.

Capacity to be responsive in the face of high volumes of demands

Councillors felt overwhelmed at times by the volume of correspondence and the level of demands being made upon them as representatives. They said they received a significant amount of correspondence, anything up to a hundred e-mails a day, connected with their political role, in addition to the other demands of the role such as attending meetings and reading documents. Dealing with correspondence could take around two hours a day for people in a voluntary role. Although in principle they were committed to dealing with all correspondence within a reasonable time, in practice sometimes only a proportion of e-mails were ever answered. Sometimes councillors were not sure that they were the most appropriate person to handle a request.

The high level of demands on them undermined their ability to be fully responsive. This is a more prosaic perspective on the representative relationship, but one which was deeply felt and grounded in experience. Councillors said they

Table 9.1: Prioritisation experiment – overall rankings of requests

Category of request	Specific request	Treatment = T	Total score/1,090 1= top priority 10 = bottom priority	Average/10 for specific request 1= top priority 10 = bottom priority	Rank/8 for specific request with treatment letters combined	Rank/4 by category of request	Rank/5 by category of request with treatment letters combined
Individual unorganised interests	Constituent/voter letter		237	2.17	1	1	1
Organised groups (distracter task)	Political group		424	3.89	2	2	2
Organised groups (treatments)	Youth group letter	T	457	4.19	5		3
	Refugee group letter	T	614	5.63			
	Dance group letter	T	755	6.93			
Civil servant requests	Equalities and Diversity workshop		577	5.29	3	3	4
	Crime meeting		599	5.49	4		
	Strategy consultation		710	6.51	6		
Local visibility requests	Community fun day		739	6.78	7	4	5
	Church fundraiser lunch		878	8.05	8		
	All treatment letters	T	n/a	5.58	5	n/a	3

Table 9.2: Prioritisation experiment – overall averages and rankings by information-poor or -rich letters

Category of request	Specific request	Treatment = T	Av. score/10 by specific request for less-professionalized group 1 = top priority 10 = bottom priority	Av. score and rank/5 by category of request for less-professionalized group	Av. score/10 by specific request for more-professionalized group	Av. score and rank/5 by category of request for more-professionalized group
Individual unorganised interests	Constituent/voter letter		2.21	2.21 1	2.13	2.13 1
Organised groups	Political group		3.70	5.21 2	4.09	5.09 2
	Youth group letter	T	4	5.72 3	4.40	5.43 3
	Refugee group letter	T	5.86		5.38	
	Dance group letter	T	7.29		6.52	
Civil servant requests	Equalities and diversity workshop		5.29	5.72 3	5.28	5.81 4
	Crime meeting		5.21		5.81	
	Strategy consultation		6.66		6.35	
Local visibility requests	Community fun day		6.75	7.33 5	6.81	7.51 5
	Church fundraiser lunch		7.91		8.21	

Table 9.3: Prioritisation experiment – Wilcoxon rank-sum test for intervention groups

Group	Sum for intervention group	Sum for control group	Z	Probability (two-tailed)	N
Dance	2,564 (2,860)	3,431 (3,135)	1.800*	0.0700	109
Refugees	2,680.5 (2,860)	3,314.5 (3,135)	1.099	0.2718	109
Youth	3,088.5 (2,860)	2,906.5 (3,135)	-1.401	0.1611	109

* = statistically significant at p. < 0.1; figures in parentheses are expected ranks

had prioritised issues considered to be relevant to their wards. Beyond this, their strategies for choosing between requests were based on which e-mails or letters were immediately easiest to reply to or physically attend, and which seemed to be happening soonest.

Perceptions of general trends in the workloads for local councillors were that the role had become increasingly professionalised, and more like a full-time role. These trends have been documented empirically in other research (Stoker *et al.* 2007). However, they did not receive administrative or sufficient officer support to perform the role in a professional way. They were also unhappy with the responsiveness of their own internal systems to their demands to resolve problems.

Individual unorganised interests

When asked how and why they had made their decisions, councillors clearly stated that constituents, as voters to whom they had an obligation to represent, were the highest priority. They described responding to individual constituents as 'casework', which is seen as a core part of the role, and features in 'role descriptors' where local authorities have these written documents in place for councillors. However, in terms of equality of treatment, it was not necessarily those who shouted the loudest who received preference. Instead, representatives differentiated between those who shouted softly or with respect, and those who shouted aggressively. Councillors across the local government areas emphasised that they were more reluctant to respond to requests, particularly from individuals and groups, if they were 'rude and abusive', or 'if they call me or an officer a liar'.

Data from the UK described earlier in this chapter showed that citizens felt representatives were 'disrespectful'. However, this perception works both ways. There is a dynamic, two-way relationship between representatives and the represented; but relationships require ground rules in order to operate, one of which was that the represented also need to be respectful of the office of the representative and behave in a way that recognises the elevated nature of democratic office.

Organised groups

Respondents said that they were very driven by their affiliation to their political groups; there are few independents in the UK, unlike in some other countries, and parties hold the key to their election and ability to influence decisions in the council. They saw this as an obligation to the groups they represented, as much as a self-interested act. Without active membership of a political group, they felt unable to promote their constituents' interests within their organisations and bureaucracies.

The other key group of organised interests was the citizen interest group. For a small number of respondents, their choices matched the conceptions of the representative relationship found in Urbinati and Warren, and Mansbridge. That is, the ever-expanding plurality of democratic spaces and insensitivity of electoral systems makes responsiveness to organised groups and garnering their insights a necessity for democratic representatives. One councillor agreed, saying she had put 'groups of young people trying to do something as the top', because: 'issues that get raised and that are in the public psyche, those groups have potential knowledge, and potential solutions, and information on the problem'. However, other representatives in this study illustrated the idea described in the chapter by Esaiasson, Gilljam and Persson, that representatives were simply fulfilling their obligations to communicate with the represented. For example, councillors who had given the youth group letter a high rank agreed with the idea, articulated by one person, that: 'if they take the time to write in, we need to value that, and respond to them'. The *quid pro quo* of the represented respecting the office of the democratic representative, e.g. by being polite, is that the representative is polite enough to respond.

Civil servant requests

A large proportion of the correspondence was internal e-mail traffic from their own bureaucracies, much of which they felt was of low importance or irrelevant, or just 'weird and wonderful', as described by one councillor. Although 'very few are total junk', they still felt that 'half [...] are rubbish', or 'half don't require a response'. Officers present in the exercises agreed with councillors that there was a tendency for officers to copy councillors in on all correspondence and documentation, regardless of its relevance, so as not to be accused of hiding information from their political masters.

Local visibility requests

There were contradictions between the motivations councillors said they had for responding to requests, and the results of the prioritisation exercise. Opportunities for communication or interaction with constituents, for example the letter offering contact time through a local church event or the community fun day, on average ranked much lower than internal meetings of the council. However, some councillors talked about wanting to get 'out and about' in their political constituencies, to meet constituents and potential voters face-to-face:

> we under-estimate how much people like to see us. They feel that their council tax is being used properly if they see us, so it's important to attend events and make contact with people even if there is no immediate function [to attending].

Councillors who expressed these views had generally ranked those activities highly, but they were in the minority.

Responsiveness as communication, not accommodation, from representatives

In the private and relatively safe setting of the group discussion, representatives agreed with Pitkin's theory that representatives have the scope to go against public opinion if they fulfil their duty to account for their actions (Pitkin 1967). For example, representatives warned against the idea that all minority interests can be incorporated into democratic representation, and argued that:

> You can't have total democracy. We don't want to be run by all the activist groups out there. Part of our job is to say no. The Government tells us to bring people in more, but it's a very delicate business, balancing needs and priorities. We need to be free to make decisions. People can be free to say their opinions, but we need to decide.

However, in a public arena, some struggled to enact this in practice, identifying their least preferred type of communication as responding to issues where they felt they were not able to give the constituent or group what had been requested. They were frustrated that when they had to turn down or deny requests (e.g. on legal grounds) this was not understood by residents: 'you have to fob them off, but people don't like it. Residents are furious if you don't respond to their needs. As far as they are concerned, they elected you, and you should help them'. This suggests that citizens had an understanding of responsiveness not as communication, but as accommodation first, and then as communication of the response to their preferences. Local councillors' perceptions of public definitions of responsiveness have some empirical support, for example in the Newton *et al.* study described earlier (2010). However, this poses a challenge both for local councillors to retain decision-making roles, and for theorists.

Conclusion

What might be seen as positive from our findings is that citizen interest groups which presented themselves as having fewer resources were not penalised by representatives. In one sense, there was equality of treatment by representatives of different interest groups seeking to make claims. However, this finding only gives small comfort for those wishing to see the full and mature operation of BED as, overall, the levels of responsiveness to organised citizen groups in the research was low. In both of our field experiments, the letter writing campaign of citizen interest groups was not very effective in getting local politicians to respond. Research presented in Chapter Three suggests that citizens in other countries perceive letter or e-mail writing by citizens as having low effectiveness. Ironically for our work, MPs in Marien and Hooghe's study saw letter writing as more effective than citizens did. This was not to say that representatives were wholly unresponsive in the field experiments. Politicians in the study did rank responding to individual constituents as a priority, perhaps preferring to deal with unorganised interests than collective bargaining. Despite expressing a willingness in principle, in practice (in the research) they rejected formal and face-to-face channels for informal interaction and communication between representatives and the represented, such as social events. Politicians in the study felt and expressed more loyalty to their political parties than to constituents.

In contrast to observational studies, experimental methods potentially offer a way of resolving classic problems of endogeneity and selection bias. Clearly, caution must be exercised in transferring these findings beyond the specific context of the respondents in this study of English local government. The limited generalisability of experimental findings beyond the specific context implies the need for more extended use of experimental studies of responsiveness and equality in different contexts. However, it is interesting that these studies, using experimental methods, perhaps provide a challenge to some existing literature. What has been argued is that there is often high responsiveness but possibly unequal treatment. The experimental studies and linked qualitative investigation described in this chapter found equality of treatment but low responsiveness. As noted by Mansbridge in relation to the United States, the empirical evidence suggests that 'the existing representative apparatus [...] does not facilitate well the processes of mutual education, communication, and influence' (2003). Empirically grounded and detailed studies like these experiments could help to create an opening to better understand why the perceptions about the quality of local democracy in different countries and contexts can be at such wide variance between the represented and representatives. They may also help to start to problematise theoretically-based understandings of responsiveness through their use of applied research on the detailed processes of day-to-day political life.

As discussed in this volume, from the between-election perspective, responsiveness requires the communication of reasons for decisions and choices, but not necessarily accommodation of citizen preferences in the short-term. In the discussions with English local politicians, they also articulated this core idea. However, by representatives' own accounts, they find it challenging to put this into practice. This is partly because of their awareness of competing citizen understandings of responsiveness as accommodation to their wishes. The key issue for normative debates about BED is that discussions about how these relationships should be constituted and operate are far from the reality of actual contact and communication. The dream that interest groups 'have the potential to compensate for electoral inflexibilities – providing high levels of targeted, information-rich representation' (Disch 2011) was not fulfilled in these field experiments in the English case.

Our research unearthed some prosaic explanations for gaps in responsiveness. Representatives in the research described lack of time to respond to overwhelming demands, and poor quality administrative support which hampered their ability to be responsive. In lieu of adequate scope to respond, they sometimes resorted to prioritising the most urgent or easy to deal with demands. Both, representatives in English local government and English citizens also showed themselves to be affected by notions of respect, politeness and civility in the representative relationship, issues which are not commonly given much credence in empirical studies. Surveys in England have found that citizens perceive politicians to be disrespectful to citizens, and self-interested. However, a two-way relationship between representatives and the represented was felt by representatives to demand that the represented needed to be respectful of the office of the representative, and behave in a way that recognised the elevated nature of democratic office. This all illustrates the very real and human risks to a more effective functioning of representative relationships. It implies suggestions for more practical remedial action are needed if the normative ideals of responsiveness and equality are to be fully enacted in practice. Beyond this, it also speaks of the bigger issues raised in this volume – namely, the dual nature of representative democracy as both egalitarian and elitist. Egalitarian-orientated citizens' style and mode of politics may be in tension with politicians' more elitist conceptions; this would be a debate worth taking out into the town or city halls and into neighbourhoods.

Acknowledgements

The author wishes to thank Prof. Peter John (UCL) as the co-author of one of the papers on which parts of this chapter are based, and for his support and help on the design and analysis of the prioritisation experiment.

References

Alonso, S., Keane, J. and Merkel, W. (2011) 'Editors' introduction: Rethinking the future of representative democracy', in Alonso, S., Keane, J. and Merkel, W. (eds) *The Future of Representative Democracy*, Cambridge: Cambridge University Press.

Atkinson, H. and Wilks-Heeg, S. (2000) *Local government from Thatcher to Blair: the politics of creative autonomy*, Oxford: Polity Press.

Bartels, L. (2008) *Unequal Democracy: The political economy of the new gilded age*, Princeton, NJ: Princeton University Press.

Boyne, G. A. (1985) 'Theory, methodology and results in political science: The case of output studies', *British Journal of Political Science,* 15: 473–515.

Chin, M. L., Bond, J. R. and Geva, N. (2000) 'A foot in the door: An experimental study of PAC and constituency effects on access', *Journal of Politics*, 62: 534–49.

Chivite-Matthews, N. I. and Teal, J. (2001) *1998 British Social Attitudes Survey: secondary data analysis of the Local Government Module*, London: Department of the Environment, Transport and the Regions.

DCLG (Department for Communities and Local Government) (2007) *Representing the Future: The Report of the Councillors Commission*, London: DCLG.

— (2008) *Communities in Control: Real people, real power, Cm. 742*, Norwich: TSO.

Dearlove, J. (1973) *The Politics of Policy in Local Government*, Cambridge: Cambridge University Press.

Disch, L. (2011) 'Toward a mobilisation conception of democratic representation', *American Political Science Review*, 105: 100–114.

Druckman, J. N. (2001) 'On the limits of framing effects: Who can frame?', *Journal of Politics,* 63: 1042–44.

Durose, C., France, J., Richardson, L. and Lupton, R. (2011) *Towards the 'Big Society': What role for neighborhood working?: Evidence from a comparative European study*, London: LSE.

Enns, P. and Wlezien, C. (eds) (2011) *Who Gets Represented?*, New York: The Russell Sage Foundation.

Eulau, H. and Karps, P. D. (1977) 'The puzzle of representation: Specifying components of responsiveness', *Legislative Studies Quarterly,* 2.

Gains, F., John, P. and Stoker, G. (2005) 'Path dependency and the reform of English local government', *Public Administration,* 83: 25–46.

Gerber, E. R. and Lupia, A. (1992) *Competitive campaigns and the responsiveness of collective choice*, Working Paper 813, California: California Institute of Technology.

Gilens, M. (2005) 'Inequality and democratic responsiveness', *Public Opinion Quarterly,* 69: 12.

Hall, R. L. and Deardorff, A. V. (2006) 'Lobbying as legislative subsidy', *American Political Science Review,* 100: 69–84.

Hansen, J. M. (1991) Gaining Access: *Congress and the Farm Lobby, 1919–1981*, Chicago: University of Chicago Press.

Local Government Association (LGA) (2008) *The Reputation of Local Government*, London: LGA [England].

Mahoney, C. (2007) 'Lobbying Success in the United States and the European Union', *Journal of Public Policy,* 27: 35–56.

Maloney, W., Smith, G. and Stoker, G. (2000) 'Social capital and urban governance: Adding a more contextualized 'top-down' perspective', *Political Studies,* 48: 802–20.

Mansbridge, J. (2003) 'Rethinking representation', *American Political Science Review,* 97: 515–28.

Newton, K. (1976) *Second City Politics: Democratic processes and decision making in Birmingham*, Oxford: Clarendon Press.

Newton, R., Pierce, A., Richardson, L. and Williams, M. (2010) *Citizens and Local Decision-Making: What drives feelings of influence?*, Urban Forum: London.

Page, B. and Shapiro, R. (1992) *The Rational Public: Fifty years of trends in Americans' public preferences*, Chicago: University of Chicago Press.

Pitkin, H. (1967) *The Concept of Representation*, Berkeley and Los Angeles: University of California Press.

Potters, J. and van Winden, F. (1992) 'Lobbying and asymmetric information', *Public Choice,* 74: 269–92.

Richardson, L. and John, P. (2012) 'Who listens to the grassroots? A field experiment on informational lobbying in the UK', *British Journal of Politics and International Relations,* 14: 595–612.

Standards for England (2009) *Public Perceptions of Ethics*, Manchester: Standards for England.

Stimson, J., Mackuen, M. and Erikson, R. (1995) 'Dynamic representation', *American Political Science Review,* 89: 543–65.

Stoker, G., Gains, F., Greasley, S., John P. and Rao, N. (2007) *The New Council Constitutions: The outcomes and impacts of the Local Government Act 2000*, London: Communities and Local Government.

Stoker, G. and Wilson, G. (1991) 'The lost world of British local pressure groups', *Public Policy and Administration,* 6: 20–34.

Urbinati, N. and Warren, M. E. (2008) 'The concept of representation in contemporary democratic theory', *Annual Review of Political Science,* 11: 387–412.

Wlezien, C. (1995) 'The public as thermostat: Dynamics of preferences for spending', *American Journal of Political Science,* 39: 981–1000.

Chapter Ten

The Impact of Social Movements on Agenda Setting: Bringing the Real World Back In

Roy Gava, Marco Giugni, and Frédéric Varone

The BED framework focuses on the citizens' attempts to influence political decision-making by means other than voting. Conversely, it also refers to how the elected representatives respond to the claims that citizens formulate outside the electoral realm. To analyse empirically the transmission of information and priorities between citizens and elected representatives beyond Election Day, we study here the extent to which protest activities influence the parliamentary agenda. Thus, we scrutinise a very specific aspect of the responsiveness dimension highlighted by the BED framework, namely the impact of social movements' mobilisation on the policy priorities of the elected Members of Parliament. However, this rather narrow focus allows us to tackle a crucial relationship in terms of democratic responsiveness. On the one hand, protest activities represent a vivid bottom-up manifestation of preferences. On the other hand, decision makers' attention is a necessary condition for policy change to happen.

How elected policy makers react to signals and preferences is central to our understanding of the responsiveness of democracies. While issues and problems are potentially infinite, individuals and political institutions have a limited carriage capacity (Hilgartner and Bosk 1988; Jones and Baumgartner 2005; Walker 1977). Attention is a scarce resource in politics and issues are permanently in competition for it. A funnelling or filtering of demands and prioritisation of issues is therefore inevitable. Political institutions and decision makers process information and react to signals, both external and internal to the political system. On the one hand, crises and unexpected events can shift priorities and open a 'window of opportunity' (Kingdon 1984) for issues that were, until then, dormant. On the other hand, political actors voice their priorities and actively seek to attract political attention. In this regard, protest activities by social movements are among the most visible expressions of issue priorities and public pressure for policy change. They are a resource-intense and privileged vehicle through which non-institutionalised actors attempt to influence the political elite and policy direction. In short, they represent a manifest bottom-up signal of discontent with the policy status quo. Nonetheless, in the process of issue prioritisation, protests are in competition for decision makers' attention along with a variety of others signals.

In this chapter, we focus on two research traditions that may enrich the current development of the BED framework: the social movement and the agenda-setting perspectives. We have a double aim. First, we point out the insights of these two research traditions with regard to policymakers' responsiveness to protests, and we also highlight their major shortcomings. Second, based on such limitations, we wish to bridge these two bodies of literature so as to encourage a dialogue between scholars working on the very same topic in different disciplines and to link their reflections to the BED approach.

Schumaker (1975) has defined five criteria of government responsiveness to the demands of social movements, which can be considered as stages of the policy process: access, agenda, policy, output, and impact (*see also* Burstein *et al.* 1995b). In this chapter, we focus on a specific stage of the policy process, namely, agenda setting. This is the first stage in having a societal issue translated into a political issue. It can be defined broadly as 'the process through which issues attain the status of being seriously debated by politically relevant actors' (Sinclair 1986: 35). This first step is a key element for the BED framework: considering a social problem to be a political priority is a necessary condition for responsiveness.

Briefly put, agenda setting is when the policy issue enters the political arena. We therefore aim to assess empirically the role and impact of social movements' activities in defining the policy makers' agenda. More precisely, we look at the effect of protest activities on the introduction of parliamentary interventions. If social movements can influence policy making, the easiest way they can do so is arguably by influencing the definition of the political agenda. Once the policy process is under way, social movements may face more difficulties in trying to influence it as each subsequent stage of this process has more stringent rules and legislative action at each progressive stage is more consequential (Soule and King 2006).

In addition, we examine the interplay of protest and three other potential explanatory factors of agenda setting: public opinion, political alliances, and real-world indicators. Public opinion and political alliances have often been considered by students of the policy impact of social movements (*see* Amenta *et al.* 2010 and Giugni 2008 for reviews). However, students of social movements have largely overlooked the role of the severity and audience of a social problem, that is, the role of the 'real world' out there. One reason for this is probably that, in this research tradition, this aspect has been subsumed under the notion of grievances. Since grievance theories have largely been rejected in the social movements literature, especially by resource mobilisation and political opportunity theorists (but *see* Buechler 2004; Useem 1998), it is not surprising that this kind of explanation has not been retained. Agenda setting theorists, by contrast, have often put this aspect at centre stage in defining the political agenda, but have paid less attention to the role of social movements and protest activities (but *see* Cobb and Elder 1972). Yet, both aspects are important in the context of the BED framework.

Thus, while students of social movements have, for obvious reasons, focused on the role of protest activities and have recently looked at how public opinion and political opportunities can mediate the policy impact of movements, neglecting the role of the real situation with regard to the issue at hand, agenda setting theorists have examined the impact of the latter, but overlooked the role of the mobilised citizenry in explaining policy makers' allocations of scarce attention.

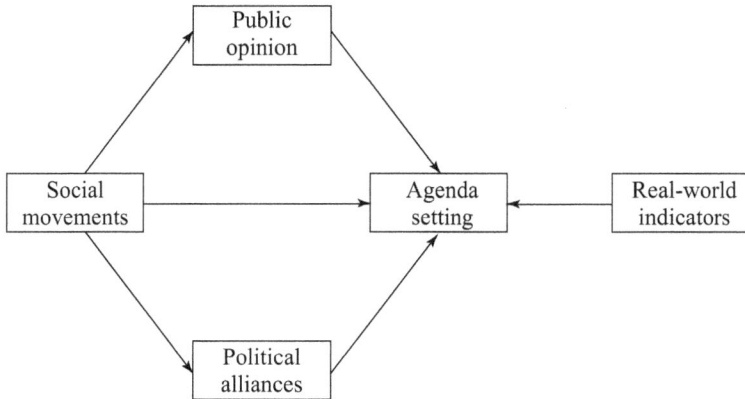

Figure 10.1: Hypothesised paths to agenda setting

In this chapter, we aim to redress this state of affairs by inquiring into the impact of social movements on agenda setting in the fields of asylum and unemployment policy, considering the mediating effect of real-world indicators, public opinion, and substantial political alliances. The latter contrasts with more formal political alliances, such as political alignments in the institutionalised arenas, and refer to public statements by institutional actors, mainly political parties, on a given issue.

Figure 10.1 illustrates the hypothesised paths through which social movements' protest activities may influence the allocation of policy makers' attention. We explore three such paths: a direct-effect path whereby social movements succeed in influencing agenda setting directly; an indirect-effect path via the role of public opinion; and an indirect-effect path via the role of political alliances. In addition, we consider the impact of the 'real world'.

The basic idea, which was stressed by agenda-setting theory, is that policy makers react to the changes in the state of the situation concerning a given issue, as shown by real-world indicators such as, for instance, an increase in the flow of asylum seekers or a rise in the unemployment rate. However, such an impact also depends on the intervention of social movements, the state of public opinion, and the positioning of parties on the issue at stake. These three factors signal to policy makers the existence of a social problem. Social movements, in turn, may influence public opinion, which can have an impact on how parties deal with the issue.

In this chapter, we present empirical evidence on agenda setting in Switzerland, combining data from different research projects. We focus on two issues belonging to different policy fields: asylum and unemployment. The main rationale for this comparison is that we expect protest activities to have a different impact across these fields.[1] The data cover the 1990s. At this stage we only present tentative results as a first step towards a more thorough analysis aimed at testing hypotheses about the differential impact of social movements on stages of the policy process.

---

1.   *See* Giugni (2004) for a more systematic treatment of how social movement outcomes may vary across policy fields.

The social movement perspective

Research on the policy outcomes of social movements has long searched for the existence of a direct relationship between movement activities, including protest activities, and some indicators of policy change. In this vein, scholars have focused on the ability of social movements to be successful and on movement-controlled variables, framing their studies along two main lines of inquiry and attempting to answer one of two basic questions (Giugni 1998): are disruptive movements more successful than moderate ones? Are strongly organised movements more successful than loosely organised ones? William Gamson's seminal book, *The Strategy of Social Protest* (1990) is exemplary in this regard. Studying a random sample of challenging groups active in the US between 1800 and 1945, he found strong evidence for the role of movement-related variables.

More recently, scholarship has moved away from the search for direct effects to examine the mediating role of certain external factors. In particular, research has focused on the role of public opinion (e.g. Burstein 1998a, 1998b, 1999; Burstein and Linton 2002; Costain and Majstorovic 1994; Giugni 2004, 2007; Kane 2003; McAdam and Su 2002; Soule and Olzak 2004) and political opportunity structures (e.g. Amenta 2006; Amenta *et al.* 1992, 1994, 2005; Giugni 2004, 2007; Soule and Olzak 2004). Among the latter, the role of political alliances has often been pointed out as a crucial facilitating factor enabling social movements to influence the policy process.

The potentially facilitating role played by these two kinds of external factors is quite easy to understand, although different mechanisms could be suggested and have indeed been proposed in the literature. For example, Burstein (1999) makes an argument about the role of public opinion based on the theory of representative democracy. In this view, public opinion would signal to policy makers that an important share of the electorate has a given policy preference or at least demands that something be done with regard to a given policy issue. The risk of not being re-elected in case of inaction would push policy makers to do something on that issue. Thus, policy makers might be influenced by public opinion when it represents a sizeable and electorally relevant share of the population, rather than by minority actors such as social movements.

Arguments about the role of political allies are perhaps even more straightforward as it is quite obvious that it is easier for insiders than outsiders to be influential. For example, for a variety of reasons, including strategic ones, political allies might have incentives to carry into the institutional arenas the issues social movements address in the public space by incorporating movements' claims into their own agenda. Once they have gained institutional access, movements' claims are more likely to impinge upon public policy.

The interplay of protest activities, public opinion, political alliances, and policy change has been conceptualised in different ways. Perhaps oversimplifying a more complex picture, we can distinguish between three basic models of the policy impact of social movements (Giugni 2004). The direct-effect model assumes that social movements can be successful without the help of external factors or conditions, as seen in the existence of a direct relationship between the presence and mobilisation of social movements and policy change. The indirect-effect postulates that movements and their activities influence policy only indirectly, following a two-step process, via their impact on either public opinion or the activation of powerful institutional allies such as parties. The joint–effect model maintains that both these facilitating external factors must be there when the movements mobilise.

Curiously enough, students of the policy outcomes of social movements have almost completely neglected one factor that is central in the analyses of agenda-setting theorists (and in the BED framework too), namely, what the latter call the 'real world'. In fact, there might be good or at least understandable reasons for that. Real-world indicators are akin to what social movements scholars call grievances. Perhaps more precisely, they form the basis for the structural stress and deprivation that breakdown theories of collective action have put at center stage. Since resource mobilisation and political process theory have largely rejected the assumptions of breakdown or grievance theories, it should not come as a surprise that students of the policy outcomes of social movements have not taken this kind of factor into account.

However, as we explain in more detail below, in the light of the impact of real-world indicators underlined by researchers in the agenda-setting perspective, we argue that this missing aspect should be brought back into the analysis. Grievances might well be irrelevant for explaining the rise of social movements and protest activities (but *see* Buechler 2004; Useem 1998), but should not be discarded from the outset when examining the impact that social movements and protest activities have on policy, including in the agenda-setting stage.

The agenda-setting perspective

Considering that the carriage capacity of political agendas is limited, policy-makers' attention represents a central and scarce resource in politics and policy processes. The literature on agenda setting explores how issues attract attention and reach political status. What is at stake is the allocation of attention by political actors and institutional arenas to diverse public problems that compete against one another in order to be dealt with. Agenda-setting studies are thus firmly concerned with the inquiry of the different factors that explain the rise and fall of issues from political agendas.

Within policy studies, the agenda-setting approach developed by Baumgartner and Jones (1991, 1993) considers that issue attention is a crucial condition for policy change. Since no policy decision can be made without prior active consideration by decision makers, agenda setting can be seen as the initial veto point in the policy-making process (Peters 2001). In consequence, it is by getting access into political agendas (e.g. parliamentary and governmental agendas) that a window of opportunity for policy change is opened (Jones and Baumgartner 2005). Following the early work of Schattschneider (1975) on conflict expansion, this theoretical perspective conceives politics essentially as a confrontation between actors (elected politicians, political parties, interest groups, social movements) seeking to get a given issue onto the political agenda against those trying to keep it out.

To analyse how agenda-setting processes evolve and eventually translate into policy change, a growing number of empirical studies rely on the mapping of political attention to issues over long periods of time (Baumgartner *et al.* 2011). The relative share of political attention to different issues is traced in diverse agendas (parliament, government, party manifestoes, public opinion, mass media, legislative production, etc.).

Policy makers face an oversupply of signals, information and demands. From a responsiveness perspective, and central to the BED framework, what is then at stake is how these diverse stimuli from the political environment are translated into policy priorities (Jones and Baumgartner 2005). Signals and stimuli, such as problem indicators, actors' claims, media attention and public opinion, are of a diverse nature. Protest activities by social movements can then be considered as one type of signal that policy makers 'weight' among others when defining their own agenda priorities.

When investigating the distribution of issue attention across policy domains, scholars have taken into consideration how 'objective' conditions or 'real-world' events that can be considered exogenous to the political system impact on the agenda (Jones and Baumgartner 2005; Soroka 2002). These include, for instance, focusing events such as accidents, natural disasters or sudden discoveries that rapidly drive actors' attention to a given issue (Birkland 1998). In some areas, the availability of systematic indicators that routinely monitor social and economic conditions (e.g. unemployment and criminality rates) provide policy makers with a tool to assess the magnitude of problems and their evolution across time (Kingdon 1984). Independently of its form, information on real-world conditions is taken into consideration when allocating attention since this enables actors to judge the severity and relative importance of issues.

The responsiveness of political actors and institutional arenas to changes in 'objective' conditions has been an element present since the early empirical studies of agenda-setting processes (Kingdon 1984; Walker 1977). Changes in real-world problems affect agenda dynamics, opening 'windows of opportunity' (Kingdon 1984) that actors can exploit to politicise and/or prioritise policy issues in institutional arenas (Green-Pedersen and Walgrave 2013).

Information about 'objective' conditions available to policy makers constitutes a signal to integrate, or at least to control for, them in empirical analysis of agenda-setting processes (*see,* for example, Kleinnijenhuis and Rietberg, 1995 on economic policy; Soroka 2002 on AIDS, crime, environmental and economic policy; John 2006 on urban riots or Van Noije *et al.* 2008 on immigration, agriculture and environment). In their longitudinal and cross-sectional (crime, economic, and welfare policy) assessment of the relationship between real-world indicators and political attention in the US, Jones and Baumgartner (2005) observe variations across policy domains. In particular, they hint that these differences are linked to the extent to which the changes in real-world indicators interact with swings in public opinion (2005).

To what extent do policy makers incorporate social movements' activities when allocating attention? Few empirical studies have been devoted to this question (for a review of US studies, *see* Walgrave and Vliegenthart 2009). A notable exception to US-based studies is Walgrave and Vliegenthart's (2009) paper on Belgium (1993–2000). The authors resorted to pooled-time series analysis to analyse the extent to which the number and size of protest demonstrations affect the attention of MPs (i.e. weekly number of interpellations and questions) and the government (i.e. weekly ministerial meetings and decisions), with media and parties' attention acting as intermediary variables. In line with previous studies, the authors substantiated that protests matter for political agendas, with their impact differing across policy domains. Furthermore, they showed that politicians react more to big events (i.e. numbers of demonstrators) than to protest frequency, and that the governmental agenda is more affected than the parliamentary agenda.

A strong asset of Walgrave and Vliegenthart's analysis is the encompassing number (twenty-five) and variety (e.g. from education to agriculture) of issues taken into consideration. Nevertheless, the consideration of such a broad number of domains represents a potential obstacle to simultaneously accounting for protest activities and 'real-world' conditions. Arguably, the existence of a broad consensus on 'unambiguous' quantitative indicators for measuring problem severity represents a high standard that makes quantitative assessments across issues difficult (Jones and Baumgartner 2005). While specific quantitative indicators are available in some policy domains, it would be hard to argue that a single indicator of reference guides policy makers at the policy area level (e.g. environment, education, health). Some other issues would simply be hard to grasp at this macro level due to the lack of quantifiable indicators (e.g. foreign policy).

In short, agenda-setting scholars have emphasised that changes in 'objective' conditions represent signals that provide policy makers with information to evaluate the existence and/or severity of a problem 'out there'. Their consideration and interplay with political actors therefore seem pertinent when exploring the impact of social movements on the allocation of political attention.

Data and methods

The analyses shown below draw on three main kinds of data. First, information on protest activities and political alliances come from two previous research projects in which claims-making data was gathered pertaining respectively to the immigration and ethnic relations and the unemployment policy fields.[2] Through the content analysis of the press, political claims analysis (Koopmans and Statham 1999) allows us to capture the timing and intensity to which actors (in this case, social movements and political parties) devoted attention to these issues. Second, information on parliamentary agenda-setting comes from the Swiss datasets of

---

2.   *See* Koopmans *et al.* (2005) and Giugni (2010) for an overview of the main findings of these two research projects.

the Comparative Agendas Project.[3] Third, public opinion data comes from most-important-problem polls.[4] Finally, real-world indicators are drawn from official sources.[5] Our analyses bear on the case of Switzerland.

Both theoretical and practical reasons justify our focus on the asylum and unemployment domains. First, in the Swiss case, these two policy domains are contrasted with regard to the politicisation and institutionalisation of debates on these issues. Second, a threshold of protest activities is required to assess these relations, and debates have been abundant on both issues. Third, cross-sectional comparisons seem appropriate given the differential impact of real-world indicators and protests reported in the agenda-setting literature. Finally, the flow of asylum seekers' requests and the unemployment rate are relatively straightforward monitoring indicators, informing policy makers about social conditions in these two domains.

We include four main variables in the analyses: claims by non-institutional actors on issues concerning asylum (i.e. unemployment) as a proxy for protest activities; claims by parties on these issues as an indicator of party intervention; the state of public opinion on these issues (i.e. most-important-problem data); and the real-world indicators of these issues. In addition, we have created a number of interaction terms aimed at measuring the joint effect of protest activities with each of the other independent variables.

To explore the connections between the intervention of non-institutional actors (protest activities), the intervention of institutional actors (political alliances), public opinion, real-world indicators, and agenda setting we adopt a regression approach to time-series analysis. Since our dependent variable is a count variable that has no negative values, we estimate coefficients based on negative binomial distributions. We regress our dependent variable (parliamentary interventions) on the independent variables following a step-wise procedure.[6] The unit of time is a quarter. The independent variables are introduced in the models with a one-period lag to make a stronger case for causality. The lagged dependent variable is included among the covariates in order to control for autocorrelation. Interaction terms are entered separately in the models to avoid multicollinearity. The series cover the period from 1990 to 1999 for asylum policy and from 1990 to 2002 for unemployment policy.

Regression analysis, however, only looks at the direct effects of independent variables on the dependent variable. In order to examine direct as well as indirect effects on agenda setting, we also use structural equations models. For each model we show the standardised solution from maximum likelihood estimation. Lags also apply to these analyses.

---

3. *See* online. Available: http://www.comparativeagendas.org (accessed 30 July 2013).

4. Most-important-problem data has been collected through public surveys by private companies. Data until 1995 has been provided by Isopublic. Since 1995, MIP data has been published annually by Gfs.bern.

5. Several publications by the Swiss Federal Statistical Office. Online. Available: http://www.statistics.admin.ch (accessed 10 May 2013).

6. Parliamentary interventions include parliamentary questions, interpellations, postulates and motions. Interventions dealing with asylum and unemployment have been identified by means of a keyword search.

Findings

We present our findings in two steps. In the first step we run a series of regression models aimed at assessing the effect of protest activities as well as the other predictors, including the interaction terms, on agenda setting. In the second step we present results from structural equations models aimed at studying direct and indirect effects as well as the paths from social movements to agenda setting. Before we move to the regression and structural equation analyses, however, we show the development over time of the variables of interest. Figure 10.2 does this for asylum policy, Figure 10.3 for unemployment policy.

Table 10.1 shows the effects of protest activities and the other independent variables, including the interaction terms on agenda setting on asylum policy. Model 1 is the baseline model, which includes all the predictors with a control for the total number of parliamentary interventions in the legislative session and the lagged dependent variable. Models 2 to 4 include the three interaction terms. The results suggest that social movements have little, if any, leverage on agenda setting as protest activities do not display a statistically significant effect. By contrast, we observe a significant effect of the real-world indicators which holds across models. All other independent variables do not have an impact either. Given previous research showing the strong relationship between public preferences and policy change (e.g. Burstein 1998b), this is quite surprising, especially with regard to public opinion.

Previous research has shown the mediating role of public opinion and political alliances to be facilitating factors for the policy impact of social movements (Amenta et al. 1992; Giugni 2004; Soule and Olzak 2004). Our findings do not provide evidence of such a joint effect of protests and public opinion, nor of protests and political alliances (as measured through the parties' public statements on the issue at hand). Nor do we observe a significant effect of the interaction between social movements and real-world indicators.

Table 10.2 shows the findings for unemployment policy. The models are the same as in the previous analysis. Although these results present some similarities, they show above all, some important differences compared with the previous ones. On the one hand, protests continue not having a strong impact. Clearly, the coefficient for this variable is statistically significant in one of the models but the effect disappears when we control for the unemployment rate. On the other hand, the real-world indicator here appears not to have an effect, be it independent or in interaction with protest activities. By contrast, public opinion seems to matter in this case as the coefficient for this variable is statistically significant, while we observe no significant effect of protest activities. In addition, unlike in the previous case of asylum policy, here, parties display a significant effect, both independently and in interaction with protests.

Also, similarly to our findings for asylum policy, agenda setting on unemployment policy does not seem to be influenced by the joint effect of protests and public opinion, nor of protests and political alliances, as neither interaction terms are significant. Again, the interaction between social movements and real-world indicators has no significant effect.

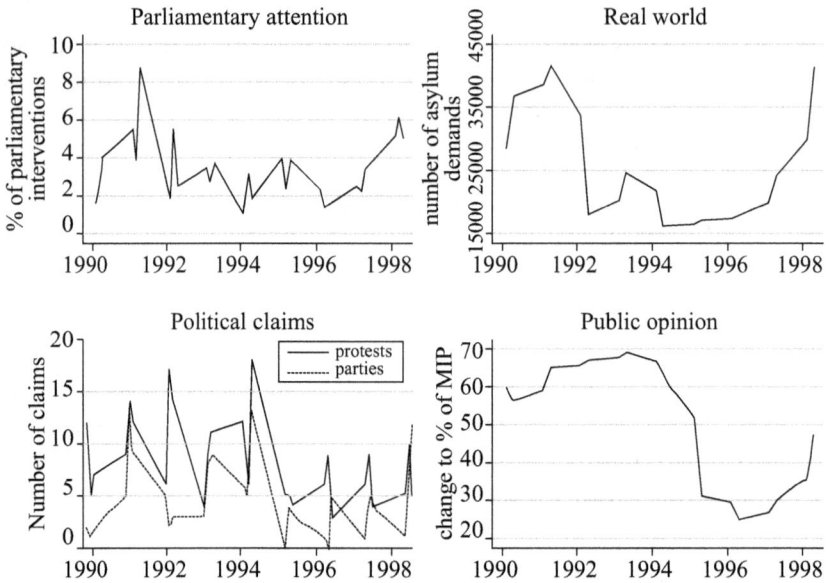

Figure 10.2: Development over time of dependent and independent variables for asylum policy

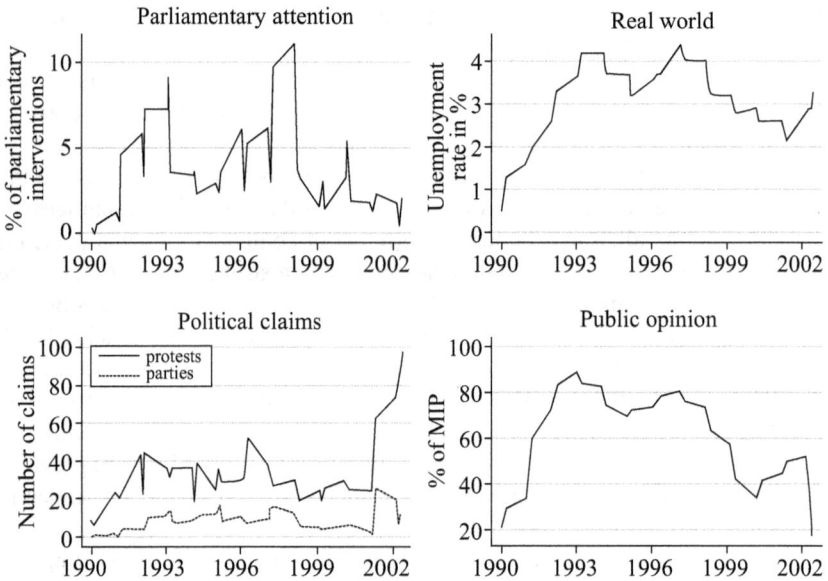

Figure 10.3: Development over time of dependent and independent variables for unemployment policy

Table 10.1: Effects of selected independent variables on agenda setting on asylum policy (negative binomial regression coefficients)

	Model 1	Model 2	Model 3	Model 4
Parliamentary interventions t-1	-0.023***	-0.001	-0.001	-0.024**
	(0.007)	(0.011)	(0.009)	(0.007)
Total parliamentary interventions	0.002***	0.002***	0.003***	0.002***
	(0.000)	(0.000)	(0.000)	(0.000)
Protest t-1	0.009	0.016	-0.057	0.014
	(0.018)	(0.140)	(0.039)	(0.048)
Parties t-1	0.0279		0.014	
	(0.018)		(0.052)	
Public opinion t-1	-0.003	0.004		
	(0.004)	(0.0179)		
Asylum requests t-1	0.045***			0.049**
	(0.009)			(0.017)
Protest * public opinion		-0.000		
		(0.002)		
Protest * parties			0.004	
			(0.004)	
Protest * asylum requests				0.000
				(0.000)
Constant	0.691*	1.232	1.518***	0.623
	(0.280)	(0.929)	(0.337)	(0.488)
lnalpha	-4.223*	-1.855***	-2.311***	-3.494***
	(1.963)	(0.390)	(0.496)	(1.030)
N	27	27	27	27
pseudo R^2	0.189	0.084	0.118	0.178

Standard errors in parentheses
*$p < 0.05$, **$p < 0.01$, ***$p < 0.001$

Thus, in line with agenda-setting theory, real-world indicators seem to be an important factor to take into consideration, while protest activities and public opinion seem to play a secondary role. However, this holds for the asylum policy field and not for the unemployment policy field, where real-world indicators do not seem to matter, while public opinion does. In order to dig deeper into the relations between all these factors, we run a structural equations model for each of the two policy domains under examination. In both cases, protest activities and real-world indicators are the exogenous variables, while agenda setting, public opinion, and party intervention are all endogenous variables.

Table 10.2: Effects of selected independent variables on agenda setting on unemployment policy (unstandardised regression coefficients)

	Model 1	Model 2	Model 3	Model 4
Parliamentary interventions t-1	0.0190[*]	0.017[*]	0.020[**]	0.031[***]
	(0.007)	(0.007)	(0.007)	(0.008)
Total parliamentary interventions	0.003[***]	0.003[***]	0.003[***]	0.003[***]
	(0.000)	(0.000)	(0.000)	(0.000)
Protest t-1	-0.002	0.022	0.022[*]	-0.004
	(0.006)	(0.017)	(0.010)	(0.007)
Parties t-1	-0.0143		0.150[***]	
	(.0199)		(0.040)	
Public opinion t-1	0.0178[**]	0.035[**]		
	(0.005)	(0.0121		
Unemployment rate t-1	-1.544			-1.987
	(0.816)			(1.578)
Protest * public opinion		-0.000		
		(0.000)		
Protest * parties			-0.003[***]	
			(0.000)	
Protest * unemployment rate				0.002
				(0.051)
Constant	0.209	-0.843	0.065	1.106[**]
	(0.477)	(0.651)	(0.447)	(0.419)
lnalpha	-1.888[***]	-1.771[***]	-1.668[***]	-1.535[***]
	(0.362)	(0.361)	(0.342)	(0.318)
N	37	38	38	37
pseudo R^2	0.115	0.116	0.110	0.081

Standard errors in parentheses
[*]p< 0.05, [**]p< 0.01, [***]p< 0.001

Figure 10.4 shows the model and estimates for agenda setting on asylum policy. The model fit is fairly good (RMSEA = 0.086) and the squared multiple correlation for the dependent variable is close to 40 per cent. However, here we are more interested in looking at direct and indirect effects than in model fit and explained variance.

Consistent with the results of the regression analysis, we observe no direct effect of protests on agenda setting. By contrast, real-world indicators display a strong and statistically significant effect, again reflecting what we found previously. However, perhaps the most interesting aspect lies in examining the indirect paths of influence of protest activities via the role of public opinion (most

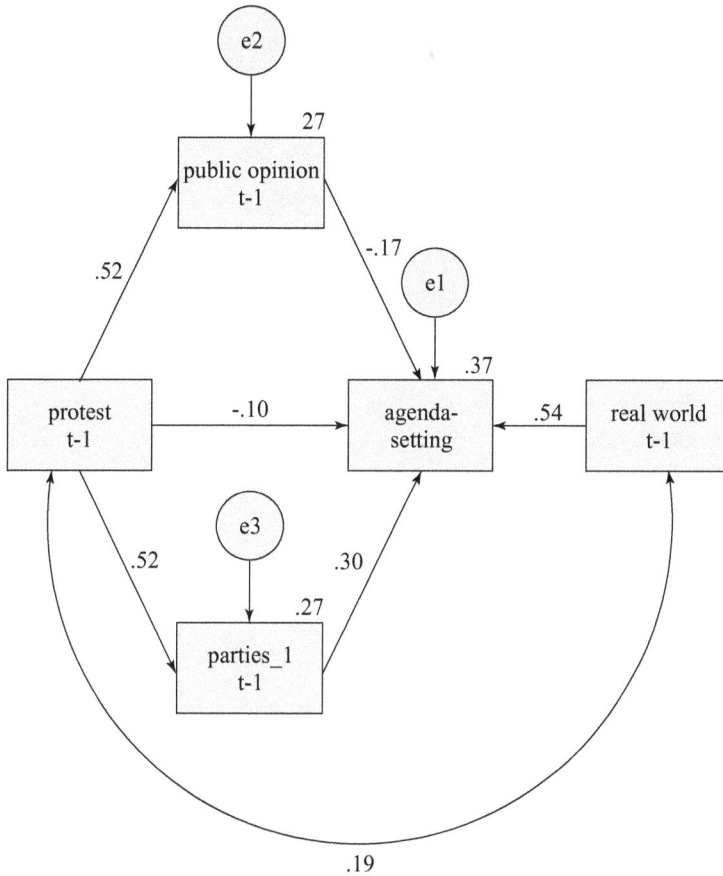

Figure 10.4: Estimates from structural equation model for agenda setting on asylum policy (standardised solution)

important problem) and political alliances (party intervention). To begin with, protests impact on both public opinion and party intervention. Here, however, we should take into account the fact that all three variables are measured in the same time unit (i.e. they all lag by one time unit). Therefore, the causal order could well be reversed, and opinion and party intervention could be causes rather than effects of protest activities.

Looking now at the remainder of the paths going from protests to agenda setting, we observe a positive effect of party intervention and a negative effect of public opinion. Again, the latter finding is somewhat puzzling in the light of previous work showing a strong impact of public opinion on policy (e.g. Burstein 1998b). We should also note that both coefficients are not statistically significant (the one for party intervention is significant at the 10 per cent level).

Do we observe a similar pattern when we look at unemployment policy? Figure 10.5 shows the results for this policy field. The model fit is particularly poor (RMSEA = 0.686), but the squared multiple correlation for the dependent variable is also close to 40 per cent. Most importantly, the answer to the above question is clearly negative. Without a doubt, protest activities are still strongly and significantly correlated with party intervention, but this is the unique similarity among the two policy domains. The effect of protest on public opinion is much weaker and not statistically significant. In addition, party interventions, and especially real-world indicators, do not seem to have an impact on agenda setting on unemployment policy, whereas they influence agenda setting on asylum policy. By contrast, here we observe a strong effect of public opinion on agenda setting.

How can we interpret these contrasting findings for the two policy fields? We suggest that they have much to do with substantial differences between the two domains. Previous work on the policy impact of social movements has argued that certain features of the issues addressed by the protests matter (Giugni 2004). Here we are dealing with two contrasting issues in several respects. On the one hand, unemployment is an 'old' issue which has been on the political agenda for several

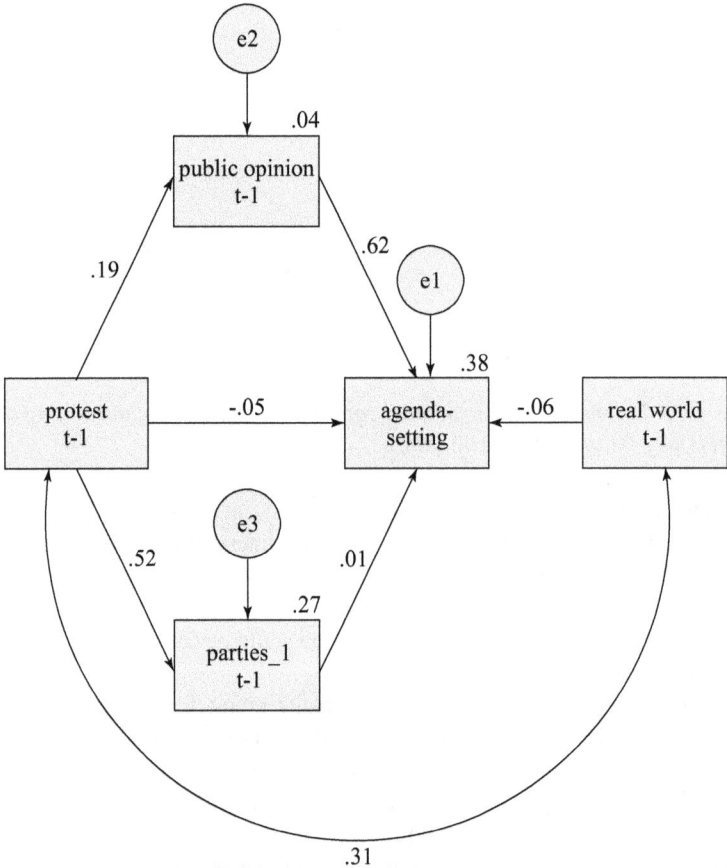

Figure 10.5: Estimates from structural equation model for agenda setting on unemployment policy (standardised solution)

decades. It is based on a traditional class cleavage and the Socialist Party is the main 'issue owner'. On the other hand, asylum is a 'new' issue which has been put on the political agenda in the past twenty years (as a reminder, our data covers the 1990s) and the radical right Swiss People's Party is the main 'issue owner'. It is based on a new cleavage opposing those who are favourable and open towards the new challenges stemming from globalisation to those who are more skeptical and closed with regard to the risks involved in it.

In addition, the two policy fields also differ from an institutional point of view. The unemployment policy field is dominated by neo-corporatist arrangements, whereas the asylum policy field sees the intervention of organisational actors, but has no institutionalised arena of negotiation. Finally, while unemployment policy sees a wide consensus concerning policy ends (i.e. to reduce unemployment), but not necessarily policy means, asylum policy is a much contested field in which both the ends and means of policy are subject to political debates and controversies.

These differences give us some clues to understanding the variation we observe in our findings and in the effects of the variables in our models among the two policy fields. The direct effect of real-world indicators on agenda setting on asylum policy points to the role of external shocks (e.g. the Balkan Wars) and focusing events (Birkland 1998) in a little-institutionalised policy field dealing with a new issue (at least at the beginning of the period under study). This calls for a direct reaction to external (often international) events that have high visibility and media coverage. In such a context, the role of public opinion becomes less crucial as policy makers do not need other signs with regard to the issue at hand. They respond directly to an 'objective' increase in the problem that the policy aims to tackle and solve.

By contrast, unemployment policy, especially in Switzerland, is highly institutionalised through neo-corporatist arrangements. Furthermore, unemployment is an old issue which, either overtly or latently, is always there. As a result, public opinion acquires a particularly important role in signalling it as a major political problem to be dealt with. More than the actual state of the situation (i.e. the unemployment rate), what counts here is the perception of unemployment (of citizens who care about their job security) as a problem. Public opinion communicates such worries to elected policy-makers.

Concerning the paths connecting protests to agenda setting, variations across the two policy fields can be traced back to the different degree of politicisation of the issues and the presence of issue ownership in one of them. The indirect effect of protests on asylum via party intervention can be linked to the role of the Swiss People's Party, which has made asylum, and, more generally, immigration, one of its main electoral topics, together with opposition efforts to better integrate Switzerland at the European level. This party clearly owns the issue and has largely contributed to politicising it through its political campaigns that are strongly opposed to immigration, forcing other parties to address the issue in parliamentary debates. Therefore, agenda setting in this policy field is influenced by party intervention. This does not occur in the unemployment policy field, which is dealt with mostly through negotiated solutions within neo-corporatism arrangements. However, in both the asylum and the unemployment policy fields, protests seem to be at the origin of the process, providing the spur that sets them in motion.

Conclusion

Our empirical findings, which should not be considered more than tentative at this stage, suggest that what we have called 'real-world indicators' (here, the flow of asylum seekers and the unemployment rate) may be an important predictor of the introduction of parliamentary interventions, depending on the policy field. This is consistent with work following the agenda-setting perspective.

From a social movement perspective, this points to the importance of objective grievances for policy change. Grievances have long been disregarded as an explanatory factor of movement rise and development (but *see* Buechler 2004; Useem 1998). However, our analysis suggests that they should be taken into account when examining the policy outcomes of social movements, more precisely their impact on agenda setting. From a BED perspective, our findings show that elected politicians appear to be more influenced by 'objective' conditions than by protest activities in some policy domains.

In our analysis, real-world indicators matter for asylum policy but not for unemployment policy, suggesting once more that the mechanisms of influence vary from one policy field to another. The existence of relatively 'unambiguous' quantitative indicators (i.e. the flow of asylum seekers and unemployment rates) for these two issues makes them the most likely cases in which we would expect a linkage between an exogenous signal and a political response. Yet, different processes are at play in these two issue areas. More precisely, real-world indicators seem to have a direct effect on asylum and an indirect effect, via public opinion, on unemployment.

A similar varying effect can be observed for public opinion. In this case, we observe an effect on agenda setting on unemployment policy, but not on asylum policy. We suggest that these variations can be traced back to differences among the two policy fields, in particular in their degree of institutionalisation and politicisation.

Finally, it is worth mentioning that our analysis does not capture the fact that information processing is considered to be non-linear (Jones and Baumgartner 2005).When considering the relation between political attention and real-world indicators, do policy makers react to absolute values, symbolic thresholds, or relative change in time? How and why is this different across policy domains?

What about social movements? Here the patterns are somewhat more similar across the two policy fields. Consistent with previous findings (Giugni 2004), in both cases protest activities do not seem to impact directly on agenda setting. We find some evidence of a direct effect on agenda setting on asylum policy with non-lagged variables (results not shown), but this effect disappears when we look at lagged variables. This suggests a reverse causal relationship: agenda setting influences social movements rather than the other way around. This is in line with political opportunity theory.

In addition, in both cases protest is strongly correlated with party intervention, although here we cannot establish a causal relationship because both variables are measured in the same time unit. However, things change when we focus on the other paths because protests have an indirect effect via party intervention in the more politicised asylum policy field, but not in the more institutionalised unemployment policy field.

Further work could follow four directions. The first direction would be to look for a possible differential impact of protest activities across stages of the policy process. This was done, for example, by King *et al.* (2005), who showed that in the case of the US, social movements have more chances to succeed in the first stages of the policy process, in particular in setting the political agenda, than in later stages such as policy adoption or implementation. It would be interesting to examine whether a similar finding applies to other countries as well and, perhaps, whether this varies across countries for that matter. In this regard, the empirical evidence from Belgian case studies (Walgrave and Varone 2009) and quantitative analyses (Walgrave and Vliegenthart 2009) leads to contradictory results. Furthermore, this is likely to vary across policy issues. More generally, such a perspective would help research move beyond a narrower focus on policy adoption (such as changes in legislation or government spending as indicators of public policy) to embrace a broader view, which also looks at what comes before and after that particular stage of the policy process (Andrews 2001; Burstein *et al.* 1995a).

However, while one could simply compare various moments in the decision-making process, assessing the differential impact of protest across stages of the policy process makes more sense if it is done by following the fate of specific movement demands during the whole decision-making process. Thus, a second avenue for further research lies in adopting a process-tracing approach that allows for a stronger case for a cause-effect relationship and helps the research by spelling out the (responsiveness) mechanisms through which movement demands are translated into legislative acts, therefore contributing to bringing about policy change.

Thirdly, we should pay more attention to the other side of the dyad formed by social movements and elected policy makers. Research on the policy outcomes of social movements have most often started from the movements' side, then looked at the conditions and, less often, mechanisms leading them to have an impact. We should consider the other side more seriously, as suggested by the BED framework too. For example, one could interview policy makers in order to see, on the one hand, to what extent they consider social movements and protest in their day-to-day work and, on the other hand, to what extent they are influenced by them. This would imply resorting to more qualitative kinds of analyses.

An alternative or perhaps complementary methodological approach would consist of implementing an experimental or a quasi-experimental design to study the impact of specific movement tactics on decision makers. For example, this was recently done in the case of lobbying tactics by interest groups (*see* Richardson and John 2012).

Finally, there is a need to expand the scope of the present analysis by comparing both across countries and possibly also across a wider range of policy issues. As we said, this might help us make sense of the processes and mechanisms at work in social movements' influence over the different stages of the policy process. This might also provide stronger external validity to the findings.

Acknowledgements

Roy Gava and Frédéric Varone acknowledge the financial support of the Swiss National Science Foundation (project *Agenda Setting in Switzerland*; ref. 105511–119245/1).

References

Amenta, E. (2006) *When Movements Matter*, Princeton, NJ: Princeton University Press.

Amenta, E., Caren, N. and Olasky, S. J. (2005) 'Age for leisure? Political mediation and the impact of the pension movement on US old-age policy', *American Sociological Review,* 70: 516–38.

Amenta, E., Caren, N., Chiarello, E. and Su, Y. (2010) 'The political consequences of social movements', *Annual Review of Sociology,* 36: 287–307.

Amenta, E., Carruthers, B. G. and Zylan, Y. (1992) 'A hero for the aged? The Townsend movement, the political mediation model, and US old-age policy, 1934–1950', *American Journal of Sociology,* 98: 308–39.

Amenta, E., Dunleavy, K. and Bernstein, M. (1994) 'Stolen thunder? Huey Long's "Share our Wealth", political mediation, and the second New Deal', *American Sociological Review,* 59: 678–702.

Andrews, K. T. (2001) 'Social movements and policy implementation: The Mississippi civil rights movement and the war on poverty, 1965 to 1971', *American Sociological Review,* 66: 71–95.

Baumgartner, F. R. and Jones, B. D. (1991) 'Agenda dynamics and policy subsystems', *Journal of Politics,* 53: 1044–74.

— (1993) *Agendas and Instability in American Politics*, Chicago: University of Chicago Press.

Baumgartner, F. R., Jones, B. D. and Wilkerson, J. (2011) 'Comparative studies of policy dynamics', *Comparative Political Studies,* 44:1–26.

Birkland, T. A. (1998) 'Focusing events, mobilisation, and agenda setting', *Journal of Public Policy,* 18:53–74.

Buechler, S. M. (2004) 'The strange career of strain and breakdown theories of collective action', in Snow, D. A., Soule, S. A. and Kriesi, H. (eds) *The Blackwell Companion to Social Movements*, Oxford: Blackwell.

Burstein, P. (1998a [1985]) *Discrimination, Jobs, and Politics*, 2nd edn, Chicago: University of Chicago Press.

— (1998b) 'Bringing the public back in: Should sociologists consider the impact of public opinion on public policy?', *Social Forces,* 77: 27–62.

— (1999) 'Social movements and public policy', in Giugni, M., McAdam, D. and Tilly, C. (eds), *How Social Movements Matter*, Minneapolis: University of Minnesota Press.

Burstein, P., Bricher, M. and Einwohner, R. L. (1995a) 'Policy alternatives and political change: Work, family, and gender on the congressional agenda, 1945–1990', *American Sociological Review,* 60: 67–83.

Burstein, P., Einwohner, R. L. and Hollander, J. A. (1995b) 'The success of political movements: A bargaining perspective', in Jenkins, J. C. and Klandermans, B. (eds), *The Politics of Social Protest*, Minneapolis: University of Minnesota Press.

Burstein, P. and Linton, A. (2002) 'The impact of political parties, interest groups, and social movement organizations on public policy: Some recent evidence and theoretical concerns', *Social Forces,* 81: 380–408.

Cobb, R. W. and Elder, C. D. (1972) *Participation in American Politics*, Baltimore, MD: Johns Hopkins University Press.

Costain, A. N. and Majstorovic, S. (1994) 'Congress, social movements and public opinion: Multiple origins of women's rights legislation', *Political Research Quarterly,* 47: 111–35.

Gamson, W. A. (1990 [1975]) *The Strategy of Social Protest,* 2nd edn, Belmont, CA: Wadsworth Publishing.

Giugni, M. (2004) *Social Protest and Policy Change*, Lanham, MD: Rowman and Littlefield.

— (2007) 'Useless protest? A time-series analysis of the policy outcomes of ecology, antinuclear, and peace movements in the United States, 1975–1995', *Mobilization,* 12: 101–16.

— (2008) 'Political, biographical, and cultural consequences of social movements', *Sociology Compass,* 2:1582–1600.

— (ed.) (2010) *The Contentious Politics of Unemployment in Europe: Welfare states and political opportunities*, Houndmills: Palgrave.

Green-Pedersen, C. and Walgrave, S. (eds) (2013) *Tracing Political Attention: A novel approach to comparative politics,* Chicago: University of Chicago Press.

Hilgartner, S. and Bosk, C. L. (1988) 'The rise and fall of social problems: A public arenas model', *American Journal of Sociology,* 94: 53–78.

John, P. (2006) 'Explaining policy change: The impact of the media, public opinion and political violence on urban budgets in England', *Journal for European Public Policy,* 13: 1053–68.

Jones, B. D. and Baumgartner, F. R. (2005) *The Politics of Attention: How government prioritizes attention*, Chicago: University of Chicago Press.

Kane, M. D. (2003) 'Social movement policy success: Decriminalizing state sodomy laws, 1969–1998', *Mobilization,* 8: 313–34.

King, B. G., Cornwall, M. and Dahlin, E. C. (2005) 'Winning woman suffrage one step at a time: Social movements and the logic of the legislative process', *Social Forces,* 83: 1211–34.

Kingdon, J. W. (1984) *Agendas, Alternatives, and Public Policies*, New York: Harper Collins.

Kleinnijenhuis, J. and Rietberg, E. (1995) 'Parties, media, the public and the economy: Patterns of social agenda-setting', *European Journal of Political Research,* 28: 95–118.

Koopmans, R. and Statham, P. (1999) 'Political claims analysis: Integrating protest events and political discourses approaches', *Mobilization: An International Quarterly,* 4:203–21.

Koopmans, R., Statham, P., Giugni, M. and Passy, F. (2005) *Contested Citizenship: Immigration and cultural diversity in Europe,* Minneapolis: University of Minnesota Press.

McAdam, D. and Su, Y. (2002) 'The war at home: Antiwar protests and congressional voting, 1965 to 1973', *American Sociological Review,* 67: 696–721.

Peters, G. (2001) 'Agenda-setting in the European Union', in Richardson, J. (ed.), *European Union: Power and policy making,* London: Routledge.

Richardson, L. and John, P. (2012) 'Who listens to the grassroots? A field experiment on informational lobbying in the UK', *British Journal of Politics and International Relations,* 14: 596–612.

Schattschneider, E. E. (1975) *The Semisovereign People: A realist's view of democracy in America,* New York: Wadsworth Thomson Learning.

Schumaker, P. D. (1975) 'Policy responsiveness to protest-group demands', *Journal of Politics,* 37: 488–521.

Sharkansky, I. (1970) *Policy Analysis in Political Science,* Chicago: Markham.

Sinclair, B. (1986) 'The role of committees in agenda setting in the US Congress', *Legislative Studies Quarterly,* 11:35–45.

Soroka, S. N. (2002) *Agenda-Setting Dynamics in Canada,* Vancouver and Toronto: University of British Columbia Press.

Soule, S. A. and King, B. K. (2006) 'The stages of the policy process and the equal rights amendment, 1972–1982', *American Journal of Sociology,* 111: 1871–1909.

Soule, S. A. and Olzak, S. (2004) 'When do movements matter? The politics of contingency and the equal rights amendment', *American Sociological Review,* 69: 473–97.

Useem, B. (1998) 'Breakdown theories of collective action', *Annual Review of Sociology,* 24: 215–38.

Van Noije, L., Kleinnijenhuis, J. and Oegema, D. (2008) 'Loss of parliamentary control due to mediatization and Europeanization: A longitudinal and cross-sectional analysis of agenda building in the United Kingdom and the Netherlands', *British Journal of Political Science,* 38: 455–78.

Walgrave, S. and Rihoux, B. (1997) *De Witte Mars: Eénjaarlater,* Leuven: Van Halewyck.

Walgrave, S. and Varone, F. (2008) 'Punctuated equilibrium and agenda-setting: Bringing parties back in: Policy change after the Dutroux crisis in Belgium', *Governance,* 23: 365–95.

Walgrave, S. and Vliegenthart, R. (2009) 'The agenda-setting power of protest: Demonstrations, media, parliament, government, and legislation in Belgium, 1993–2000', unpublished manuscript.

Walker, J. (1977) 'Setting the agenda in the US Senate: A theory of problem selection', *British Journal of Political Science,* 74: 423–45.

Index

agency theory 8, 78–80
  see also under candidate nomination
    analysis
agenda-setting theory 6, 10, 189, 190,
  193
  BED framework and 190
  definition of 190
  issue attention and 193–4
  see also under social movement
    organisations (SMOs)
Arab Spring revolts 38
Austria
  electoral system in 60
  issue uptake analysis 60, *72*
  participation study *41, 43,* 44, *45, 48*
  protest in 135 n.2

Balkenende, J.-P. 159
Belgium
  issue uptake analysis 60, *72*
  participation study 40ff.
  protest impact studies and 195
  voter turnout analysis 108 n.4
Bentham, J. 36
between-election democracy (BED)
  7–11, 15–22, 29, 77, 103, 185, 189,
  190
  citizen preference communication
    and 20, 185
  collective decision-making and 16,
    17, 18
  contours/boundaries summary 21, *22*
  democratic quality, criteria of 29
  electoral authorisation and 16, 20
  equality, value of in 171
  representatives, identification of
    16–18, *22*
    formal/informal relationships
      and 17

line of delegation and 17–18
  represented, identification of 18–19,
    22
    associational life and 18–19
    issues/decision stages study and
      20–1
    territorial ties and 18
  systems perspective and 9–10
  see also candidate nomination
    analysis; responsiveness
Bos, W. 159

campaigning 3, 79–80, 84–5
  citizen engagement in 19
  party-centred and 77, 78, 81
  professionalisation of 84
  promissory representation and 57
  see also under candidate nomination
    analysis
candidate nomination analysis 8,
  77–97
  agency theory and 8, 78–83, 95
    accountability, concept use of 79,
      80, 81, 83
    delegation chain and 78–9
    ex post monitoring/sanctioning
      and 79–80
    responsiveness and 80, 81, 83,
      95–6
  between-election democracy
    concept and 77–8, 97
    institutional setting, effect of 78,
      79, 97
  campaigning styles 77, 78, 80,
    81–2, 84–5, 96, 97
    candidate centred (US) and 77,
      78, 82, 84
  electoral system and 78, 79, 80, *81,*
    84, 85, 86, 95–6

open systems and 81, 85
  PR systems and 81–2, 84, 85, 96
media, role in 79, 84
party culture/traditions and 78
party leader's role in 8, 81
representational roles, effect on 77,
  82, 83, 85, 96
  focus and style of 85–6, 96, 97
  party nomination and 78, 81, 82,
    85, 86, 96
  role orientation, concept of 86
  voter nomination and 78, 81, 82,
    85, 86, 96
selection methods and 77, 78, 82–3
see also campaigning; study under
  Norway
CentERData 160
citizen participation 8, 20, 35–48, 103
  arenas of 128–9
  boycotts/buycott and 8, 20, 36, 39,
    42, 129
  as democratic duty 36
    accountability and 36, 37
  effectiveness, country analysis
    37–48
    PARTIREP data, use of 39, *41,
      43, 45, 46, 48*
  elections, importance of 38–9, 47
    turnout, decline in and 105
  internet discussions and 8, 39, 42, 47
  non-electoral and 35, 37–9, 40, 42,
    103
    cross-national effectiveness study
      43, 44, 45, *46*, 47
  party activism and 39, 40, 42, 47,
    155
    see also study under United
      Kingdom
  symbolic/cultural meaning of 37
  see also demonstrations; internet
    activism; petitions
civil disobedience 104
Civil Rights Movement 38
cleavages, social 54
  globalisation, effect on 132–3

collective action 132, 133
  breakdown theories of 193
Comparative Agendas Project 196

deliberative democratic theory 6, 8
democracy 1, 35–6, 46
  Ancient Greece and 1, 5
  concept of 1
  egalitarian-liberal view of 154, 158
  elitist theory of 154
  ideal of 35–6
  see also representative democracy
demonstrations 9, 36, 38, 39, 46, 104,
  107, 127
  effectiveness study and 39, 40, 42, 46
  illegal and 39
  news media coverage of 136 n.4
direct democracy 5, 15

Egypt 38
elections 38–9, 80, 103, 129–30, 152
  citizen/leader relationship and 3, 4
  participation decline in 36, 47, 105
  political effectiveness study and 40,
    47
  representational mechanisms of 3
  second order and 134
  as signalling instrument 151, 154,
    158–9
  as voter sanctioning devices 80
    electoral systems and 80
  voter turnout 105
electoral arena 128–30, 131, 132
  mass media, role in 131
electoral cycles 152–4
electoral volatility 54
European Social Survey (ESS) 9, 108

Finland 86
France
  campaigning system in 84
  1968 protest revolt and 38
  party protest analysis 9, 127, 135,
    136, 137ff

Gallup, G. 151
Germany
  candidate nomination in 86
  issue uptake analysis 60, 61, *72*
  participation study *41*, 42ff.
  party protest analysis 9, 127, 135,
    136, 137ff.
globalisation, economic effect of
  132–3
governance 6, 10

Hungary
  issue uptake analysis 60, 61, *72*
  participation study *41*, 42ff.

IDEA database 108 n.4
India, elections in 134
interest groups and organisations 6, 9,
  62, 172
  responsiveness, equality of and 173,
    184, 185
  see also lobby groups and lobbying;
    study under United Kingdom
interest intermediation 132–3, 135, 140
internet activism 37
  effectiveness study and 39, 42, 46, 47
Iraq war protest 18
Ireland 58 n.2
  issue uptake analysis 60, 61, 63, 70,
    72
Israel
  campaigning in 84–5
  candidate selection in 83, 84
  electoral system in 70
Italy
  issue uptake analysis 60, 61, 70, *72*
  participation study 40ff.

John, P. 186

LISS project 160, 167
lobby groups and lobbying 53, 172, 205
  field experiments and 175, 185
  see also study under United
    Kingdom

Luxembourg, voter turnout analysis
  108 n.4

mass mobilisation 128–31
  see also protest politics; party street
    protest analysis; social move-
    ment organisations (SMOs)
media, mass
  electoral arena and 131
  issue uptake and 8, 53
  political impact of 39, 40, 47
    issue attention and 194, 203
  political mobilisation and *129*, 131
  political protest, coverage of 135–6
Mill, J. S. 154
MZES 88 n.8

Netherlands, the
  electoral system in 151
  issue uptake analysis 60, 61, 70,
    71, *72*
  party protest analysis 9, 127, 135,
    136, 137ff.
  political history (2006–10) and
    159–60
    financial crisis (2008-), effect of
      163, 165–6, 167
  political polls signalling study 9,
    151–2, 159–66, 167
  Statistics Netherlands and 160
Norway
  campaigning in 87
    individualised and 90, 96, 97
    party centred and 87, 90, 96
    style and 78, 87, 90, 93, 96
  candidate nomination analysis 8, 78,
    86–95, 96–7
  cleavages in 86
  electoral system and reforms in
    86–7
    PR, use of 86
    multiparty system in 86
  issue uptake analysis 60, 61, 63,
    70, *72*
  parties in 86, 87, 97

Norwegian Candidate Study (2009) 78, 88 n.8

opinion polls, signalling and 9, 156–67
 as anticipatory representation 157
 bandwaggon effect of 156
 as a between-election signal 158
 characteristics of 156–7
 information depth and scope in 156, 158

parliamentary systems 84, 85
 responsible party model and 85, 97
parties, political 8, 19, 54, 130
 collective accountability and 56
 collective preference alignment and 132
 identification/confidence and 54
 interest representation and 54, 127, 132–3
  differentiation hypothesis and 127–8, 133
 issue linkage, role in 130
 membership decline and 47
 nomination procedures of 77
  see also candidate nomination analysis
 protest politics, sponsorship of 127, 131–2
  see also party street protest analysis
 representation, role in 19, 47, 97
 see also campaigning
PARTIREP survey
 citizen participation analysis and 39, 41, 43, 45, 46, 48
 interest uptake analysis and 54
party street protest analysis 9, 127–45
 BED perspective, use of 127, 131, 145
  between-election hypothesis and 128, 131–2, 133–4, 135, 142–4, 145
  party sponsorship and 127, 131, 134–5, 137, 145
 'street', use of term 130

see also parties, political
petitions 9, 36, 39, 46, 104, 109, 121, 151, 154, 155, 172
Poland, issue uptake analysis 60, 61, 63, 70, 72
policy feedback theory 6, 10
political consumerism 20, 36, 46, 47, 109
political opportunity structure approach (POS) 9, 103, 106
 see also under social movement organisations (SMOs)
political participation analysis 9, 20, 21, 29, 103–6
 associational involvement and 112, 122
 between elections and 105, 106, 107, 111–13, 114, 119
 electoral participation and 103, 106, 107, 113, 115, 116–17, 118, 119, 121
  cross-national variations in 106, 120
  proportional electoral systems and 107, 111, 115
  voter turnout and 108, 118, 119
 institutional openness and 9, 106–7, 109–11, 112, 113, 115, 118, 119
  country scores 111
  institutional linkages and 109–11, 114, 115, 117
  measurement of 109–11
  notion of 106
 institutional structure and 105–7, 112, 119
  decision-making powers and 106, 109–10
  incentives and 103, 107, 112, 119, 120
  patterns of participation, effect on 105, 107
 institutionalised/non-institutionalised distinction and 103, 105, 106–7, 120
political trust 20, 21, 27, 29, 37, 55

polling analysis 151–67
    elections and 151, 154, 155–9
        as signals of voter intention 151,
            152, 158, 159
    representativeness, levels of *156*,
        157, 158
        perceived responsiveness and
            158
    voter/representative relationship and
        152–4, 157–8, 167
        between-election period and
            152–3, 154, 158
        interaction model of 153–4
        perceived responsiveness and
            157–8, 163
        as triad of communication 152–3,
            154, 167
    see also case study under the
        Netherlands
Portugal
    issue uptake analysis 60, 70, *72*
    participation study 40ff.
preference formation 23, 57, 66
protest politics 5, 10, 23, 129, 130,
    134, 154, 155–6, 189
    arenas, concept of 128–9, 130
        issue linkage and 129, 130
    citizen participation in 8, 20, 130
    electoral politics, link with 131, 134
    illegal protests and 8, 9, 42
    impact of 130
    mass media, role in 130–1
    party involvement in 127–8
    see also social movement organisa-
        tions (SMOs); party street protest
        analysis
public opinion 56
    articulation of 56
    mass media, role in 56
    organised interests and 56
    research 10, 17
    as signal to policy makers 192
    social movements and 190, 191
    see also under representative
        relationship

representation 1, 11, 19
    anticipatory view of 39, 54, 104,
        105–6, 152, 157
    definition of (Pitkin) 1–2, 24
    promissory view of 57, 71, 152
    style and focus of 85
representation theory 6, 15, 16–17, 20, 23
    electoral district delineation and
        16–17
    substance of representation and 19
representative democracy 1–4, 15,
    38–9, 104
    accountability and 106, 151, 152
        n.1, *153*, 184
    collective/individual and 55–6
    constituency interests and 53, 54–5
        bottom-up/top-down perspectives
            and 57
        dissent, role in 54
    egalitarianism and 1, 3–4, 186
    elitism and 1, 2, 3, 23, 186
    institutional structure and 105–6
        electoral mechanisms and 2,
            38–9, 104
    origin of 1
    see also citizen participation;
        elections
representative relationship 2–11, 53,
    54–5, 104, 171
    between-election mode and 2–3,
        4–5, 7–11, 15, 19, 22, 29
        accountability concerns and 7
        responsiveness mechanisms and
            3, 6, 9, 171
        see also between-election
            democracy (BED); responsive-
            ness
    citizen preferences and 2, 20, 23, 24
    communication, role in 172, 184
    disagreement opportunities and 54
    election mode and 4, 5, 7, 19
    interactionist model and 153
    issue-specific character of 6, 53
        see also issue uptake analysis
    lobby groups, role of 172

see also study under United
Kingdom
public opinion and 1, 2, 3–4, 5, 23
n.4, 24
deliberation, role in 55
research and 5–6
dynamic systems approach and
10, 23
territory delineation and 16–18
see also citizen participation;
elections
responsiveness 3, 6, 7–8, 10, 15, 20,
22–5, 28, 106, 152–3, 171
BED framework and 190, 194
citizen interest and 23–4
communicative view of 6, 7–8, 11,
24–6, 28, 104, 185
citizen opinion and 24, 28
majority/minority distinction and
25–6, 28
elections/electoral systems and 80
limitations of 172–3, 183
issue prioritisation and 6, 172–3,
177, 189
signals and stimuli and 194
opinion polls, role in 157–8
perceived vs objective and 157–8,
185–6
preference formation dynamics and
23–4, 189
procedural fairness and 25
representative relationships and 3,
6, 7, 15, 22–3, 171, 179
bottom-up approach to 23–4,
104, 189
interests, perception of and 53,
171, 184–5, 189
study methods of 174–5, 185
see also between-election democracy (BED)
Rousseau, J.- J. 3, 4, 35
Rutte, M. 159, 160

Schmitt, H. 88 n.8
social choice theory 2 n.1, 132, 133

social interaction theory 153
social movement organisations
(SMOs) 5, 19, 106, 130, 133, 137,
189–205
agenda-setting analysis 189, 190–1,
193–205
agenda definition, use of 190
data and methodology 195–7
findings and 197–8
objective grievances and 204
paths to (hypothesised) *191*
real-world indicators as predictors 204
regression models and 196, 197
structural equation model *199,
201, 202*
variables of interest and 197
see also under Switzerland
as bottom-up signals 189
mobilisation and 106, *129*
institutional openness and 106
political alliances, role of 190, 191,
192, 197, 201
policy, impact on 6, 189, 192–3,
197, 202, 204–5
issue attention and 193–5, 202
party intervention and 204–5
political claims analysis and 195
political opportunity theory and
204
three models of (Giugni) 192–3
public opinion, role of 190, 191,
192, 196, 197, 199, 201, 202,
203
real-world indicators and 10, 190,
191, 193, 194–5, 196, 197, 199, 203
research and 9, 10, 20, 23, 25, 28,
103, 106, 119, 131, 190–2, 204–5
agenda-setting theory and 10,
189, 190–1, 193, 205
BED framework, use of 189,
190, 193, 204
grievance theory 190, 193
opportunity structure approach
and 9, 103, 106, 120

see also agenda-setting theory;
case study under Switzerland
responsiveness criteria of (Schumaker) and 190
Sweden
communicative responsiveness
analysis 26–7
political effectiveness study 44–5
Swedish National Election Study 26 n.6
Switzerland 39 n.3
cantonal system in 61
issue uptake analysis 60, 61, 71, *72*
participation study *41*, 42ff.
protest activities analysis 10, 135
n.2, n.3, 139 n.7
protest agenda-setting study and
191–205
asylum policy and 190, 191,
196ff
data and methodology 195–6
issue ownership and 203
politicisation of issues and 203,
204
unemployment policy and 190,
191, 196ff
Socialist Party 203
Swiss People's Party 203

Tunisia 38

United Kingdom
campaigning system in 84
issue uptake analysis 60, 61, 63,
70, *72*
lobby groups, equality study 172,
174–85
data/methodology and 174–5
prioritisation experiment and
177–82, 183–4
local government in 172, 173
centralisation in 173
communication/information and
174, 184
public perception studies and
174, 184

representative interaction and
173–4, 182, 183, 184
organised interest groups and 183
participation study 40ff.
party protest analysis 9, 127, 135,
136, 137ff.
representation relationships in 9–10,
58 n.2, 173–4, 179, 186
equality of treatment in 174,
179–80, 182, 184, 184
United States
campaigning in 84
candidate selection in 83
use of primaries and 84
Congress and 85
election studies 17
participation research in 19
leader responsiveness and 38
political attention research in 194,
195
political protest in 136 n.4
public opinion, notion of and 56
representation relationships and
16–17, 28, 85, 185

Verdonk, R. 159
voting 3, 7, 129, 151, 153, 157 n.7
key characteristics of *155*
as signalling preferences 153–4,
155
see also elections

Wilders, G. 160

www.ingramcontent.com/pod-product-compliance
Lightning Source LLC
Chambersburg PA
CBHW072119020426
42334CB00018B/1652